P9-DNB-981

THE VITAL DIFFERENCE

Unleashing the Powers of Sustained Corporate Success

Frederick G. Harmon
and Garry Jacobs

amacom

AMERICAN MANAGEMENT ASSOCIATION

Library of Congress Cataloging-in-Publication Data

Harmon, Frederick G.
   The vital difference.

   Bibliography: p.
   Includes index.
   1. Industrial management—United States.
2. Success in business—United States.   I. Jacobs,
Garry.   II. Title.
HD70.U5H36   1985   658.4'09   85-47674
ISBN 0-8144-5569-7

Printing number

10 9 8 7 6 5 4 3 2 1

This book is dedicated to
Nancy M. Harmon,
who has made a vital difference
in many lives, and to
the future heroic business leaders
of the United States

Acknowledgments

We are indebted to some 100 managers from 15 companies who took time for interviews with us. In as many cases as practical, we have attempted to acknowledge such individual contributors in the text of the book. In many of these companies, dedicated corporate communications specialists set up appointments for us, provided detailed information, and checked hundreds of facts and figures. In this regard, we extend our special thanks to:

Bobbi Blake, Regis McKenna Inc. for Apple Computer, Inc.
Lyle D. Percy, Bata Limited
Taggerty Patrick, Chrysler Corporation
Thomas E. Gray, The Coca-Cola Company
Clint G. Sweazea and James L. Ewing, III, Delta Air Lines, Inc.
George Palmer, E. I. du Pont de Nemours & Company, Inc.
Terry J. Thompson, General Mills, Inc.
John T. Britton, Hertz Corporation
James W. Jarrett, Intel Corporation
Robert J. Siegel, International Business Machines Corporation
Joyce Bustinduy, Levi Strauss & Company
Robert T. Souers, Marriott Corporation
A. B. Fiskett, Merck Sharp & Dohme
Thomas W. Towers, Northwestern Mutual Life Insurance Company
Gene L. Harmon and Donna C. Peterman, Sears, Roebuck & Company

Despite this assistance, we remain fully responsible for the editorial matter as it finally appears and for the interpretation we have given to the histories and strategies of these companies.

At the American Management Association, we are indebted to several people, particularly to AMACOM Publisher Robert A. Kaplan, whose early enthusiasm and sustained support for our project were important at every stage. Our editors, Barbara Horowitz and Janet

Frick, managed with good humor to be both patient and demanding, helping us strengthen our manuscript in several key ways. John Anderson of the AMA Presidents Association and Virginia O'Connor of the AMA Membership Department provided useful opportunities for us to test our ideas before audiences of managers. Grace Crawford worked on her own time to give us greatly needed administrative and secretarial support.

In India, G. Panneer and V. G. Thyagarajan spent months reading, collecting, and processing material for the book.

Contents

A Note from Peter F. Drucker

Some months ago, I received a copy of the manuscript of *The Vital Difference* with a request that I write a foreword for it. After reading the manuscript, however, I decided against writing the foreword. My reason for the decision was that I felt it would be redundant. In fact, I felt that it would detract from the book, because the book is so well done and there is so much in it. A foreword always implies that the book needs a boost. This one does not—and one should not give the impression that it does.

Fred Harmon and Garry Jacobs have managed to write a book that is easy—indeed captivating—reading full of profound insight, indeed wisdom. They do not offer the "quick fix" but they show every business and especially the CEO of each business how one looks at a business, how one thinks about it, and how one plans and executes action that produces achievement, ability to grow, willingness to change, and corporate health and longevity.

—*Peter F. Drucker*

Introduction: The Issue

Sustained corporate success that extends over decades and continuously expands without apparent end or limit has thus far been a luxury enjoyed by very few companies. So unusual is this phenomenon that when it does occur, we tend to look upon it in awe and admiration rather than closely scrutinizing its origins and history for a clue to the process. In fact, we are so sure that this high achievement is the result of some exceptional talent or extraordinary luck that we rarely even ask the most fundamental question: "What is the process by which sustained corporate success is achieved?" Some may even wonder whether there actually is a process at all. But science assures us that there is a process behind all phenomena—physical, social, psychological, and even spiritual.

This question that we have asked first is actually the last that can be answered. Before we ask how an organization grows, and grows continuously, we must ask several other questions. If organizations grow, there must be an energy or force that drives that growth. What is that energy? Where does it come from? How is it converted into achievement? How does it generate growth?

Our search for answers to these questions spanned more than a decade and literally circled the globe. Drawing inspiration from such diverse sources as the philosophy of Indian yoga, the process of social development, and the psychology of personality, we caught a glimpse of a wider vision, arrived at a hypothesis, and applied it to a study of some of America's most successful corporations.

Our aim was to trace the historical development of these companies from their early days, to identify the most prominent factors, both internal and external, responsible for their growth, and at the same time to examine each of these companies at different levels from top to bottom and in cross section of their activities in order to identify characteristics common to the entire organization. Our work involved an extensive research of literature and more than 100 interviews in 15 leading companies.

The first and probably the most important of our findings is the all-pervasive role of human energy in the development of individuals, companies, and societies. We observed that this energy is converted by successful corporations into an atmosphere of intensity, which other companies lack. We have sought to discover the origins of that energy and the process of its conversion into intensity for a clue to the secret of enduring success.

The generation and conversion of energy is the key to corporate development. But who or what accomplishes this great transformation? In answering this question, we have to introduce the reader to the most important personality in the life of any company—the personality of the corporation itself.

Personality is a comprehensive term that includes several component parts. We found that the parallel between the individual and the company is far more than a metaphor. It contains a deeper truth. All the pieces of the corporate puzzle began to fall into place, and a pattern of interrelationships emerged. Values, organization, people, systems, skills, technology, machines, materials, and money are not isolated components; they are parts of an integrated, living whole—a personality.

Each of these parts contains a vast reserve of untapped energies and potentials, which the coporate personality releases and utilizes for its growth. We are all familiar with the power of money and technology, so much so that we easily overlook other powers of the corporate personality that contain equal or greater potentials. Henry Ford started with $28,000 and tapped one of these powers to fuel a 25,000-fold expansion of his company in 25 years, without any additional investment. J. Willard Marriott and his son exploited another of these powers to convert a few small drive-in restaurants into the eighth largest U.S.-based hotel chain in the world. A considerable portion of this book is devoted to exploring the rich creative potentials of the powers of corporate personality.

It is very easy to get lost in admiration of one or two powers of the corporate personality and lose sight of the whole, of which they form only a part. But much of the power of organization results from the interrelationships between these parts, the golden gaps that have to be bridged to combine them into a single, unified whole. Merck & Company, Inc. rose from sixth place to first in the American pharmaceuticals industry by bridging the gap between research and marketing. C. E. Woolman—a simple, friendly, lovable man—transformed

Delta Air Lines, Inc. from a crop-dusting operation into the world's most profitable airline by building bridges between people. We have tried to focus in on these organizational interrelationships and illustrate how they have been built up by successful corporations.

The whole we have been describing is itself a part of a greater whole. The living organization is a child of society. The difference between the individual and the company is that people grow by becoming independent of their parents, while corporations grow by forging a more intimate relationship and interdependence with the society that fostered them. A stationmaster who recognized this truth 100 years ago founded what is today the largest retail operation in the world, Sears, Roebuck and Company. Tomas Bata, an uneducated shoemaker who discovered it, expanded his company 15-fold in 5 years and built it up into the largest shoe manufacturer in the world. A couple of young computer buffs made it the springboard for the 1,500-fold growth of Apple Computers, Inc. in a period of 8 years. Shy, inarticulate Robert Woodruff used it to build up The Coca-Cola Company into the most articulate marketing organization and the most popular soft drink in the whole world. Later in the book we explore some of the infinite potentials of this perpetual child-parent relationship.

Finally we come to the process that leads to enduring success. It is the process by which personality develops. We have sought to discover and explain the intimate relationship between the growth of individual personality and the development of the corporation and show how both are expressions of the same process. By consciously following this process, any manager can become a significant individual in the life of the organization, and any company can energize itself and embark on a course that leads to endless expansion and enduring success.

For those who seek the ultimate boon of endless corporate expansion, we invite you to that great adventure and to share our glimpse of a vision of the process. For those who seek a more limited boon like doubling your profits or sales, the book presents specific strategies for achieving your goal.

CHAPTER 1

The Driving Force

When we arrived at the headquarters of Intel Corporation in Santa Clara, California, to begin our initial round of interviews, we were struck by the intense energy that seemed to supercharge the atmosphere. Evidently we were not the only ones to perceive it. For when we began our very first interview with Intel's manager of corporate communications, Jim Jarrett, his very first word in reply to our opening question was *energy*. What did he first notice when he joined Intel? "Energy. Energy is certainly one of the striking characteristics of this company and this industry."

Nor were Jim Jarrett and Intel unique in this respect. In fact, our experience at Intel was repeated over and over again as we visited a cross section of highly successful companies around the United States. From Silicon Valley to Atlanta, from companies barely a decade old like Apple to centenarians like Coca-Cola, from breakfast foods to life insurance, wherever we found high achievement, we found high energy, too. "There is an energy here. Everybody feels it," declared Doug MacMaster, president of Merck Sharp & Dohme, the nation's largest manufacturer of prescription drugs. There is "a kinetic energy that flows through all of us," said Jere Whiteley of Northwestern Mutual, America's most admired life insurance company.

Energetic People

What is this thing that is so tangible and palpable to the experience of these companies and yet does not find even the slightest mention in textbooks or university courses on management? Energy is basic to all life. Wherever there is greatness, great energy abounds. Many who

have been in the presence of a great personality have noted the aura
of intensity such an individual radiates, the unbounded and overflowing energy of a Napoleon, a Churchill, a Beethoven, a Carnegie, or a
Henry Ford. After meeting Theodore Roosevelt, an Englishman once
remarked, "Do you know the two most wonderful things I have seen
in your country? Niagara Falls and the President of the United States,
both great wonders of nature!"[1] One writer described Roosevelt as "a
perpetual flow of torrential energy, a sense of motion even in stillness
. . . thrilling to be near."[2]

Energy is the basis of all creativity. It is the fuel that feeds the
fire of inspiration. Honoré de Balzac, one of the greatest French writers,
possessed a vitality as imposing and fascinating as the life depicted in
his stories. "Everything he did seemed to have a tenfold intensity.
When he laughed the pictures on the walls trembled; when he spoke
the words came cascading forth; . . . when he worked there was no
difference between day and night as he sat writing round the clock
and blunted a dozen pens in the process."[3] Balzac was a firm believer
in the store of energy concentrated inside people, and his life gave
credence to his belief. During 1830 and 1831 he poured out approximately 150 short novels, stories, articles, and commentaries—a feat
unparalleled in the annals of literature—and over the next 20 years,
he completed 40 full-length novels.

Energy spurs innovation. No other individual has been responsible
for striking the springs of so much wealth as Thomas Alva Edison.
Edison was an indomitable worker who frequently went days on end
without sleep in the process of producing 1,100 patentable inventions
and giving birth to several entirely new industries—the motion picture, phonograph and recording, and electric and household appliance
industries. The General Electric Company, which Edison founded, is
today the tenth largest industrial corporation in the United States,
with $23 billion in assets. In 1907, when Edison was 60, Hearst's *Cos-
mopolitan* magazine urged him to authorize a serialized autobiography.
"When I go into senile decay I may consider the autobiographical
scheme," Edison replied, "but as long as I can put in eighteen hours
daily, I don't want to waste any time on it."[4]

Energetic Entrepreneurs

Business leaders, especially those who have created great enterprises
within a single lifetime, are also noted for their energy. In 1940 a

psychology student named Mort Feinberg went into an IBM office in Manhattan to process some punch cards for his Ph.D. thesis. A fairly old gentleman came over to offer his assistance. Feinberg was struck by "the tremendous energy, the tremendous strength exuded by the guy." It was Thomas Watson, Sr., the founder of the International Business Machines Corporation. Feinberg's description was identical to the one given by *Fortune* magazine in an article published the same year. John C. Johnston, the founder of the Northwestern Mutual Life Insurance Company, was known as a man of boundless energy who migrated from the East Coast to the frontiers of Wisconsin and set up the first life insurance company west of New England in 1857.

Most of these leaders channeled their high energy into endless hours of hard work. When J. Willard Marriott opened a small A & W Root Beer stand on a busy street in Washington, D.C., in 1927, he was launching the billion-dollar Marriott Corporation. Biographer Robert O'Brien described Marriott in his early days:

> His managers never knew what time of day or night he'd show up at the kitchen door and go bird-dogging almost at a half-run through the kitchen, the pantries, the storage rooms, the refrigerators, the restaurant itself, running a finger over the shelves to check for dust, checking under tables and in cutlery drawers, checking the ranges, the storage rooms, the trays about to be served, sampling the root beer, and raising hell if everything wasn't spotless, neat, clean, bright, polished, done efficiently, done well.[5]

Sometimes an enterprise has received its greatest impetus not from the founder, but from energetic people who came afterward, like Julius Rosenwald and General Robert Wood at Sears. Wood, who inspired and directed Sears' entry into the retail store business in the 1920s, was a tower of strength with a military bearing and a sparkle in his eye. Donald Craib, chairman of Allstate Insurance Company, whose father was a close friend of the general, says Wood was an energetic man who exuded confidence. "You knew you were in the presence of a man who could wield considerable power."

Energy is not the exclusive possession of the great. It is an attribute shared by most successful CEOs who have made a significant impact on the companies they directed. In fact, we all have times when our energies and productivity are far higher than normal. Often this occurs when we are faced with a difficult problem that must be overcome or an extraordinary opportunity that calls for an all-out effort. High achievers are set apart from the rest by the way they use the energy available to them. Mort Feinberg, who is now professor of industrial psychology at New York University as well as consultant and confidant to some of America's leading executives, says that energy is an "enormously important" factor in their success, but not energy alone. "With the energy comes discipline. These men have a tendency to be highly disciplined. They are not out to parties. They go to sleep on time. They rarely drink. Very few of them smoke. They exercise regularly. They are very disciplined people. Their energies are focused." These individuals are able to accomplish more than the average because they channel all their available energies into activities designed to achieve the goals they have set for themselves instead of allowing that energy to flow in many different and unconnected directions not governed by a clear central focus. Not only is their energy more disciplined and focused, it is also more constant and consistent— because it is not expended in an extravagant or wasteful fashion on unproductive activities. As a result, highly disciplined and intensely focused energy becomes a characteristic of all that they do. It becomes a conspicuous mark, a presence that can be felt by those around them.

Corporate Intensity

In some fashion the energy of an individual can be transferred to the organizations he or she founds and become a characteristic of the company as well. One of the most important findings of the McKinsey study of America's best-managed enterprises reported by Peters and Waterman in their book *In Search of Excellence* was the presence of a palpable intensity in the companies they studied. The authors noted that they could "feel it."

Our own experience has been much the same. In company after company we were struck by the intensity of the atmosphere we found. It was not just the energy of countless individuals, but a solid mass of radiant power that seemed to pervade the entire organization, supporting and energizing its individual members at least as much as it was supported and energized by them.

But in each company this intensity had a different quality. As Feinberg says, "There is a big difference in the energy of different organizations." At Intel we found the energy disciplined and tense. At Apple it was buoyant youthful enthusiasm. At General Mills, Inc. there was a dynamic exuberance. At Merck it felt like the controlled power of a well-oiled machine. At Coca-Cola it had vibrancy and charm. At Delta it was the intense warmth of a close-knit family. At Northwestern Mutual it was a smooth, quiet hum, yet very active and alert.

Not only does the quality of the energy differ from company to company, but so does the quantity and what one might call the stability of intensity it produces. In Apple and Intel one had the feeling of a young and as yet unstable foundation that had to be maintained by a conscious effort and constant straining. By contrast, at Delta and Northwestern Mutual the intensity seemed to be fully and firmly established, almost self-existent, and no longer dependent on any effort to support it.

Disciplined Energy

What is the difference between this youthful energy of a successful company still in its adolescence and the stable intensity of a mature institution? The best analogy we could think of is a comparison with a famous professional athlete like Jim Connors, Roger Staubach, or Mary Lou Retton at three different stages of their lives. First, imagine our future stars as children trying to learn how to hit a tennis ball, throw a football, or master the parallel bars. They are boundless and endless fonts of energy without measure or mission, running and jumping everywhere, restless, excited, exuberant. Their movements are clumsy, uncoordinated, and abrupt, because they are not yet masters of their own energies. The energy overflows in every direction but accomplishes very little, because the youngsters lack the skills necessary to control and direct it. This is the stage of many entrepreneurial companies still in their infancy. They subsist on excitement, enthusiasm, and the sheer thrill of the challenge. Now imagine our athletes in adolescence as stars on the high school team. They have gained a measure of control over their energies. Their movements are better coordinated. They have acquired many skills. Yet still, every action requires the utmost effort and concentration. They lack the confidence that comes with long experience. They are as yet nervous, jumpy, anxious, straining, and unsure of themselves. Like Apple they have won a lot of games and surpassed all their peers but have still to prove that they can survive in the big leagues. Finally, think of them as professional athletes at the peak of their careers. They have a calm bearing and steady poise. Every movement is well measured and precise without the slightest unnecessary expenditure of energy. They are in full control of their energies and have perfected their skills. They have a clear knowledge of and a confidence in their abilities. Those who meet them are awed by their very presence, as the computer industry is by IBM.

In the child, energy is a raw force—uncontrolled, undirected, sporadic. It comes in sudden bursts of motion and ends in motionless exhaustion. In the professional, on the other hand, the energy is constant and stable, a solid state of radiant power. Between the uncontrolled raw energy of nature and the pure, power-packed intensity that is the summit of human achievement, there is a *vital difference.* We see this difference all around us. When energy is brought under control, focused in a particular direction, and harnessed for productive work, it generates intensity. The raw energy of Niagara Falls is converted into an intensity that can illuminate an entire city. The crushing force of millions of tons of water is captured and tamed by human invention and made productive. It is channeled through a carefully designed structure. Its kinetic energy is used to drive giant turbines, which convert it into electrical power. The electricity is directed through an extensive network of systems and delivered over long distances to the ultimate points of consumption, where it may be sharply focused as a tiny beam of electrons passing through the hair-thin filament of an incandescent bulb to illuminate a small room.

A very similar process takes place within companies. All available energies must be harnessed by the organization, controlled by authority, and directed to work through systems and skills to achieve the desired goals. The greater the energies collected and harnessed, the more effectively they are controlled and directed, the more coordinated and integrated the systems through which they pass, and the more perfect the skills with which they are expressed, the greater is the productivity of the organization and the intensity it generates. As Feinberg put it: "Great corporations focus disciplined energy. They channel their energies and avoid fragmentation, diffusion, and nonfocused activities, which are often characteristic of organizations that have lost their goals."

Sources of Energy

It is not just energy that makes for corporate excellence. It is human energy converted into organizational intensity. An organization is a huge repository of latent and potential energies. Where do these energies come from? They come from people. Initially, it is the energy of the founder that gives life to an organization. The founder pours forth his or her energies onto the new creation much as a mother lavishes affection on her infant child. He or she devotes personal attention to every small detail of work, often doing the most mundane tasks himself or herself in the early years like Bill Marriott, Sr., who did the cooking himself in the first Hot Shoppe. The founder works endless hours giving form and substance to the company—hand-selecting employees, training them, designing systems and procedures, establishing priorities and goals, setting a personal example of the values he or she wants to instill in others.

By giving attention to the new recruits, teaching and training them, delegating authority, assigning responsibilities, and rewarding good performance, the founder builds up a core of employees who feel involved and dedicated to the company. They contribute not only their physical energies but their psychological energies as well. Their interest, excitement, enthusiasm, ambition, loyalty, and pride are channeled into the work. By attitude and example, the founder may also foster a spirit of cooperation and teamwork, as C. E. Woolman did at Delta during the early days when he had to pass the hat among employees to collect enough money to fuel the plane for the next flight. To the extent that people begin to feel part of a collective effort and a greater whole, they dedicate even more of their energies to the enterprise.

As the company grows, it requires a steady influx of new energy, talents, and capacities. Some of the early recruits lack the education, technical background, or managerial experience the work demands. A greater emphasis is placed on recruiting bright, educated talents with alert minds and new ideas. At a relatively early stage, the founders of Apple recognized the need for highly trained professionals to build up efficient production and marketing facilities that could effectively deliver their innovative products to large numbers of people at competitive prices. This influx of mental energies adds to the growing reservoir of corporate strength.

The young, developing company also forges relationships with the world around it. It wins some loyal customers who appreciate its products or services. It finds reliable suppliers that appreciate its regular business. It may attract investors willing to risk funds on the strength of the company's achievements and prospects. These people, too, contribute their energies to the growth of the organization.

Though all growing enterprises draw energies from these various sources, companies do differ in the energies they possess. Much depends on the quality of the people they recruit—the importance the company places on selecting people with good health, enthusiasm for work, strong nerves, dynamism, expansiveness, education, and intelligence. But companies differ even more in the extent to which they are able to release, harness, and channel the various energy resources at their disposal into productive work. People are not a limited, finite resource like so many kilowatts of power or pounds of salt. People are a nearly limitless reservoir of physical, psychological, and mental energy and talent. The key is in knowing how to utilize peoples' capacities to the full or, rather, how to motivate people to give themselves entirely to their work.

Shoe Power

Tomas Bata was a man who possessed this key. He was the ninth generation in a family clan of shoemakers from the town of Ziln, in what was then Austria-Hungary, now Czechoslovakia. Tomas and his brother founded a shoemaking "factory" in their house at Ziln in 1894 with two sewing machines and some hand tools. Despite this rather modest beginning, Tomas's ambition was to transform shoemaking from a cottage handicraft into a modern industry run with shoe machinery. Inspired by the American system of mechanized production, which he studied during two visits to the United States, and by Henry Ford's idea of an inexpensive car for the masses, Bata dreamed of producing shoes in quantities large enough and at prices low enough to shod the feet of all humanity. By the end of World War I, he had built up a medium-sized shoe industry employing 2,000 workers and producing a half-million pairs of shoes annually, part of which was exported to other European countries.

In 1922 Europe was in the midst of the first great postwar depression, which drastically cut Czechoslovakia's export trade, creating widespread unemployment throughout the country. The newly formed Czech government adopted a policy of tight monetary controls to fight inflation on the home front, resulting in a 75 percent devaluation in the currency in a single year. As a result of these factors, demand fell, purchasing power declined, and exports decreased to a fraction of their former level. Debtors, which included most businesses that had expanded on bank credit during the war, were suddenly faced with high levels of debt and falling incomes. Production declined. Layoffs multiplied. More than 400,000 Czechs were unemployed. Bata's business suffered badly. His exports dropped by 75 percent. Stocks were accumulating until his warehouses were full to overflowing. There was enormous pressure to cut production and lay off workers.

In August of 1922 the national manufacturers' association of Czechoslovakia called an urgent meeting of its members to discuss the government's policies and formulate recommendations to avert economic disaster. Those who attended felt they were helpless victims of external forces and government actions. They were nearly unanimous in condemning the government and demanding relief, but none could propose a viable solution to the problems facing the nation.

On the second day of the conference. Tomas Bata rose to speak. Bata saw the futility of the government's policy and industry's response to it. He believed that some radically new strategy was needed to break the vicious cycle of economic decline. He was a man who firmly believed in seizing adversity by the horns and wrestling it into submission. He was also motivated by a deep sense of commitment to the thousands of people who depended on him for their livelihood and very survival. When Bata addressed the conference, he did not strike the familiar refrain demanding government action. Rather, he called on the business community to act courageously for its own preservation. He ended his speech with a dramatic announcement that startled the entire gathering. Bata refused to lay off a single worker. He chose instead to seize the initiative and act decisively. The first necessity was to stimulate market demand. "Gentlemen," he said, "we are going to cut the prices of our shoes in half and we are going to sell them for half the present price."[6] Bata's announcement brought a hushed silence, which was followed by squeals of derisive laughter. He was dismissed as a lunatic or a fool. How could a company cut its prices by 50 percent and survive? How could it ever repay its creditors by lowering prices?

Bata returned to Ziln and explained his radical decision to his employees. It was the only possible solution to save the company and preserve their jobs. All costs had to be reduced to the absolute minimum. Waste of all description had to be completely eradicated. Efficiency and productivity had to be raised to much greater levels. He imposed across-the-board 40 percent wage cuts for all employees, despite the opposition of a powerful union, but he promised to supply all workers and their families with food, clothing, and other necessities at half the present price to ensure their maintenance. He divided his factory into profit centers and promised incentives for higher productivity. Having put his internal operations on a war footing, Bata launched a national poster advertising campaign depicting a huge fist crushing the Czech word *drahota*, which represented the high cost of living.

The public response was overwhelming. Shoe stores that had been languishing for months were suddenly invaded by mobs of people seeking an affordable pair of shoes. Police had to be called in to restore order and regulate traffic. Orders poured into the warehouses until they were almost empty of stock. The workshops were geared up to full production capacity. Within a week, the sense of uncertainty and despair was replaced by one of urgency, excitement, and purpose. In the coming months Bata not only maintained full employment but actually started to expand. He continuously introduced improved production techniques, administrative systems, and employee incentives to increase productivity.

Over the next five years, employment in Bata's factories more than doubled, and production multiplied 15-fold. Between 1922 and 1932 the average retail price of Bata shoes fell by 82 percent, while wages in Bata factories rose by 200 percent. Like Henry Ford, Bata succeeded in producing so efficiently that a former luxury became accessible to the masses for the first time. By 1928 Bata operated the largest tanneries, shoe-making factories, and shoe machinery industry on earth. Czechoslovakia led the world in footwear exports, and the Czech people were the best shod in Europe.

During this period Bata succeeded in releasing enormous energies latent within his small company and in tapping equally great energies from the world around him. He was a man who knew how to mobilize some of the infinite powers of an organization.

Levels of Energy Utilization

If you look at various companies in any field, you can see how much they differ in their capacity to mobilize and harness the human resources at their disposal. Some waste a large portion of their energies by internal conflicts, pursuit of goals that turn out to be dead-end alleys, inefficient production techniques, and endless indecisiveness. Others conserve their energies through rigorous discipline and systematic controls, eliminating waste of all types, keeping costs down, staffs lean, and inventories low. Still others succeed in actively utilizing available energies in a constructive fashion for gradual but steady growth. Their employees perform well. They are open to suggestions and new ideas. They make every machine and system yield its maximum. Then there are those companies that expand at a very rapid pace by constantly releasing latent energies from within the organization and drawing fresh energies from outside. They enthuse their workers to make extraordinary efforts. They offer employees constant opportunities to acquire new skills and take on greater responsibility. They draw inspiration and ideas from their customers, attract the best talent in the field, and are sought after by investors.

At the pinnacle of corporate life are those companies that have discovered the secret of fashioning the human resources of which they are composed into an integrated and cohesive living organization. They have evolved to their present position through a long process of trial and error under the leadership of a few dynamic individuals who have imposed the imprint of their own dynamism and enthusiasm on the company. These companies utilize the energies at their disposal with consummate *skill* and constantly seek to develop new skills so that latent talents can emerge. They channel these highly skilled energies through carefully designed *systems*. These systems are precisely coordinated with each other and perfectly integrated with the structure and functioning of the *organization*. The organization acts like an optical lens to focus all these energies for the fulfillment of the company's central *purpose*—its values, mission, and objectives.

Intense Crises and Opportunities

Every individual and every company have known periods when their energies reached peak levels of intensity. Such periods may come in response to a severe crisis, as the economic conditions in Czechoslovakia did for Tomas Bata and his company. During a crisis every drop of energy is mobilized to cope with the danger and ensure survival. When Chrysler Corporation found itself at the edge of the precipice in 1979, the threat of impending catastrophe released a great reservoir of pent-up energies from within the organization and brought forth unexpected reserves of support from suppliers, labor unions, bankers, and governments. Lee Iacocca was able to mobilize and utilize all these available energies for a dramatic revival of the company.

Peak periods of intensity also occur in response to the opening up of new opportunities in the environment. In 1978 such an opportunity thrust itself on Merck, the most admired pharmaceuticals company in the United States, according to three successive *Fortune* surveys.

The largest drug companies launch a major new product about once in two years and spend the remaining time promoting its use. But in 1978 Merck Sharp & Dohme, the United States prescription-drug manufacturing and marketing division of Merck & Company, Inc., found that three major new products would be ready for introduction at virtually the same time. Rather than delay the introductions to provide more time for preparations, MSD decided to launch all three products within a period of 90 days, and it mobilized all its energies, talents, and resources for the effort.

.

No pharmaceuticals company had ever introduced three major products in three different therapeutic areas in such a short time. MSD's professional representatives set industry records in taking information on the new drugs to U.S. physicians. The company's representatives traveled more than 5 million miles in nine weeks. In the first week they called on 90 percent of all the opthalmologists in the United States—some 9,000 of them—to present the first of the three products, "Timoptic." The operations department worked round the clock in 12-hour shifts, six days a week for almost three months to prepare 2.5 million special dispensers for that drug. In order to launch the second product, "Clinoril," more than 110 million packaged tablets had to be prepared within a little over a month. Measured by the number of prescriptions filled in the first two months alone, it was the fastest-selling new prescription drug introduced in the United States in 20 years. During the third month, MSD representatives met over 50,000 physicians to discuss the new broad-spectrum antibiotic "Mefoxin." In addition, 3.2 million pieces of promotional literature were printed and distributed for the three drugs in 61 days—a process that normally takes 90 days for a single new product.

What was the result of Merck's intensive effort? Six years later Timoptic is one of the world's leading medications for the treatment of glaucoma, Clinoril is one of the most widely used drugs for the treatment of arthritic conditions, and Mefoxin is the largest-selling antibiotic in the United States.

Intense Challenges

Some companies do not wait for a crisis or an opportunity to generate maximum intensity. They consciously induce and maintain peak levels of intensity by setting goals or accepting challenges that can be achieved only by a constant, all-out effort. Milwaukee has never been regarded as a very exciting place to live. Nor is the life insurance industry thought of as a very exciting field. Nor would it appear that there could be anything very exciting about a life insurance company in Milwaukee that calls itself "The Quiet Company." Yet appearances can be deceptive.

There is something exciting about life at 128-year-old Northwestern Mutual, the nation's tenth largest life insurance company, which ranks first in the industry by almost every performance criterion other than size. It is the most admired in its field according to *Fortune*'s surveys of corporate reputations in 1983, 1984, and 1985. *Best's Review* rates it first among the 71 largest life insurance companies year after year on a variety of technical criteria. The largest business enterprise in Wisconsin, with $16 billion in assets, in 1984 Northwestern Mutual earned nearly $1.2 billion on its investments. Yet it remains restless and ambitious even at this ripe old age and is never quite satisfied with its achievements.

In 1984 Northwestern Mutual set a goal for itself that generated waves of excitement throughout the company and its 4,500-person agency field force and caused a few ripples in the rest of the industry as well. In January of that year, Northwestern Mutual's president and CEO, Donald Schuenke, announced what he termed the "$100 billion challenge." He called on the employees and agents to raise the value of the company's in-force insurance policies from $93 billion to $100 billion before the July annual meeting. To accomplish this goal, the firm would have to accelerate new-policy issues by roughly 30 percent during this period, which would require a dramatic increase in sales as well as in all the administrative paperwork involved in evaluating and issuing policies. For a company that was already the most productive among industry leaders in terms of amount of insurance written per employee and per dollar of operating costs, an additional 30 percent increase would be no mean achievement.

The $100 billion challenge demanded not only a tremendous effort and dedication but also extremely high levels of coordination between the field and office staff. "Quiet days" were instituted, during which the new-business department did not answer any telephone calls. Productivity on these days rose from the normal average of processing $78 million of business a day to $105 million. At the July 23 agents' annual meeting, Schuenke announced that the company not only had reached the target but had done so two weeks early, making Northwestern Mutual only the fourth company in the industry to cross the mark of $100 billion of individual life insurance coverage.

A Celebrated Challenge

A far cry from quiet Milwaukee, with its Germanic work ethic and traditional conservatism—until a few years ago, drinking coffee (except at lunch) was forbidden at Northwestern Mutual—there is another company where creating challenges to generate intensity has become a way of life. On April 24, 1984, San Francisco's Moscone Center became the focal point for a $2 million dealer extravaganza. Some 3,500 people, including 2,000 North American dealers and 1,500 sales reps and software and peripheral-product developers plus members of the press, gathered for the launching of Apple's new IIc computer, amid flashing lights, stereo music, stirring speeches, and hoopla. And as if all that were not intense enough, the celebration was perfectly timed to coincide with an earthquake that registered 6.2 on the Richter scale.

The IIc introduction formed part of a carefully conceived and well-executed strategy, which Apple calls "event marketing" and which involves such functions as sales support, public relations, software development, and so on. Besides the excitement, the Moscone event also generated 50,000 orders for the Apple IIc, making it one of the most successful single product introductions in the history of the computer industry. Like the "$100 billion challenge," "Apple II Forever" was an attempt to release energy and channel it into productive work.

Apple has accomplished its meteoric rise by capturing the imagination of the American people with a unique combination of sophisticated technology and an almost playful people-orientation, which the company's logo—a rainbow-colored apple with a bite taken out—calls to mind. Apple's real strength is its appeal to a vision of the future in which people and machines can live harmoniously and happily together. The Moscone event was designed to release the enthusiastic energies of Apple's staff, sales channels, and third-party developers of software and peripherals.

Event marketing at Apple is far more than a mere publicity stunt. It is clearly attuned to the realities of a highly competitive, rapidly changing market where limited retail shelf space has forced a narrowing of the field to a few major brands and failure to become a total success may be tantamount to total failure. A highly motivated and directed workforce and an enthusiastic customer base are critical not only to growth but even to survival in this industry. Event marketing is "a way that we can all focus on what we have to accomplish internally within Apple to make it happen." says Del Yocam, executive vice-president of the Apple II Division; "and it's also a way that we can bring all of the external forces together—our dealer base and rep firms, vendors, press, and analysts." Apple is consciously releasing and focusing energies, internally and externally, for its growth.

Intensity Versus Excitement

While acknowledging the success of Apple's strategy, we must be careful not to confuse focused intensity with agitated excitement. Corporate intensity is a rich, highly productive atmosphere based on alert, brisk, harmonious physical functioning, supported by dynamism, enthusiasm, cooperation, and expansiveness, in pursuit of clear values and objectives, whereas an effervescent excitement is a high-pitched, short-lived burst of undirected energy, basically unstable and unproductive, a form of feverish movement that shoots up rapidly and later crashes down. It is the intensity of destruction. For lasting achievement, excitement must be transformed into productive energy and institutionalized as corporate intensity.

Effervescent energy and agitated excitement are a common response to the sudden expansion of new markets, such as the explosive growth in demand for video games between 1979 and 1982, when profits grew by 600 percent, or the nearly tenfold growth in the personal computer market from 1980 to 1983. When the market suddenly opens up like this, hundreds of companies rush forward to share in the windfall. The number of American personal computer makers doubled to over 200 between 1981 and 1983.

During the initial period of expansion, demand far exceeds supply, customers clamor for the product, sales boom, and profits soar for every company that happens to be in the field. Activision, Inc. began manufacturing video game cartridges in 1979 with $700,000 in capital and by 1982 had sales of over $60 million. Apple, which had assets of $5,309 at the beginning of 1977, had a stock market value of $1.79 billion by the end of 1980. Intoxicated by fantastic predictions of exponential growth of demand, exhilarated by the rapidity of their rise, companies hurry to grab a larger share of the profits and work with desperate speed to produce and sell more than the competition, without thought for the morrow.

During this phase the customer will buy anything he or she can lay hands on, regardless of quality. Companies prosper even if their product is poor, price high, service indifferent, and attitude rude or arrogant. In the scramble for rapid expansion, most companies ignore the basics of sound management. Systems are absent or only partly functional. The hierarchy of authority is ill-defined or frequently bypassed. There is no insistence on perfect quality, since the market will take anything the firms produce. There is no need to try to please the customer, since the customer is happy just to get the product. Standards for recruitment fall, because there is a shortage of quality personnel in the marketplace. Training of workers is abridged by the urgent demand for greater production. Normal levels of cleanliness and orderliness in office and factory give way to dirt, disorder, and sloppiness generated by the rush to meet deadlines. In such an expansive and buoyant climate, even minimum levels of efficiency are enough to earn high profits. Standards are low, lapses are tolerated, and sales gimmicks work wonders.

When everyone is reaching for the moon, there are a few companies that keep their feet on the ground, their nerves steady, and their eyes leveled on the horizon. When everyone else is excited and jubilant, they remain calm and keep their heads. At a time when even the minimum is enough, they insist on giving their maximum. These few exceptional companies understand that those who take temporary advantage of temporary movements will be temporary companies. They go out of their way to please the customer, even when it is not required to make the sale. They strive to develop the best technology, and they insist on quality, even when the market neither demands it nor rewards it by a higher price. They continue to display courteous behavior during the pressure of heavy work. They try to maintain prompt payment schedules, even when suppliers are fighting with each other to sell them goods on any terms. They take pains to carefully build up their organization, even though it distracts them from production to meet waiting demand. They insist on systematic functioning through appropriate channels, despite the temptation for urgent on-the-spot personal management by the CEO. They maintain high standards of cleanliness and orderliness, as if they were in no big hurry. They recruit their staff with great care, even if it means taking on fewer new hands. They refuse to abridge the training process to catch a few extra worker-days for production. These companies make an enormous psychological effort to adhere to the basics when others are rushing after gold. They work extremely hard and methodically, expending more energy than the situation demands, and this effort creates the foundation for corporate intensity.

When the period of mushrooming growth is over, when sales peak and begin to decline and prices start to drop, when the giant corporations in the field move in to take over from the hundreds of small fries, companies begin to fall as rapidly as they rose. The effervescent ones disappear. The excited ones totter. Those that ignored quality find no market. Those that ignored the customer find they have none. Those with low efficiency cannot compete at a lower price. When, like the South Sea bubble, the boom starts to collapse, companies scramble for survival. They cut production, reduce prices, discharge staff, close facilities, introduce countless gimmicks and giveaways to get rid of swelling inventories. This is 1983 for the video game industry, when Atari, Inc. lost half a billion dollars and cut its payroll by 30 percent, when Mattel Inc.'s electronics division lost around $400 million and pushed the entire company close to bankruptcy before Mattel sold it off, when the Timex Group Ltd. slashed prices on its personal computer by 50 percent and still saw its sales cut in half within two months before it finally bailed out of the market altogether.

Now the honeymoon is over, and only the very best can survive. Unless you please the customers, they will not buy. Unless your quality is high, the product does not sell. Unless operating costs are low, every sale generates a loss. As companies fold, the competition thins out. Those that stuck to the basics during the boom find that their customers remain loyal, their markets remain healthy. They still earn profits despite falling prices because their efficiency is high and systems are fully operative. Apple survives and continues to surprise the experts, while countless others fade from memory. This is the phase when giant companies dominate the field. Growth is slow. It requires a hundred times greater energy to survive than it did during the initial period of expansion. Those companies that have been faithful to the seminal values that nourish an organization are able to survive and grow. They pass the test in a million details of everyday functioning.

During the ascending spiral of the market, when it is commercially unnecessary and psychologically difficult to stick to the basics, these companies maintain them as a religious ritual. During the downward spiral, when it is a physical necessity to do even ordinary things perfectly, these companies are able to, because the habit of perfection is already deeply ingrained. The effort these companies have made to stick to essential corporate values through all the vicissitudes of the market cycle has generated an intensity that saturates the organization and overflows on all sides. This intensity is a vast reservoir of productive power that could eventually carry the company to the top of its field.

One That Made It

Apple began in the mid-1970s, like hundreds of other garage operations, with few expectations, no resources, and no clear direction, knowledge, or experience to guide it. Yet early in Apple's career, it began to differentiate itself from the pack. In the first year it was probably held together more by "a relentless pressure" than by anything else.[7] There were plenty of the errors that youthful exuberance is prone to, but "the early gaffes were concealed by the forgiving nature of an expanding market."[8]

At a very early stage, Apple began to reach out for the knowledge and expertise its founders lacked. Much of its success must be attributed to its ability to recruit highly qualified professionals with greater talents than the immediate situation necessitated or warranted. The influx of experienced executives helped instill a sense of discipline, while the informal, unconventional atmosphere fostered innovation and expansiveness.

The dramatic response of the market to the Apple II reinforced the vision of the founders that the personal computer was revolutionizing society—and gave the company an inspiring mission around which to rally all its energies. The structure, systems, and skills brought in from outside provided a means to channel these youthful energies into productive work. A succession of talented, hard-nosed presidents managed to instill a nontraditional type of order and discipline without killing the company's idealism and enthusiasm. Within eight years a garage operation had been transformed into a publicly held, divisionalized, multinational corporation holding revenues of $1.5 billion in 1984.

Attention to the Smallest Customer

Energy is the starting point; intensity is the result. But how does that intensity express itself? It is expressed in every action a company initiates, in the smallest and least significant as much as in the largest and most important. In fact, the greater the intensity, the smaller the act in which it is manifested. It is not the grand, dramatic events— the crises and the challenges—that are the truest measure of corporate intensity. It is in the way a company attends to its ordinary customers, the way it relates to its lowest-level employees, the way it performs its most ordinary routine daily acts.

Most companies dote on their biggest customers and smother them with VIP service. Every letter receives a prompt, courteous, and proper reply. Every complaint is listened to with due sympathy for the customer's viewpoint. Every error is generously compensated. Every appointment and time schedule is adhered to with perfect punctuality. The company displays great thoughtfulness in anticipating its most important customer's needs and preferences as well as a strong desire to please in every way possible. All this requires a very great effort by the entire company, from the CEO at the top, who may have to personally call on the customer to take an order or handle a problem, all the way down to the shipping department, which must follow the customer's special packing instructions without error and deliver merchandise at short notice on a high-priority basis, bypassing other customer orders to do so. In dealing with the VIP, everyone's energy and enthusiasm are at a high pitch, cooperation between people and departments is at a maximum, the organization puts on its best performance.

But when it comes to the small customer, how many companies extend the same consideration and treat them with the same sense of importance? The common experience of small customers is that their orders are the last to be filled, their letters often "misplaced" and never answered, and their complaints most frequently ignored. The effort required to extend VIP service to the smallest customer is truly enormous. Every staff member must be continuously full of enthusiasm and on his or her best behavior. Every system must work smoothly and flawlessly. Punctuality must be maintained as an established routine, no longer a special effort. All this requires a tremendous expenditure of energy.

For C. E. Woolman, the founding patriarch of Delta, every single customer was precious. "Get me one more passenger," he was always saying. Add one more passenger to every Delta flight and you are adding $50 million in revenues a year. Jim Ewing, Delta's director of national media and internal publications, recalls that one time when he boarded a flight with Woolman, a flight attendant informed them that the plane was overbooked. Woolman turned to Ewing and said, "Jim, it looks like you and I are going to have time for a cup of coffee back in the terminal." When a newly employed executive called up Delta's station manager in New York ordering him to hold the next flight for ten minutes till he could reach the airport, the station manager contacted a flight controller who called Woolman for clearance. Woolman replied, "Have I ever asked you to hold a flight for me? Send her off on time."

Woolman's attitude toward the customer pervades the Delta organization from top to bottom. Flight attendants Chris Hendrix and Lynn Gauwitz could both recall occasions when they gave their own food to hungry passengers on flights without meal service. When an elderly disabled woman showed up unescorted for a Delta flight, another Delta flight attendant, who was just leaving duty for a few days off, volunteered to fly for another eight hours as a passenger in order to escort the woman safely home.

Keeping to the flight schedule is a commandment at Delta. Delta mechanics often assist in loading baggage to ensure that flights take off on time. If a Delta flight is behind schedule for whatever reason, any available employee, including executives, may pitch in to clean the cabin so the plane can leave sooner.

Delta's marketing division is constantly striving to improve the speed and courtesy of its phone reservation agents. Recently Delta has brought down the average time for answering phone reservation calls to the very low level of 20 seconds, even during peak hours.

As a result of such a persistent and dedicated effort to serve the customer best, the entire organization rises to a peak level of performance and maintains itself there. The enormous energy expended—or rather, invested—is converted into a constant state of organizational intensity.

Attention to the Lowest-Level Employee

At the higher levels of management, most firms maintain respectful and cordial relationships among colleagues, with people adjusting for each other's convenience, tolerating mistakes, and refraining from open confrontations. How much greater effort is required to display the same patience, courtesy, understanding, and tolerance when dealing with subordinates as we express in dealing with colleagues and superiors.

Bill Marriott, Jr., president and CEO of Marriott, says that one of the real keys to his father's success in building up what eventually became a major multibillion-dollar corporation from a single root beer stand was the way Bill, Sr., related to his hourly employees. "In establishing the culture of the company, there was a lot of attention and tender loving care paid to the hourly workers. When they were sick, he went to see them. When they were in trouble, he got them out of trouble. He created a family loyalty."

During the early 1930s, when Bill Marriott, Sr., was operating six Hot Shoppes in the Washington, D.C., area, he and his wife would frequently drop into the restaurants at off-hours to chat with the manager, cooks, and waitresses. He firmly believed that if you want to please the customer in a service business, "you've got to make your employees happy. If the employees are happy, they are going to make the customers happy."[9]

C. E. Woolman recognized from the outset that Delta was in the people business, dedicated to serving people, and to carry out that mission, the key ingredient was people. Delta's president, Ron Allen, says of Woolman: "He showed so much interest in the individual. For example, it was not unusual to find him in the hangar talking to the mechanics, just seeing how the day was going." Woolman took great pleasure in bringing his homegrown orchids to the office for the ladies.

Woolman's attention to employees has become institutionalized at Delta. Every year teams of top executives go around to meet with every group of employees in the country to discuss the company's current objectives and hear whatever employees have to say. We pressed Hollis Harris, senior vice-president for passenger service, to tell us what it is he tries to communicate during these meetings. "The main thing we are trying to communicate to our people is that we are interested in their problems and their suggestions. We are concerned with them personally. We believe that if we do communicate that, they will communicate the same attitude to our customers."

Delta considers each and every employee so important that even before hiring an agent in Seattle, the company will fly the final candidate all the way to Atlanta for a final round of interviews. Delta's open-door policy enables virtually any worker in the company to meet the chairman or president with a suggestion or a complaint. To listen carefully and consider every idea that comes from anywhere within the organization requires genuine openness, considerable psychological effort, and enormous patience. How much easier it is to just keep the door closed!

When each employee in an organization is treated and treats others with respect and importance usually accorded only to top management, the very best attitude and behavior are brought out. Cooperation, coordination, and harmony grow to a far higher level. Every employee exhibits a far greater sense of commitment and responsibility. The employees' full energies and enthusiasm are released and get magnified by reverberation. A positive milieu is built up within the organization that becomes a permanent culture of the company and a rich, supportive atmosphere of intensity.

Success in Small Matters

The intensity generated by serving the smallest customer and relating to the lowest-level employee also results from giving full attention to every routine detail of work.

Roberto Goizueta, chairman and chief executive officer of Coca-Cola, really believes that "God is in the details."[10] Francis Rodgers, a recently retired vice-president of IBM, says, "above all we want a reputation for doing the little things well."[11]

Julius Gwin, comptroller at Delta Air Lines, told us: "One of the reasons the company is so successful is that people pay attention to small details." C. E. Woolman set the tone by his own words and actions. Elimination of waste was one area where Woolman was really a fanatic for detail, and everyone knew it. When a relay tower was being dismantled, the supervisor was concerned about how to dispose of 70 feet of rusty wire that had been used as a support. He knew Woolman would not approve of discarding it. While the supervisor was contemplating what action to take, Woolman arrived on the scene and inquired how the wire was going to be used. The supervisor replied, to Woolman's approval, that he planned to sand it down and reuse it. A week later Woolman visited the workshop to ask the supervisor about the wire. The supervisor assured him that it was being sanded. The next morning Woolman returned with the secretary-general of the United Nations, whom he was showing around the premises. Woolman was pleased to find the supervisor sanding the wire himself. "It's good," he remarked, "to see people who attend to details."

Expenditure is another area where Delta is obsessed with small details. That is part of the reason why Delta has earned the title of "the world's most profitable airline." Cost control at Delta is both comprehensive and minutely detailed. All items of expenditure above $1,000 in this $4 billion company must be approved by an executive committee headed by the president, which meets every Monday. Lesser amounts can be sanctioned by a senior vice-president but are still reported to the committee on a list the following week.

Item: Typewriter rental, $95
Item: Snacks for employee meeting, $90
Item: Dishwasher repair, $309

Just how small an expenditure is of concern to Delta? Gwin says that he and Frank Chew, the treasurer, "can spend up to $25 with impunity!"

It is in the small, routine items of work that the most successful companies surpass the rest. It is not very difficult for staff members to be punctual for a conference addressed by the chairperson of the board or a sales meeting with a $10 million customer. But to maintain punctuality for routine daily meetings with subordinates is very rare in most companies. It is easy to clean factory floors and polish machinery in anticipation of a scheduled visit by the CEO, but to constantly maintain high levels of cleanliness requires a tenfold effort. Many companies reply to important phone calls and letters on a high-priority basis, but to respond to every call and letter the same day requires a highly disciplined, well-organized, and dedicated staff. Important correspondence and documents are usually kept safe and are "only occasionally " misplaced in most organizations. But how many companies maintain faultless systems for filing the least important piece of paper?

Even after Marriott Corporation had grown to include hundreds of facilities around the country, Bill, Sr., vowed he would personally inspect every restaurant and hotel at least four times a year. Don Mitchell, vice-chairman of Marriott and former president of Sylvania, called Bill, Sr., "a perfectionist of the most avid type." If during a tour he saw a few cigarette butts on the floor, he would pick them up and say, "The restaurants are filthy." Today the company is far too big for any single individual to visit all its facilities even once a year. But Bill, Jr., and other senior executives try to visit as many as possible and to continue the tradition. What is the smallest thing they look for when they visit a Marriott hotel? Fingerprints on the brass door rails, dirt in the light fixtures.

Everyone makes an exceptional effort to perform well under exceptional circumstances, but the truest test of efficiency is how an organization carries out small, recurring routine tasks. Even in very successful companies, 25 percent of routine work may not be done properly on a regular basis. If the *smallest* work at the lowest level is always to be done well, it is not enough that employees are motivated, or that supervisors are attentive, or even that middle-level managers take interest in it. It is only when top management is fully committed to perfection at the lowest level that it can be achieved and maintained. Proper performance of routine work in each department depends on proper execution of routine work in other departments to which it is related. Consistency between departments depends on the establishment of uniform standards at a higher level that are passed down, monitored, and enforced. That is why the drive for perfection must pervade the entire organization from top to bottom in order to be successful.

Companies like Delta and Marriott that make an extraordinary effort to do ordinary things promptly and perfectly raise their normal level of performance to a high pitch of intensity and release a hundredfold greater energy for growth.

Effort Releases Energy

Where does all this energy come from for investing in excellent performance and building up organizational intensity? The more energy an individual or organization expends on constructive work, the greater the energy at its disposal and the greater its strength. How does a bodybuilder build up his or her body? By constantly expending more and more muscular energy in constructive physical exercises. How does a runner build up endurance for longer races? By constantly running farther and harder each day. Every runner and every successful executive knows the phenomenon of "second wind." You run and run, work and work, until you have exhausted your last breath, and suddenly a miracle happens. A full breath of fresh air fills the empty lungs, a burst of fresh energy fills the tired limbs or dull mind. The gold-medal runner is one who is constantly exhausting every ounce of energy and constantly getting "second winds," and companies that generate high intensity are much the same.

The founders of successful companies are only rarely people of exceptional talent. But they are almost universally people who work very hard and are able to inspire others to work hard, too. They are sharply focused and highly disciplined and direct all their energies to give life to something greater than themselves.

Conclusion

Creativity, achievement, and enduring success are associated with high levels of energy. Successful individuals and companies somehow are able to release, mobilize, harness, and control these energies through an effort of will and self-discipline and channel them into productive and carefully executed work. In the process, these unstable raw energies are converted into a steady state of radiating intensity that saturates the organization. This process involves not only the physical energies that move our bodies but also the psychological energies that excite, motivate, and enthuse us and the mental energies that inform and inspire our thoughts. The intensity that results may be expressed as a dynamic power for focused action, as at Merck; a calm, steady, unagitated drive to excel, as at Northwestern Mutual; a rich, cheerful, overflowing enthusiasm, as at Delta; or a clear perception and firm commitment to the realization of a high and distant goal, as at Apple.

Perhaps the ultimate example of this state in the individual is the self-mastery, perfect harmony, and grace of ballet dancers. Compared to the energetic, clumsy, and uncontrolled gestures of children, the movements of mature dancers are poetry in motion. Every muscle of their body is under perfect self-control. The nerves are absolutely calm. There is no trace of excitement or agitation in the expression on their face or in the rhythm of their dance. Their mind is alert, concentrated, still. They are able to move from a state of tranquil repose to dynamic action in a flash, to suddenly freeze animated in midair and again resume their dance with perfect form and graceful ease. Calm, power, harmony, and perfection are the attributes of excellence in dancers and in companies.

The highest art of dancers is expressed in the gestures that accompany their movements—a slight turn of the hand, the blinking of their eyes, the faint glimmer of a smile on their lips. The highest art of corporate excellence is expressed in the smooth, graceful execution of the least significant routine acts—a warm, cheerful tone in the service agent's voice, a letter promptly and properly answered, a file in its correct place, a storeroom or light fixture immaculately clean, a genuine concern for the lowest-ranking person in the organization.

The conversion of energy into intensity and the expression of that intensity in the perfect execution of work are the keys to the achievement of enduring success. But who is to generate this intensity, and how is it to be done? To answer these questions we must first introduce ourselves to the most important person in the life of any organization—which some may be surprised to learn is not the founder or even the CEO.

CHAPTER 2

Psychoanalyzing the Corporation

Who is it that can tell me who I am?

—Shakespeare[1]

"One mark of a great man is the power of making lasting impressions upon people he meets," wrote Churchill.[2] Johann Wolfgang von Goethe was one of the greatest literary figures the world has ever known. A poet, playwright, scientist, statesman, philosopher, novelist, journalist, educationist, critic, painter, and theater manager—he was one of the last outstanding Renaissance personalities. Goethe and Napoleon were contemporaries, two giant figures of their age, both intellectual geniuses. Goethe followed Napoleon's career and admired him as the greatest mind that ever lived. But Napoleon knew very little of Goethe and had no inkling of his greatness until they met for the first time at a peace conference in 1808. Napoleon was seated at a breakfast table surrounded by guests when Goethe appeared in silhouette before the open door and was invited to enter by the emperor. When Goethe stepped in, Napoleon fell silent, full of amazement at the sight of the man before him, too full of admiration to speak. Only three words escaped his lips: "Voilà un homme!" ("Here is a man!")

We have already seen in Chapter 1 that great individuals possess great intensity. But it was not Goethe's energy alone that so impressed Napoleon. It was the beauty, harmony, and graceful majesty of Goethe's personality reflected in the radiant expression on his face. Energy is only a force—which can be used for creation or destruction, depending on how it is directed. Personality determines the direction in which the energy flows and the manner in which it is expressed. It is personality, not just energy, that distinguishes the great builders from the great destroyers, Augustus Caesar from Attila the Hun; the great emancipators from the great tyrants, Abraham Lincoln from Adolf Hitler; the great benefactors of humanity from the great enemies, Albert Schweitzer from Al Capone.

Human personality is an enigma that is more easily experienced than explained. There is something about it that eludes definition. It is that in a person which makes a unique individual. Yet although it defies description, the experience of it can be quite overwhelming. A friend of Goethe's once wrote to him of her first meeting with Beethoven. "When I saw him of whom I shall now speak to you, I forgot the whole world."[3] After meeting Teddy Roosevelt, a visitor remarked: "You go to the White House, you shake hands with Roosevelt and hear him talk—and then you go home to wring the personality out of your clothes."[4]

The Corporate "I"

Individuals have personalities; corporations do, too. "I think almost every enterprise—even the smallest ones—have personalities," says Thomas J. Bata, chairman of the world's largest shoe company. "I don't believe, even if you take two service stations, that they are entirely the same." Jim Weaver, vice-president and treasurer of General Mills, agrees, "Every company has a personality." In company after company that we visited, we talked with dozens of people, and always the answer was the same as that of Brooke Tunstall, corporate vice-president of American Telephone & Telegraph Company: "Absolutely, there is a corporate personality."

At Intel the company is conscious of a corporate personality and teaches new employees about it. "Every organization has . . . a personality that develops and evolves over time."[5] Larry Hootnick, senior vice-president at Intel, described the company as "tough, demanding, honest, result-oriented, self-critical, a little paranoid—I think you have to be paranoid to succeed in a field like this—insecure, bright, aggressive people, very fast moving." Jim Jarrett added, "spartan, non-paternalistic, straight-ahead focus, goal-oriented." Dick Sermone, personnel manager, used three terms to describe Intel's personality: "Energy, discipline, high intelligence." What about family feeling, of which we hear so much nowadays? "I don't know if I like the word *family*," he replied. "I think it's a very business-oriented environment here, very open."

We were struck by the similarities and differences between the personality of Intel and that of its younger crosstown cousin, Apple. Jay Elliot, Apple's vice-president for human resources, depicted Apple as "very bright—it's almost like an adolescent—free spirited, having great ideas, fighting this Goliath in the marketplace. It doesn't think it can't win, which is sort of incredible when you think of 5,000 people versus 400,000. It sort of has this brash attitude that it can do anything it wants. The people here love it. We're headed by Steve Jobs, who is almost like a messiah to us, a very bright young person having the vision of where we're going. It's a place where you can be free, you can express yourself and do things you've never been able to do before."

Del Yocam, executive vice-president of the Apple II Division, commented: "The personality shows itself as being young, aggressive, risk-taking, bright, intelligent. You know we are going to give it our all. If we fail, we'll fail together. But we are going to succeed, and we're all going to share in that success. We think we allude to the American dream. We think we can do it, and we all believe that. I've read in the paper that it's a cocky or ego-oriented situation, but it's not really that way from within. We really believe in what we're doing, so I think you get that kind of feeling and personality about the company."

Sue Espinosa described her first impression on joining Apple in 1980: "I didn't have to wear a business suit or anything special to establish a credibility there. Apple cared more about what you could do than what you looked like. Getting the job done, and doing it really well, and really creatively, was what Apple was all about." How does Sue describe Apple's personality? "We dare to do things that we should never have dared to do. There has never been an attitude at Apple that we're not big enough to do this, or we're not important enough to do this, or not well enough known. Somehow in 1978, '79, and '80, we were able to create a *cult*. Apple is a cult now. There is something beyond the machine, which is *magic*. I don't know how we did it, but there is something. It happened." Sue frequently repeated a word used by every person we talked to at Apple—*fun*. "It's just fun to be here. We're encouraged to have fun. Work hard, play hard. We are a force!"

The contrast between Intel and Apple is strongly influenced by the differences in the personalities of their founders and their products. Intel was founded by scientists Robert Noyce and Gordon Moore. The products it makes, silicon chips, are mass-produced and sold in a highly competitive market where even a few cents in production cost can mean the difference between big profits and heavy losses. The company operates with clockwork precision and discipline, necessitated by the

technical complexity of the production process and by competitive pressures, principally from the Japanese. It is informal and free from external status symbols. Hootnick's office is an immaculate cubicle. Not
even the chairman has a reserved parking space. Everything is measured to the nth degree—even the number of square feet that a janitor
can clean—to keep costs at the absolute minimum.

Apple, on the other hand, was started by Steve Wozniak and Steve
Jobs, the latter having recently returned from wandering around India
in search of spiritual enlightenment. It entered a market where the
customer is an individual consumer, not another manufacturer. Competition was very intense here, too, but the primary factor was not
cost—Jobs and Apple President John Sculley debated back and forth
on whether to price the Macintosh personal computer at $1,995 or
$2,495.[6] The primary factor is customer appeal. Being able to attract
the buyer through marketing was the key. Apple set out to capture
the imagination of the consumer with its vision of the future. To do
so it had first to capture the imagination of its own employees through
a combination of inspiring ideas, exciting challenges, enormous freedom for individual initiative, lucrative compensation, and fun. At
Apple "many employees see their work as an evangelical calling to
bring computers to the masses," reports *Business Week*. In the words
of John Sculley: "At Apple we have a chance to change society."[7]

Personality and Culture

What people described to us at Intel and Apple was a varied assortment
of beliefs, values, attitudes, customs, and behaviors that are frequently
referred to these days as the main constituent elements of corporate
culture. But there is something more than just culture here. The word
culture, as it is generally applied to a company, refers to "the amalgam
of shared values, behavior patterns, mores, symbols, attitudes and nor-
mative ways of conducting business that, more than its products and
services, differentiates it from all other companies."[8]

What we found was something much deeper than beliefs and behavior, though encompassing them both. Beliefs and behavior are characteristics of a living being, but who is that person who so believes
and so acts? We come face to face with what Don Schuenke, president
and CEO of Northwestern Mutual, described as "something living here,
a personality."

Every human being has a rich assortment of ideas, values, attitudes, and various recognizable ways of conducting himself or herself. The person's beliefs and opinions are influenced by education and life experience, by people met, books read, movies watched. His or her patterns of behavior also change according to the time and place, the people he or she is with, the social and work environment. But through all these changes of thought and action, the basic personality—the individual's motives, character, temperament, habits—remains the same.

Personality: Energy and Direction

Beliefs and values strongly influence the formation of personality, individual or corporate, but they are not the personality itself, only attributes of it. In *Personality and Organization*, Chris Argyris writes: "Personality is something different from the sum of the parts; it is an organization of those parts."[9] Personality tells us who a person is, not just what the person thinks or how he or she acts. Personality is the source of the energy that drives the individual. As Argyris put it, "Personality manifests energy."[10] It is also the character or will that channels the energy into action. It includes the traits and skills through which the energy is expressed in behavior and that give a distinct personal color to each gesture and action.

To the extent that the personality is developed and integrated around some central core of values and goals, it controls and directs all the available energies, channels them through its traits of character, expresses them through its habits and skills in actions aimed at the fulfillment of its life purpose. In the process, raw energy is converted into intensity. The more powerful and well integrated the personality, the higher its aims, the stronger its organizing will, and the more varied and developed its skills, the greater is the energy it can harness and the intensity it can generate, and the greater the results it can achieve in life.

Napoleon was one of the most powerful and well-integrated personalities of all time. Will and Ariel Durant describe him as "an exhausting force, a phenomenon of energy contained and explosive."[11] But energy in him ceased to be a raw, unbridled force of nature. It was tamed and trained, restrained and disciplined, made orderly and obedient by an indomitable will and a strong, unified character. He was gifted with many skills and capacities. All his energy, will, and talent were directed toward the fulfillment of one lifetime goal—the quest for power. His ambitious character developed, mobilized, coordinated, harmonized, and integrated all of his manifold skills, talents, capacities, and traits to achieve this single aim. Napoleon, as Will and Ariel Durant put it, "was the finest master of controlled complexity and coordinated energy in history."[12]

In physics the resultant effect of a physical force is determined by its energy and its direction. The force of a personality in life is also determined by its energy and direction. Napoleon had one direction, Mahatma Gandhi another. Gandhi was also a powerful and integrated personality, a man of incredible energy and endurance, but his motives and goal were quite different. He directed all his energies toward the liberation of India from British rule. Like Napoleon, Gandhi was absolutely fearless. During battles Napoleon often rode along the front lines of his army and exposed himself to enemy fire without any apparent concern. In Wellington's judgment, "his presence on the battlefield was worth forty thousand men."[13] Gandhi walked unarmed into Indian villages where raging communal warfare between Hindus and Muslims had taken thousands of lives and quelled violence by his very presence.

Napoleon tried to create a new empire by force of arms, and in the end he failed. Gandhi tried to destroy an old empire by force of words and ultimately succeeded. Napoleon, unsatisfied with being ruler of France alone, craved dominion over all of Europe. Gandhi's sole ambition was to see his country free; when absolute power was offered to him at the time of Indian independence, he turned away from politics. Both men possessed energy, willpower, and total dedication to the mission of their lives—one to serve humanity, the other to make humanity serve him. Gandhi, like Napoleon, harnessed the raw energies of nature; disciplined, mastered, and directed them with an unflinching will toward the achievement of one goal; and generated in the process an intensity of personality that inspired an entire nation and won the admiration of the whole world. These two great personalities differed mainly in the directions their souls pursued for self-realization.

Corporate Personality

Individual and corporate personality are constituted in much the same way. Both are living forces characterized by energy and direction. Direction in the individual is determined by the dominant values, motives, and goals that constitute the core of personality that psychologists call the self or psyche. Each corporation has a psychic center, too, which consists of the beliefs, values, mission, attitudes, and objectives that determine its long-term direction and short-term goals. Its organizational structure and hierarchy of authority act, like character and will in the individual, to harness the available energies and direct them in pursuit of the company's aims and objectives. Its systems, like the temperamental traits in the individual, are the channels through which the energies flow and the habitual ways in which the organization responds to recurring situations. Its skills are the means by which it refines the energies and expresses them in well-measured and precise actions. All these things together—beliefs, values, mission, attitudes, objectives, structure, authority, systems, and skills—are components of the corporate personality, which also possesses a physical body, consisting of the facilities, machinery, and other assets at its disposal.

As in the individual, the effectiveness of the corporate personality depends upon the extent to which energies are released by some powerful centralized motive or goal, harnessed by the organization, clearly focused in a given direction, disciplined by authority, expressed through coordinated and integrated systems with the necessary skills, and thereby converted into a controlled intensity for constructive action. The more developed and integrated the corporate personality is, then the higher are the values and goals it aspires to, the more powerful the energies it releases and harnesses, the more effective its control and direction of those energies, the greater its coordination of activities and skill in their execution, and the more powerful the intensity it manifests in work. The corporate personality is the most important person in the life of an organization—the person we alluded to in the previous chapter. The corporate personality holds the key to the process of converting energy into intensity.

Companies, like individuals, vary enormously in the quality of their personalities. We are all familiar with one great corporate personality that looms large today on the American scene—a vigorous, assertive hero to respect and admire, a giant tower of strength and self-discipline, a protective parent to its friends, an awesome opponent to competitors, as systematic and methodical as the machines it makes, of prodigious intelligence and varied skills, with an indomitable persistence and consistency, prudent and thoughtful, ambitious without limit, exuding confidence and inspiring trust, hard-driving, persuasive, and practical—Big Blue, the spirit and substance of IBM.

By contrast, the best way we can characterize the personality of Delta is as a happy southern country family. A warm friendliness and wholesome feeling permeate the atmosphere at Delta. There is an abiding sense of security and acceptance. There is strong pride, but it is not arrogant or assertive—a family pride based on loyalty and a sense of belonging. There is a simplicity and thrift—the executive briefing room is furnished with molded lounge chairs removed from Convair aircraft 20 years ago—yet no sense of deprivation or asceticism. There is an informality that masks but cannot conceal a high level of skill and professional competence. There is a keen practical intelligence, free of pretensions but perceptive and shrewd, that only rural folk possess. There is a deeply rooted work ethic, intense energy, and an unceasing drive for higher performance motivated by a commitment and dedication to people.

The Individual and the Corporation

The kinship between individual and corporate personality is more than just an analogy. It is a symbiotic relationship. Hal Geneen, former CEO of the ITT Corporation, observed, "All organizations, large and small, . . . reflect the personality and character of the man or men who lead them. The chief executive establishes the personality of the whole company."[14] Usually it is the founder's personality that is the dominant influence. A vice-president of IBM once said of Tom Watson, Sr., "His personality and force have saturated . . . IBM until now the personality of the man and the personality of the corporation are so closely identified as to be practically one and the same."[15] IBM's enormous energy, high intelligence, limitless ambition, strict self-discipline, serious demeanor, tough and driving nature, methodical approach, premier marketing skill, conservative social values, and sober and conventional conduct are direct reflections of its patriarchal founder's personality.

Psychologists tell us that personality is a product of many influences—biological, familial, social, educational, environmental, and experiential. Geography and timing certainly played a significant role in the development of Delta. Delta was founded in Monroe, Louisiana, in 1928. Monroe was located near the vast cotton fields of the Mississippi Valley, which served as the market for Delta's original business as an aerial crop duster, and the company has never fully lost the rural flavor of it origins. Delta's first commercial flight was in June 1929, just months prior to the crash on Wall Street. The strained financial conditions of those early years undoubtedly contributed much to its proverbial cost-consciousness.

But the personality of C. E. Woolman probably had much more to do with it than the Great Depression. Woolman came from a Scottish

Presbyterian background and had a passion for thrift and efficiency that was legendary. Assistant Vice-President Clint Sweazea still types on a 50-year-old black Underwood and fondly refers to Woolman's resistance to purchasing new typewriters. Woolman believed in spending lavishly on the customer and airplane maintenance but sparingly on everything else—a tradition Delta continues to this day.

Thrift was only a small part of Woolman's legacy to the personality of Delta. The founder bestows not only ideas and values on the company but also his or her ways of dealing with people and exercising authority. Woolman was a big, broad-faced, good-natured man with a homespun manner reminiscent of Will Rogers. He was hearty, outgoing, and gracious in public but quiet and humble in private—a description equally appropriate to a company known for its warm in-flight hospitality to the customer and unassuming management style at home. Woolman was fond of affecting an innocent, gullible, country-boy manner that veiled a shrewd mind and an inexhaustible ambition. The same informal manner, keen shrewdness, and incessant urge to excel characterize the company today.

The founder influences the corporate personality not only by his or her own traits but also by the type of people the founder recruits as subordinates. Woolman recruited individuals like himself—hearty, open, unassuming, and hardworking. Even today you could hardly mistake a Coca-Cola* executive for one from Delta—they are people of different casts. Woolman worked incessantly but told others to spend their weekends at home. His preoccupation with the safety and welfare of his employees won their loyalty and dedication to the company, released their energies and enthusiasm, and resulted in the creation of a friendly, secure, and highly productive work environment, where there has never been a strike or a significiant layoff. In the words of corporate biographers Lewis and Newton, "In a paternalistic tradition already well established in the South, Delta became not simply a business corporation but something of an extended family as well."[16]

A Southern Aristocrat

In some cases it is not the founder, but subsequent leaders with greater vision and more developed personalities who mold the corporation and

---

* In quotations Coca-Cola and Coke are used interchangeably to refer to The Coca-Cola Company and to its cola product; we hope the context will make it clear which is meant each time. In text Coca-Cola denotes the company name, and Coke is the name of the beverage.

leave the stamp of their personalities upon it. Such an individual was Robert Woodruff, the grand old patriarch of Coca-Cola, who headed the company from 1923 to 1955 and was chiefly responsible for its growth into a multinational, worldwide phenomenon.

Across town from Delta at the headquarters of Coca-Cola, we felt we were in the presence of a wealthy, aristocratic southern plantation owner with strong ties to the nobility of Europe. The luxurious executive offices—which one journal referred to as a "southern mansion," with elegant high-backed chairs, plush carpets, spiral wooden staircases, and oil paintings on every wall—contributed something to this feeling; but it went far deeper than the decor. Carlton Curtis, assistant vice-president for corporate communications, explained: "The overall culture and style of a southern institution is far more European than it is northeastern. The best analogy is the one of the duck floating placidly on the water, looking so serene and gentle, until you look underneath the water and see its feet beating away. It is part of the culture here that everything is more genteel and gentlemanly." Coca-Cola is polished, gracious and charming, sophisticated and formal—staff members button their jackets just to walk through the executive floor here, while at Delta they come in shirt sleeves to meet the president. Coca-Cola is cosmopolitan and conservative, honest, patient and reliable, extremely intelligent, highly professional, a stickler for quality, private, but still dynamic despite its long history of supremacy in the world of soft drinks. There is somehow an incongruity in this unusual blend of aristocracy and soft drinks that is reinforced by the custom of serving paper cups full of Coke in elegant surroundings, where one might rather expect crystal glasses full of champagne.

From the beginning Coca-Cola was characteristically southern. The product was invented by an Altanta patent-medicine maker, Dr. John Pemberton, a century ago, with its successive owners all having deep southern roots. Back in 1931 *Fortune* commented facetiously that "The Pause That Refreshes" was ideally suited to the South because "The Southerner exhibits an inexhaustible capacity for pausing and an equally inexhaustible capacity for being refreshed."[17] The aura of an aristocratic plantation owner can be traced back to Robert Woodruff, the son of a wealthy financier and the grandson of a self-made nineteenth-century millionaire, who bought a 30,000-acre plantation in southern Georgia for hunting and recreation about the same time he took over as president of Coca-Cola.

Woodruff was known as "Mr. Anonymous," always putting Coca-Cola in the limelight and himself behind. He was a vigorous, energetic, robust man, always very private and reserved, a man of few words, who had a warm personality and a good sense of humor. "Laugh with others, laugh at yourself, don't let anything get you down." There was nothing very exceptional about him, other than his exceptional success. One of his successors as president, who saw the company as a reflection of Woodruff's personality, described him about 35 years ago: "Bob has no particular talents. He's not a technical man or an advertising man. He is fumbling in his talk, and when he tells you something's wrong and you ask him what, he simply can't explain, though he nearly always turns out to have been right. But he has an ability for finding good men and for binding them to him, for developing in them an extraordinarily deep sense of loyalty. I am dedicated to Woodruff as to no other man alive."[18]

Although Woodruff did not assume charge at Coca-Cola until it was more than 50 years old and handed over the reigns to his successor 30 years ago, his influence was alive in company affairs at the time of his death in early 1985. "His presence is still very much felt," Coca-Cola President Don Keough said a few months before Woodruff's death. "If you look around at the worldwide Coke system, his stamp is still on the system. It is a very real one."

Coca-Cola's perennial dynamism derives partly from the energetic line of entrepreneurs in the Woodruff family and partly from the present and relentless efforts of Pepsico, Inc. to overtake the leader. But there is another driving force behind Coca-Cola's century of continuous growth to become a $7 billion a year enterprise—the product itself.

For decades the enormous popularity of the drink was as surprising and inexplicable to the company's owners as to anyone else. A mystique grew up around the product, since no one was really sure whether it was the drink itself, or the shape of the 6½-ounce bottle, or the tradename, or a combination of them all that was responsible.

Coke established an image of quality and an aura of mysterious appeal that enabled it to withstand the onslaught of more than 1,000 competitive products—most of them lower-priced imitations—that attempted to make inroads on its domain. Somewhat on a parallel with King Midas, everyone who touched Pemberton's secret formula turned to gold (except the inventor himself, who sold it for $2,300). Coke has made untold numbers of shareholders, bottlers, and distributors rich beyond their dreams.

Coke was once described as "a sublimated essence of all that America stands for, a decent thing, honestly made, universally distributed, conscientiously improved with the years."[19] But today Coke represents more than just America. This is the century of the common people. All over the world people have emerged from centuries of hard labor and suffering with a passionate aspiration for success, leisure, and enjoyment. Coke is "the common people's champagne"—refreshing, pleasant, and affordable. In every country where it is sold, it is identified as a symbol of the values of that nation.

One executive described Coke's personality this way: "In my view the personality is the American flag in America. In Brazil it is the Brazilian flag. In Argentina it is the Argentine flag. The world owns Coca-Cola. One time some visitors from a foreign country who had never been outside their country came into Atlanta, and they said, 'Oh, you've got Coca-Cola too!' It is a symbol of what is good and growing in each country." In fact, Coca-Cola is an even more dominant force overseas. It controls from 40 percent to 70 percent of the carbonated soft drink market in most the countries where it is sold—in Japan the figure is 67 percent—compared to its 38 percent market share in the United States. As *Fortune* wrote 50 years ago, "Coca-Cola is not so much a drink as an institution."[20] Coke has become a symbol of the better life in an age when people everywhere are moving up. As Woodruff liked to say, it is "the people's drink."

The symbolic identification of the product with humanity's aspirations is a key to the personality of Coca-Cola and its phenomenal success. "There is an absolute fascination that people have with Coca-Cola," says Keough. "It is a sort of mystique which surrounds this particular product. That name, *Coca-Cola*, has somehow penetrated the psyche of hundreds of millions of people around the world." Doug Ivester, one of the few finance people we met who spoke more about other things than about money, said, "The Coca-Cola business is a little bit of a religion." Coca-Cola's chairman insists, "It's more than a religion. The people here have Coca-Cola in their veins instead of red blood."

During our visit to Coca-Cola, we were frequently reminded of another company three thousand miles away that belongs at a dramatically opposite end of the product spectrum—Apple. What could a hundred-year-old soft drink manufacturer and an eight-year-old computer maker possibly have in common?—A streak of mysticism. On hearing us repeat Sue Espinosa's comment that "Apple is a cult," one Coca-Cola executive replied, "Well, when they grow up, they can become a religion, too." For all their differences, we came away with the conclusion that Apple is in some essential respect a younger version of Coca-Cola, appealing to the deeper aspirations' of people in a new age in much the same way as Coca-Cola has done since the beginning of the century.

Coke addressed people's need for relaxation and enjoyment, for relief from the nervous stress and the straining pace of modern life. Apple addressed a deeper psychological need in society. In an age when people are in danger of becoming mechanized by the impersonal machine, Apple has humanized the machine and made it not only personal but personable as well. Apple has converted the machine from a dehumanizing threat into a source of enjoyment. Apple's biggest strength is its identification with a fundamental need of modern society, which opens up to a company the possibility of endless expansion. Such needs and possibilities exist in every field and can be served by any company—no matter how small it may be—that has the vision to perceive them.

Changing the Corporation

When Coca-Cola introduced its new low-calorie soft drink in 1982, it broke with a hundred-year-old tradition by attaching its precious trade name to another product for the first time and called it Diet Coke. The same year, the company ventured into an entirely new industry with its acquisition of Columbia Pictures Industries, Inc. Then, in April 1985, Coca-Cola astonished American business by changing the secret formula of the world's largest-selling soft drink.

These moves have been labeled by outsiders as evidence of a dramatic change in Coca-Cola's corporate culture. A Merrill Lynch analyst said that Chairman Roberto Goizueta has "transformed Coca-Cola." *Beverage Digest* described it as "an extraordinary metamorphosis."[21] *International Management* ran a cover story on the shake-up in Coca-Cola's corporate culture.

Does a change of product or entrance into a new field really reflect a fundamental change in the character of an organization? When an individual changes jobs, his or her dress and actions may change—the person may shift from being a tax collector to running an orphanage—but the individual's basic personality remains the same. Changes in product line are more like the annual model changes at Detroit. The appearance and price are different, but the engine and the chassis remain pretty much the same.

Roberto Goizueta has no illusions about it. He loves to point out the degree to which things at Coca-Cola remain exactly the same. "I think that the idea of a new Coca-Cola company has been overplayed in the press. We have the same strengths today that we had ten years ago." To him, the company's diversification into pictures is a logical extension of a process that began in the early 1950s. Coca-Cola has always been a company that excelled in marketing images, and that is precisely the business Columbia Pictures is in. The entertainment industry provides relaxation and enjoyment for the mind, as Coke does for the nerves. When Goizueta first discussed the idea of entering the entertainment field with Woodruff 3½ years ago, the 92-year-old man replied, "If I were 50 years old today . . . this is precisely the sort of thing I would be doing."

People frequently change their opinions, their behavior, sometimes even the values and beliefs they espouse, but their personalities remain essentially unchanged. The same is true of companies. Psychologists have always been leery of sudden conversions, because they usually prove quite superficial and temporary. Permanent changes are most often very gradual and rarely radical. This, of course, does not mean that people and companies do not change. They are constantly changing. But deep-rooted changes are not brought about merely by a change in the goals top managment seeks, the strategies it adopts, or the actions it initiates. A company's personality is rooted in every one of its beliefs, values, and attitudes; in its structure; in the way it motivates and controls people; in its systems; in the type of people it recruits; in the way it trains them; in its relationship with suppliers, customers, and shareholders; and in the products or services it markets. Management can and must act to constantly modify, and hopefully improve, functioning in all these areas. In the short run, it can motivate people to work hard through greater rewards or greater discipline, it can shuffle managers or fire them, it can reorganize divisions and enter new fields, it can buy or sell subsidiaries—but none of these actions necessarily has a deep and lasting impact on the basic personality of the company. Institutions do not evolve by themselves. They need leaders who extend and widen their vision, who release and mobilize their energies, and help them evolve. The challenge faced by all leaders is whether their personalities are going to imprint a greater vision, dynamism, discipline, and expansiveness on the personalities of the organizations they guide in order to foster company growth, or whether the company is going to impose its own personality on the leader in order to preserve its present character.

The Great Dame

The most dramatic example of a sudden, radical change in the life of a major corporation was brought about by the breakup of the Bell System at the end of 1983. Until that time, AT&T was the largest corporation in the history of the world and the greatest corporate personality of them all.

Each of us has felt the presence of that personality in our own lives. She has been a mother to us all—kind, attentive, courteous to a fault, rich in talent, laden with skills, huge beyond conception but not overbearing, wealthy beyond calculation but not snobbish, confident of her strength and knowledge and capacity but neither arrogant nor vain: Ma Bell—for 107 years, the heart and soul of AT&T.

AT&T's personality was a natural product of the kind of people who guided its early development, the field of the company's activity, and the business environment of the day. When Alexander Graham Bell filed his patent application for the telephone in 1876, several other men were working on similar inventions, and it has never been clearly established whose was the first. But Bell and Gardiner Hubbard, who organized the original Bell Telephone Company, were the first to devise the system for utilizing this invention that has subsequently been adopted throughout the world. At that time, the only model available was the telegraph system devised by Western Union Corporation. But Bell had an even more ambitious system in mind. He envisioned installation of phones in every home and office in the country and gathering the local lines at local offices, which would be interconnected by cables. Hubbard knew that financing such a system would be impossible, so he conceived the plan of selling franchises to local telephone companies, which would raise their own capital, use the Bell patents, and pay royalties to the Bell company.

It was Theodore Vail who drew up a program to create a national telephone system interlinking all the local companies by providing long-distance services between them. AT&T was incorporated in 1885 as a separate company with Vail as its first president. Vail also proposed to affiliate local companies with the Bell organization by exchanging equity with them. In 1907 the various Bell companies were consolidated under AT&T, and Vail assumed leadership of the new firm. In the structure that emerged, a highly centralized parent organization controlled many regional operating companies on which it imposed common values, objectives, policies, standards, strategies, and behavior.

Just at the time of AT&T's emergence as the dominant force in the industry, events were taking place that very powerfully influenced the development of the company's personality. It was a time of great public outrage against the ruthless, illegal, and corrupt practices of giant trusts like Standard Oil, culminating in the breakup of the Standard Trust under the Sherman Anti-Trust Act.

Vail was keenly aware that in order to survive, a corporation had to do much more than just amass huge profits; it also had to be accepted and valued by the community, which the Standard Trust never was.

He perceived service, not profit, as the guiding mission of AT&T and established as the corporate credo, "One system, one policy, universal service." His idea was to make AT&T a monopoly that would not behave as if it were one—a "publicly owned but privately managed institution," as one of his successors phrased it. Instead of using its position to extort greater profits from the public, Vail strove to distribute the benefits of AT&T's size by giving lower phone rates to the company's customers. Instead of concentrating ownership in the hands of a few, he succeeded in creating a very broad-based ownership. He also established a steady dividend policy in bad as well as good years to make the stock attractive to small shareholders as a lifetime investment that could be passed on to their descendants. He wanted the company to be perceived as a good neighbor and succeeded so well that while the public had angrily demanded the breakup of Standard, it hailed AT&T as a responsible corporate citizen and Vail as an enlightened entrepreneur. Ma Bell became the ultimate symbol of a benevolent corporation working in and for the public interest.

The personality of AT&T was strongly influenced by the personalities of the individuals who founded it. Most of them were wealthy Bostonian aristocrats. Hubbard was a regent of the Smithsonian Institution and founder of the National Geographic Society. AT&T's conservative, respectable image undoubtedly had its roots in the cultured background from which it sprang. Vail was an outgoing and open man, who moved smoothly with others, freely delegating authority. He was the first of a new breed of managers who helped create the style of the modern corporate executive. Up to that time, it had been common to view the company as merely an extension of the individual who founded it. But Vail believed the founder is there to serve the company and willingly subordinate himself or herself to its interests. Vail was certainly ambitious, but he knew the limits of power, was sensitive to the growing public concern over big business, and voluntarily curtailed AT&T's expansion, restricting it from entry into several related fields. He was a cautious man. "I don't believe in ghosts, but I am afraid of them."[22] From Vail, AT&T acquired both the thrust for expansion and the prudent self-restraint that have sustained it over the decades.

The rapid and continuous expansion of the U.S. telephone system throughout the first half of the twentieth century generated a constant need for additional employees and qualified managers trained in the Bell organization. Employment security, lifetime careers, and promotion from within naturally followed from this situation and imbued the corporate personality with the characteristics of a secure and accepting mother. "You know, you can laugh about 'Ma Bell' and that sort of thing," said Brooke Tunstall, corporate vice-president, organization and management systems, "but nobody ever felt that their job was in jeopardy. This benign protector, the thing called Ma Bell, made people feel secure. A workplace was created where the interest of the individual could be sublimated to the interests of the company, because people felt secure." When Tunstall appeared for a job interview at one of the Bell operating companies in 1948, he was so overwhelmed by the friendliness and cheerfulness of everyone he met that he said to himself, "I'd work for this company for nothing." The same atmosphere pervaded the entire system from coast to coast. AT&T evolved into a harmonious environment characterized by highly disciplined people working in an atmosphere of trust and committed to "something that was a little larger than the company."

As a regulated company, AT&T was freed from many of the pressures of the competitive marketplace. Yet it still was able to operate the cheapest and most efficient telephone system in the world. It did this by encouraging internal competition between 20 Bell operating companies, which were evaluated and compared with each other every month on at least 100 specific measurements of productivity and quality of service.

The major characteristics of AT&T's personality were closely linked to its stated mission of providing universal telephone service to all customers in the United States. The values it adopted, the attitudes it fostered, the organizational structure it created, the standardized systems it established, the uniform policies it enforced, the type of people it recruited, the skills it imparted through training, the internal atmosphere of coordination and teamwork it fostered between different departments and divisions and companies of the system, and the way it attuned itself to be in harmony with the needs of a changing society over nearly ten decades—all these were related to its mission of being the one company that provided all telephone services to practically every customer in the country.

Whatever Happened to Ma Bell?

In the past few decades, dramatic changes in the environment have altered many of the external conditions under which AT&T grew up. The development of computers and satellite communications eliminated the necessity of one telephone system to meet the needs of the entire country. AT&T's corporate mission has become outdated. The breakup of the Bell System was the result.

After divestiture, AT&T has had to adjust to the shift from a regulated to a competitive environment. It has had to turn its attention away from interactions with regulatory agencies of the government to competition with other communications companies in the marketplace. Divestiture has necessitated a reformulation of corporate mission; a change in structure; a comprehensive review of corporate attitudes and policies toward employees, customers, and society.[23] These changes have generated shock waves of disturbance throughout the company as well as deep anxiety among employees and have helped to popularize Chairman Charles Brown's remark, "Ma Bell doesn't live here anymore."[24]

If ever there were a classic case of an organization's having to change its personality beyond all recognition, this is surely it. To those intimately involved in the process and sentimentally attached to the old AT&T, the changes appear like mortal blows falling on a dear friend. But in reality, the core of AT&T's personality remains intact. It still possesses a highly motivated, dedicated, and committed workforce, which is perhaps even more motivated than before. "The energy level is higher," Tunstall observes. It still operates through the same communications network, though no longer exclusively anymore. It still possesses the most sophisticated industrial research laboratory in the world. It still possesses an impressive array of technical, managerial, organizational, and interpersonal skills. It is still one of the largest and wealthiest corporations in the world.

It is true that AT&T now faces heavy competition in the marketplace, that its assets are diminished, that its research budget is under far tighter constraints, and that is must acquire marketing skills that it did not possess earlier. But these things do not touch the core of the company's personality. It may be true that the culture at AT&T is changing from a care-taking, secure environment to a more risk-taking, competitive one, but this is still a relatively superficial type of change. Culture is only a way of living and acting. Personality is the being that lives and acts, and the corporate personality remains essentially intact. Ma Bell still lives at AT&T.

Twenty-five years ago Frederick Kappel, then president of AT&T, wrote a book entitled *Vitality in a Business Enterprise*. He defined vitality as "the power a business generates today that will assure its success and progress tomorrow." What makes a vital business? "Vital people make it. . . . It is not to be found in things, in machines, or dollars, or material resources of any kind. Vitality is something people demonstrate through sustained competence; through creative, venturesome drive; and through a strong feeling of ethical responsibility, which means an inner need to do what is right and not just what one is required to do."[25] Certainly AT&T still possesses all those attributes today.

AT&T's greatest strength lies in its highly skilled and dedicated workforce, its ability to put service to the customer ahead of profitability as a corporate priority, and its capacity to identify with the larger national interests of the country. These are the roots of its historical growth and its incredible accomplishments. They remain intact. If only the top management does not abandon the company's greatest strengths by casting off what is of lasting value in the process of shedding outmoded attitudes, policies, and structures, then Ma Bell is virtually assured of a future as impressive and accomplished as her past.

Conclusion

Corporations are as varied in their personalities as people are. Yet all successful corporations release, harness, direct, and convert human energy into corporate intensity through one or more of the powers of personality. It may be through the power of discipline, like Intel; through systems and skills, like IBM; through cooperation and loyalty, like Delta; through service, like AT&T; through harmony with a social need, like Apple and Coca-Cola; or through any combination of these powers. The powers of corporate personality are not the monopoly of the large and successful. All of these companies had small, entrepreneurial beginnings—Coca-Cola 100 years ago, Apple in 1977. They have reached their current status because these powers are present in every organization, though often unseen and untapped. Companies that mobilize one or more of them surpass others in the field and establish a record of enduring success.

CHAPTER 3

The Heart of the Matter

Alice went on, "Would you tell me, please, which way I ought to walk from here?"

"That depends a good deal on where you want to get to," said the Cat.

"I don't much care where," said Alice.

"Then it doesn't matter which way you walk," said the Cat.

—Lewis Carroll[1]

Energy and direction are the primary attributes of personality. Energy comes from willpower and effort. Direction comes from ideas. Ideas inspire. They possess the power to release energy and channel it in a creative direction. There are several types of ideas that give direction to a company and constitute the core of its personality, its psychic center. These ideas include the beliefs, values, mission, goals, objectives, and attitudes that influence its thoughts, guide its decisions, mold its policies, and determine the course of its actions. The psychic center consists of those ideas that actually influence corporate behavior.

There is a tale from the *Arabian Nights* entitled "Barmecide's Feast," about a prince who decided to amuse himself by inviting a beggar to an imaginary feast of words. The beggar was led into a grand dining hall laden with ornately decorated covered dishes. The prince went around the table describing each dish in mouth-watering terms one by one before uncovering the empty plates. The beggar eventually caught on to the prank and pretended to eat and drink from the empty dishes. Feigning drunkenness, he then got up, stumbled across the room, and punched his host in the face.

It has become fashionable these days for some companies to publicize idealistic statements of corporate philosophy, which are essentially feasts of words. This has evoked a natural and justifiable response of skepticism and cynicism from many people who are reluctant to assume that a company's pronouncements necessarily reflect its intentions. The relationship between words and deeds is the crux of the issue. To what extent do a company's stated beliefs actually determine the way it acts?

An Extraordinary Act

When a man died of gunshot wounds, the coroner's investigation found that it was a case of suicide. The man had taken out a Northwestern Mutual life insurance policy, which did not provide coverage in the event of suicidal death. But Northwestern Mutual was not quite satisfied by the coroner's report and decided to launch an investigation of its own. The company concluded that there was a reasonable doubt about whether it was a case of suicide and paid the full value of the policy to the deceased man's family.

Why on earth would a company act contrary to its own financial interests when law had freed it of any possible liability? Such acts, numbering in the hundreds, maybe thousands, are characteristic of Northwestern Mutual's personality. They are expressions of the company's mission, which is stated in a corporate credo dating back to 1888: "The ambition of the Northwestern has been less to be large than to be safe; its aim is to rank first in benefits to policyholders rather than first in size." In practice, this means that the company is highly selective in underwriting new policies but extremely liberal in awarding benefits even under doubtful circumstances. A century-old credo, a simple idea, charts the company's course of action. But there are still questions that remain unanswered: Why? Who? and How? Why does a company adopt idealistic values and then seek to follow them? Who determines a company's guiding values? How are the values actually translated into action?

Testing Values in a Crisis

There is an old proverb that says, "Thought is the soul of act." Ideas determine decisions; decisions dictate actions. There are virtually hundreds of ideas that influence the behavior of a corporation. The impact of ideas depends on their inherent validity, the extent to which management is committed to them, and the level at which they are implemented. A real test of an individual's or a company's commitment to an idea is the way it behaves during a crisis.

Such a crisis descended on Johnson & Johnson in the fall of 1982 when seven people died in Chicago of cyanide poisoning after consuming extra-strength Tylenol capsules. A company whose products had become a byword for quality, gentleness, and the finest in health care for nearly a century was suddenly associated in the minds of millions with the very antithesis of the values it had tried to embody. At stake was a $400 million a year product and the reputation of one of America's most respected companies.

Tylenol began its rise to fame around 1975, when Johnson & Johnson's McNeil Consumer Division began aggressively marketing the product as an alternative to aspirin. In what *Fortune* termed "one of the headiest success stories in the last decade,"[2] Tylenol had captured 35 percent of the $1.2 billion market for analgesic drugs by 1982, contributing 7 percent to Johnson & Johnson's worldwide sales and 15 percent to 20 percent to its profits. When news of the poisonings broke out, Johnson & Johnson was faced with innumerable decisions that had to be made by management on the spur of the moment under the glare of nationwide media coverage. From the beginning of the crisis, the company opened its doors to the media in recognition of its responsibility to keep the public fully informed of the events. The major issue concerned 31 million bottles of extra-strength Tylenol capsules that were on drugstore shelves around the country. It soon became evident that the cyanide had been introduced into the capsules only after they had reached the stores and that the problem was localized in the Chicago area. Nevertheless, news of the poisonings had reached the entire country, and a wave of fear hit drug consumers everywhere. Tylenol sales plummeted to 20 percent of their previous level, and opinion polls revealed that 61 percent of Tylenol users would probably never buy the product again. Madison Avenue marketing experts predicted that the product would never recover.

The FBI and the Food and Drug Administration counseled Johnson & Johnson not to take any precipitous action. Despite that advice, Johnson & Johnson decided to immediately recall the 31 million bottles of Tylenol at a cost of $100 million. The company's second major decision was made a few weeks later—to relaunch the product in triple-sealed, tamperproof packages. Contrary to the consensus of the experts, within a year the product had regained 90 percent of its previous market share.

Looking back on the events, Johnson & Johnson's president, David R. Clare, remarked: "Crisis planning did not see us through this tragedy nearly as much as the sound business management philosophy that is embodied in our credo. It was the credo that prompted the decisions that enabled us to make the right early decisions that eventually led to the comeback phase."[3] Chairman James E. Burke confirmed that "the guidance of the credo played the most important role" in the company's decision making.[4]

Johnson & Johnson's credo, which was written by General Robert Wood Johnson 40 years ago, is based on two central beliefs. The general expressed the first of them in these words:

> Institutions, both public and private, exist because the people want them, believe in them, or at least are willing to tolerate them. The day has passed when business was a private matter—if it ever really was. In a business society, every act of business has social consequences and may arouse public interest. Every time business hires, builds, sells or buys, it is acting for the . . . people as well as for itself, and it must be prepared to accept full responsibility.[5]

From this belief arose the text of the credo, which sums up the responsibility of the company to its customers, employees, the community, and its shareholders. It states that the company's *"first responsibility* is to the doctors, nurses and patients, to mothers and all others who use our products and services." On the basis of this belief, the company felt the obligation to withdraw $100 million of product from the market—not only to eliminate even the slightest possibility of any further poisonings but also to alleviate the widespread anxiety arising from the events. It acted to protect the public's safety and also to bolster the public's emotional security.

The second belief on which the credo was based is that paying attention to social responsibilities is beneficial to business. Burke said, "I have long harbored the belief that the most successful corporations in this country, the ones that have delivered outstanding results over a long period of time, were driven by a simple moral imperative— serving the public in the broadest possible sense better than their competition."[6] To the management of Johnson & Johnson, the unexpected recovery of Tylenol is a vindication of that belief.

The company's actions during the crisis won the confidence of the public. One poll taken three months after the tragedy showed that 93 percent of the people felt the firm had handled its responsibilities well. It also won accolades from the press. *The Wall Street Journal* wrote of it: "Without being asked, it quickly withdrew extra-strength Tylenol from the market at a very considerable expense. The company chose to take a large loss rather than expose anyone to further risk."[7] Winning the confidence of people is not merely a question of convincing their minds that you have done the right thing; you must convince their feelings, too. A clear understanding does not create as much confidence as a satisfied feeling. Johnson & Johnson succeeded in providing both.

A Bitter Truth

On the night of March 1, 1984, the lights were burning a little brighter than usual at the New York headquarters of *The Wall Street Journal.* A news story was about to break, and the editorial staff was carefully examining the facts as they came in, sifting substance from rumor, trying to arrive at the truth. The largest-selling newspaper in America, published by one of the most admired companies in the country, which over the last ten years has earned an average 26.3 percent return on equity (second best in the United States), a close observer of the business world, a relentless seeker after the secrets of corporate failure and success—perhaps the *Journal* has learned more from watching others than it reveals to its readers. Its appeal is not the alluring excitement of sensationalism and scandal but, rather, authoritative and factual reporting backed by integrity, reliability, and a commitment to the highest ethical standards of journalism.

But on this particular occasion, the big story *was* a scandal, and the subject of investigation was the *Journal* itself. That day the Securities and Exchange Commission had notified the *Journal* that one of its reporters for the "Heard on the Street" column, R. Foster Winans, was under informal investigation for periodically leaking market-sensitive information to a stock trader that may have affected trading in the shares of 21 companies.

At stake was the *Journal's* most precious possession—its reputation for integrity and impartiality. It had to make a difficult choice—to chase after the story and reveal all of the facts or to hide behind the screen of legal precedents that provide journalists with a certain degree of immunity from public scrutiny. The *Journal* made its decision immediately. The next morning it came out with a feature article on market leaks, in which it disclosed the SEC investigation of Winans. A few weeks later, after the first round of investigations was over, it published a front-page article headlined "Stock Scandal" in which it revealed all available information on Winans and the investigation. Meanwhile, Winans had been fired.

The extent of the *Journal's* openness and cooperation with the SEC evoked both praise and anxiety from other newspapers. An editor of *The Washington Post* was quoted as saying, "The *Journal* has done a fine job of reporting the story."[8] A *New York Times* columnist suggested that the *Journal* may have actually been too open, when it provided even personal records and reporters' notes to the SEC. "Does the *Journal's* cooperation with the SEC investigation jeopardize First Amendment guarantees of a free press?"[9] But the *Journal* remained adamant in its decision to reveal all the facts. Dow Jones Chairman Warren Phillips explained the idea behind the *Journal's* actions: "The only consideration in our coverage was what we owed our readers. We felt we had an obligation to give all the facts in precisely the same way we do when wrongdoing occurs at other institutions. . . ."[10]

These two incidents do not prove that companies always act in the public interest. But they do illustrate how a company's central beliefs give direction to the decisions and actions of top management during a crisis. Such crises are, of course, rare. Of more practical importance is the impact of a company's central ideas on its normal day-to-day functioning.

An Honest Merchant

One corporation that has become renowned for living up to its word is Sears. The most striking characteristics of Sears are its size and its plainness. With 798 retail stores and 2,389 catalog-sales centers, with 60 million Sears credit card holders representing half of all American families, with nearly 450,000 employees worldwide and almost $39 billion in annual sales, the company is gigantic and possessed of enormous reserves of vitality.

Yet, in spite of its size, Sears is somehow very ordinary. The company is still grounded in the simple values and levelheaded common sense of middle America's rural heartland, and this is by far its greatest strength. As the corporate director of human resources, Mary Kay Kennedy, put it: "We are about as U.S.A. America as anybody can be." Sears' personality is rooted in values like utility, reliability, consistency, and worth. Its patient, unpretentious, nonaggressive demeanor has often misled people, especially sophisticated northeasterners, into seriously underestimating its capabilities and intelligence. But Sears is not lacking in either, as its remarkable history amply demonstrates and its present diversification into financial services will undoubtedly confirm.

One thing nobody doubts about Sears is its integrity. Just before the turn of the century, Julius Rosenwald introduced a policy at Sears that was highly instrumental in the growth of the fledgling mail-order business into the largest retailer in the world. That policy, which can be found printed in bold letters above the front door of every Sears store in the country, reads "Satisfaction Guaranteed or Your Money Back." There is nothing very high-sounding about this policy today, primarily because Sears popularized it so widely over the decades that most major department store chains have been forced to adopt something similar—at least in words, if not in practice. But in 1895 such an idea was far from common.

When Rosenwald joined the company, he found that Richard Sears, the founder, had quite a penchant for poetic license in advertising his wares. At a time when the company was barely known outside of Chicago, Sears emblazoned the cover of his catalog with the modest claim: "Cheapest Supply House on Earth. Our Trade Reaches Around the World." The catalog included obesity powders to get rid of superfluous fat and a hair restorer—hardly products any company would like to back by a guarantee. Rosenwald recognized that in order to win the confidence of conservative and skeptical farmers living in the rural areas, the catalog had to be factual. He curbed Sears' literary impulses, introduced clear, factual descriptions of each product, and established the famed policy.

The policy itself is based on two values—the value of trust and the value of reliability. It says, in effect, that Sears is a company you can trust because it sells reliable, quality merchandise. The idea of a trustworthy and reliable merchant is certainly appealing. But the power of the idea arises from the fact that it has been converted into a policy that is enforced.

A few years ago a man walked into the Sears store at Wayne, New Jersey, with an old beer carton containing some five- to ten-year-old Craftsman tools and asked the service counter representative to replace them because they were rusty. The service representative called over the store manager, Bill Collett, to speak with the customer. The man explained that he had just moved to another house and in the basement he found these tools, which had obviously been abandoned by the previous owner of the house. He saw that they were Sears' Craftsman tools, which he knew carried a lifetime guarantee. Since they had rusted, he had come in to exchange them. Collett was a little stupefied by the customer's request, but after ascertaining that the man was both serious and adamant, he exchanged the tools for new ones.

Hatchets with smashed heads that are sold with clear instructions not to use them as hammers, broken screwdrivers that have been used as crowbars, shoes that are nearly worn out, even furniture purchased six months earlier—all are brought back to the Wayne store for adjustment. Collett says that in 24 years he has never refused an adjustment to a customer.

Sears' money-back guarantee is not just a policy enforced by the manager in extreme circumstances. It is communicated down the line from manager to the sales floor and to customer service as a guideline for everyone to follow. Mike Minetti, who had been working as a sales clerk at the Wayne store for only six months, could recall installing entire kitchens for customers exactly according to the specifications of a written contract and approved plan, then ripping them out and changing things around at no extra charge because the customer was not happy with the layout. "The bottom line with Sears is that if the customer is not happy—even when the conditions of purchase are explicit and clear—satisfy him."

Employees carry out the Sears policy even when they know the customer is taking unfair advantage of the company. Since the policy is clearly written above the door, there is no alternative but to comply. Kim Newburg, a college student and part-time customer-service representative at the Wayne store, says: "The company wants us to make sure the customers are satisfied and they get whatever they need. . . . We take back almost anything, even if there is no receipt, even if it is the customer's fault. We take back clothing, even if it is a year old."

Many companies have liberal return policies, but few have converted the ideas of trust and reliability into a living tradition that is transmitted from management to part-time hourly workers and translated into practice on a daily basis in stores all over the country. According to a recent article in *Time*, much of the positive feeling toward Sears even today is a result of this policy. "Sears will take almost anything back, for almost any reason" and "sometimes get taken itself in the process of taking back goods. . . . At a time when many companies cannot resist the temptation to take the money and run, Sears continues to show how to succeed in business by really trying."[11]

Edward Brennan, Sears' president, explained the significance of the policy this way:

> Most companies will be very quick to give the customer his money back on a $2 tie. If it's a $20 shirt, most retailers will be fairly quick to give the money back. If it's a $200 lawn

mower, many companies will take care of that. If it is a $2,000 central air conditioner, then there are fewer that are going to be responsible. And if it is a $20,000 remodeling of a house, there are not very many *at all*. It is the principle of the thing. I've never seen the profit and loss account of a store significantly impacted in a negative way by a liberal adjustment policy. It also brings in more customers, no question about it. It is the spirit that has created that reputation for integrity.

A Pragmatic Idealist

Johnson & Johnson has a credo that guided the decisions of its top management during a crisis. Sears has a policy based on certain values, which it communicates to its employees and which serves as a guideline for their conduct in the day-to-day operation of the business. These are two different levels or expressions of value implementation. At Merck Sharp & Dohme, we found another.

Values were not the first thing we thought of when we visited MSD's facilities at West Point, Pennsylvania. There was a cool air of military discipline about the place as we struggled to pass through security and were rushed along to our first meeting. Merck has a strong, assertive personality, highly professional, hard-driving, very intelligent. It has a systematically organized character, undoubtedly a legacy from the company's founder, George Merck, whose family had run a pharmacy and drug-manufacturing business in Germany for more than two centuries prior to his move to the United States in 1891.

This first impression hardly prepared us for what we encountered during our meeting with John Lyons, a former president of MSD who has since been promoted to executive vice-president of Merck & Company, Inc. In fact, we were quite taken aback as Lyons waxed eloquent on the value of integrity. He believes that the company's credibility with physicians is one of the most important factors in its success:

> The key to our productivity is our credibility. It can take years to build it, and it takes just an instant to destroy it. If the sales force asks what they should really be doing, I tell them: "You should just make believe that your mother is the next patient to be diagnosed by the physician. How would you like the physician to be informed about the product? You want to make sure the physician understands when

not to use the product; or if they are going to use it, you want to make sure that the side effects, if any, are understood by the patient."

Quite frankly, we did wonder for a while whether we were being treated to a Barmecide feast like the beggar. But all doubts were very soon dispelled. Lyons warned us not to take his word for it. What we discovered was that his obsession with credibility was only one expression of the company's preoccupation with integrity. At MSD credibility is not just an idea or even a policy. It is a value that has been converted into a top-priority goal to be pursued at every moment in every department at every level of the company.

Credibility at MSD starts with training. The professional representatives who meet physicians to present information on new drugs are inculcated from the first day of training with the doctrine of "fair balance." *Fair balance* means that the representative must present the strengths and the weaknesses of each product in an absolutely objective manner, with no exaggeration of positive claims about a drug and no understatement of its side effects. Eugene McCabe, vice-president of marketing, explained: "From the very beginning we explain to the representative that it is in his or her interest and our interest and the patient's interest and the doctor's interest that we be very, very much aboveboard, that we present things in a balanced way, and then we drill them on this."

Credibility begins with training, but it does not end there. The representatives are also evaluated monthly on the fair balance of their presentations to physicians, and this is one of the criteria for determining their performance ratings. A recent study by Scott-Levin Associates found that MSD's representatives scored highest among all major U.S. pharmaceuticals firms on the quality of their presentations to physicians.

MSD also has a rigorous system for ensuring that all literature presented to the medical community passes the test of fair balance. Every single communication that is sent out of the company—including letters to physicians, sales bulletins to representatives, and prescribing information contained in the drug package—must first be cleared by one of the half-dozen medical-legal review boards, each consisting of a lawyer who reports to corporate headquarters and a physician who reports to the research division. Representatives are not even permitted to write out a note at the doctor's office containing any product information. "That's strictly forbidden," says McCabe, because "we must have trust among the medical profession that what we tell them is truthful and honest."

Maintaining and enhancing credibility at Merck is not just the responsibility of the review boards or the training department. It starts with the CEO and includes just about everybody. Every manager at Merck is responsible for preserving the image and credibility of the company and for everything that is done by those who work under him or her. Managers have to be informed and alert regarding every detail. "Details are important in this business," says McCabe, "because it is in the little details that you can get in trouble. It is little facts, overlooking little things, which can hurt patients." In addition to the responsibility of managers, there is also an intense peer pressure from colleagues to maintain the company's high standards.

Merck does not have a high-sounding credo to draw inspiration from, but most people trace the origin of its insistence on integrity to the founder's son, George W. Merck, who became president of the company in 1925. Merck once said, "We try to remember that medicine is for the patient. We try never to forget that medicine is for the people. It is not for the profits. The profits follow, and if we have remembered that, they have never failed to appear. The better we have remembered it, the larger they have been."[12]

Those words were spoken in 1950. To what extent have they proved true since then? According to John Huck, chairman of Merck & Company, Inc., "every time." In the midsixties the firm started putting an extra emphasis on its obligation to the community and on fair balance. This coincided with a period of rapid growth that took the company from sixth in the industry to its present position as No. 1. As MSD's president, Doug MacMaster, put it: "It made good sense to be ethical. To tell the full truth about your product makes you all the more believable. Our success in selling is really based on very good products and having tremendous credibility." The company's integrity has earned it not only the confidence of the doctors but the loyalty of its own employees as well. As one executive commented: "It is very, very nice to work for a company in a marketing job where the underlying philosophy is to be as honest as you possibly can with the customer. That is a nice thing, because I think it is the right thing to do."

Value implementation at Merck is based on a lofty idea, to which top management has very seriously committed itself. This idea has been translated into a formal program that includes a clear statement of policy, explicit standards for conduct, training, and a series of systems designed to control, monitor, and evaluate behavior to ensure that it is consistent with the value. Responsibility for value implementation goes right down the line and is reinforced by pressure from peers.

Safety Pays

The most powerful corporate values are not the ones that are preached and practiced by top management. They are the ones that penetrate through all the layers of the organization down to the bottom, where they are implicitly followed, often unconsciously.

When Eleuthère du Pont immigrated to America from revolutionary France in 1790, he had to abandon the property and privileges of his aristocratic past. But he did carry with him two valuable assets—a technology and an idea. The technology was for making the best gunpowder in the New World. Du Pont established a gunpowder factory alongside the Brandywine River at Wilmington, the seed for what is today the seventh largest industrial company and most admired chemicals producer in the United States. Du Pont's formula for gunpowder is no longer valuable, since the company left that business long ago; but the idea he brought along with it is more valuable than ever before.

His idea is summed up in the philosophy of E. I. du Pont de Nemours & Company, Inc.: "We will not produce any product unless it can be made, used, handled and disposed of safely."[13] That philosophy expresses a very lofty idea even by today's standards. But it is absolutely incredible to think that it originated 200 years ago from a manufacturer of gunpowder, especially in the days when powder mills had the nasty habit of blowing to smithereens now and then.

Du Pont started a safety tradition at his powder mill that has long outlived its founder or the mill and become a core value of the company. He designed his first powder mills to minimize the danger in the event of an explosion. He tested new gunpowder formulations himself before permitting other employees to handle them. He established a rule that no employee was allowed to enter a new mill until he or his general manager had first operated it safely. But more than all these precautions, he demonstrated his commitment to safety by living with his family on the plant site beside the mills along with his employees.

Two hundred years later Du Pont's safety record is truly impressive. Its workdays-lost rate (related to accidents) in the United States is 69 times better than the average for all U.S. industry and 17 times better than the average for the U.S. chemicals industry. Even the worldwide rate for Du Pont's 146 facilities is 67 times better than the U.S. average. In the wake of the recent disaster in Bhopal, India, where 2,500 people died and more than 100,000 were injured due to leakage of gas from a chemicals plant, Du Pont's performance takes on far greater significance. During the past five years, Du Pont's 157,000 employees have been involved in only 253 lost-workday injuries. If the company had been typical of U.S. industry, it would have had more than 12,000 such injuries.

How does Du Pont do it? It begins by converting the corporate *value* of safety into an explicit *objective*—zero accidents. This objective is based on the *belief* that all accidents are preventable. One Du Pont plant with 2,000 workers actually went for 445 days without a recordable injury. At Du Pont safety is a line management responsibility. All managers, from the chairman of the board to the supervisors who manage groups of workers in plants or offices around the world, are responsible for safety in their departments. If an injury occurs in any Du Pont plant, it is reported to world headquarters within 24 hours. If a death occurs, it is reported to the chairman. At Du Pont the CEO is also the chief safety officer, and at all executive committee meetings, safety is first on the agenda.

The same importance is given to safety by plant managers. Every plant defines standards, sets goals, designs a safety program, and conducts regular safety audits. Training is a key element. The first thing taught in every training program is safety. Studies have shown that safety performance is proportionate to the level of training of the workforce, so training is continued as an ongoing activity. More impressive than all these things is the fact that all supervisors in Du Pont facilities must review one safety feature every single day with each of their subordinates. Every sales and administrative department also conducts regular safety meetings. An open file drawer in a Du Pont office is considered a safety hazard and attracts immediate attention.

There is also a specific set of safety-related rules. Wearing seat belts in company vehicles while on company business is mandatory. Defensive-driving courses are given to employees who travel on the job by car. When one traveling employee in Florida was identified by his manager as a problem driver, an outside driving expert was flown down from Wilmington the next day to give him special instruction.

Safety is the responsibility of every employee at Du Pont, not just managers. Rules are enforced by discipline, and violations are a serious matter. Leon C. Schaller, section manager in the employee relations department, says, "Anyone working for Du Pont knows the fastest and surest route to getting fired is to repeatedly violate safety rules and procedures."[14] The company tries to positively involve workers in the safety program.

Safety at Du Pont does not end at 5 P.M. There are off-the-job safety programs, too. According to the National Safety Council, in 1983 off-the-job accidents cost the nation $25 billion, of which $8.5 billion was borne by employers. Although it is still many times safer to work at

Du Pont than to play off the job, the company has managed to reduce off-the-job accidents by 58 percent over the last 30 years. Through special programs at some locations, the percentage of Du Pont employees wearing seat belts during nonwork hours has been raised to 70 percent, compared with a 20 percent national average. In fact, as you drive out of a Du Pont parking lot, the guard could ask you to buckle up.

Does Du Pont's obsession with safety really justify the cost? According to John Page, director of safety and occupational health, "Safety is good business." The average cost of a disabling injury in the United States works out to about $17,000. On that basis, Du Pont would have spent an additional $48 million last year if its safety record were at the all-industry rate. The company's workers' compensation costs measured in dollars per employee are about one-tenth the all-industry level. That translates into annual savings of about $30 million.

Safety pays in other ways, too. Page says:

> It is an outstanding human relations tool. What better way is there to show concern for people than to show concern for their safety and health? It pays in the protection of the skills that they have built up and in the elimination of suffering. It pays in the reduction of workers' compensation and maintenance rates and in the loss of property. Show me a manager who cannot protect his people from hurting themselves, and I'll show you a manager who is not a good manager in anything he does. Show me a manager who manages safety well, and I'll show you a manager who manages quality well, production well, costs well, too. The technique that you learn in managing safety applies to any parameter. There is a tremendous payback, and the biggest payback is in the efficiency of management.

We have said that corporate intensity is generated by perfect attention to small details. We asked Page what is the smallest detail that is considered important for safety at Du Pont. "A toothpick or paper clip on the floor is a safety hazard," he replied. At Du Pont value implementation has been taken another step further down the line. It includes conversion of the value into a policy and the policy into an objective for each facility, commitment and active responsibility by top management, establishment of standards and rules, ongoing training, systems for monitoring and enforcement, middle- and lower-level management responsibility, regular meetings, and involvement of all personnel on a daily basis.

This is an excellent example of comprehensive value implementation. Not only is implementation done through formal systems and procedures but the value has become so fully institutionalized that it is a custom or culture of the company. As a value becomes more institutionalized, the formal structures for implementation fade out of use.

An Idea Becomes an Attitude

In December 1975 a 32-year-old stockbroker, a married man with children, failed to pay the quarterly premium on his $100,000 life insurance policy with Northwestern Mutual. In spite of repeated reminders from the company, the policy owner allowed his policy to lapse. Six months later the man's wife phoned the Northwestern Mutual agent who had sold the policy to her husband and informed the agent that her husband had been hospitalized with a brain tumor. The doctors said he had only one or two years to live. She was informed by the agent that the policy had lapsed. The agent was quite upset and started dwelling on the case in his mind. He recalled a casual statement of the man's wife that her husband had been making irrational business decisions for several months, perhaps because of the tumor. The agent referred the matter to the Northwestern Mutual head office, asking if anything could be done. The company agreed to reopen the case for investigation. Months went by, then one day the policy owner's wife received a call from the agent. The company had decided that her husband had been disabled by his illness prior to the lapse of the policy and was entitled to a waiver of premiums from that time. The policy was reinstated at no cost. On hearing the news the woman replied, "Oh, my God!"

Why does a company behave in this manner? The simplest answer is because its mission says it should, but that reply only begs the question. Why should a company have a mission that states, "The aim is to be first in benefits to policyholders rather than first in size"? Partly the mission reflects the fact that Northwestern is a mutual company, which means that its policyholders share in its earnings and elect its trustees. Serving the policy owners is equivalent to serving the shareholders. But this is also true of at least a dozen of the largest American life insurers founded after 1842, which differ significantly in the way they conduct their business. As John Gurda wrote in *The Quiet Company:* "Mutual companies . . . assume lives of their own. They vary widely in personality. . . ."[15] Partly it is because the company was founded in Wisconsin and situated in Milwaukee, a city dominated by European immigrants, mostly of German extraction, and known for its ethic of hard work. Northwestern Mutual was the only one of the ten largest life insurance companies born west of Philadelphia. Gurda observed, "The roots of its character go deep into the substance of Milwaukee. . . . Both the company and the city are frugal, slow to change, somewhat complacent, somewhat parochial. Quality is more important to both than size."[16] One other important factor in molding the company's personality was the financial difficulty that beset it during its early years. The Wisconsin economy was primarily agricultural, whereas life insurance companies had hitherto prospered in industrial areas with surplus capital. When John C. Johnston, the founder, died in 1860, the company took four years to pay off his claim. Financial pressures made it essential for the company to minimize claims by issuing policies only to very good risks. While other companies were relaxing their standards for underwriting new policies, Northwestern Mutual was tightening its own.

These were the dominant factors influencing the company at the time when Henry Palmer was elected president in 1874 and drafted the company's credo. Palmer, who had been a judge prior to joining the company, was a conservative man even by Milwaukee standards. He established four basic principles that still govern Northwestern Mutual today—simple products, low expenses, high risk standards, and cautious investments. "When Palmer arrived, Northwestern had a personality. When he left, it had a character, and that character has endured to the present."[17]

During Palmer's term of office, which covered 3½ decades, the company's agency field force developed a high reputation for professional skill and an intense loyalty to the company. Northwestern Mutual's agents became noted for high ethical standards and an almost religious zeal for serving the customer, which prompted one president of Metropolitan Life Insurance Company to comment: "You can tell an Equitable agent by his checkered vest, a Prudential agent by his kit, and a Northwestern Mutual agent by his halo."[18] When the life insurance industry was subjected to close scrutiny by a Senate committee during Teddy Roosevelt's presidency, many of the large eastern companies were indicted for a variety of abuses ranging from bribery to illegal investments. About the worst accusation against Northwestern Mutual was that its management was self-perpetuating, which was certainly true during Palmer's 35-year reign.

All these factors help to explain the character and conduct of the company, but there is one more that stands out from the rest—the credo itself. Being better in order to be bigger may be considered a sensible idea by which to run a business, but being better instead of being bigger is not a business idea at all. It transcends business. It is an ethical ideal. Taken as a mission for corporate behavior, it is a goal that challenges management and every one of the employees in every activity they undertake in each and every minute of every day—in dealing with each other, in dealing with the company's agents, and in dealing with the policy owners—to strive for qualitative excellence rather than quantitative gain. The acceptance of such a goal, however imperfectly it may be carried out in practice, imposes an ultimate discipline on the company that no system of authority can match. It demands a constant effort to think always of what is best for the customer and to act according to that knowledge.

Two incidents illustrate the practical impact of this idea. During the late 1970s, rising interest and inflation rates and intense competition within the life insurance industry prompted most companies, including Northwestern Mutual, to offer significantly better protection to new policy owners than had been offered in the past. Alone among the major insurers, Northwestern Mutual felt obligated by its code of fairness to offer the same terms retroactively to all its existing policy owners through a massive, costly, and time-consuming program called Update '80. In a period of sagging business for the industry, the program helped Northwestern Mutual achieve its best year on record and to reap a rich harvest of goodwill from its policy owners. As Gurda wrote, "Update '80 made Northwestern a highly visible champion of mutuality and fairness."[19]

During 1983 the company conducted a similar amendment program that offered the owners of policies issued before January 1, 1982 an opportunity to receive higher dividends on the unborrowed cash values of their policies. This dividend feature is a part of all Northwestern Mutual's permanent insurance policies issued after January 1, 1982.

Another test of Northwestern Mutual's operating principle arose when the prime rate touched 20 percent in 1980 and policy owners rushed to apply for loans on their policies at the stipulated 5 percent interest rate. The demand for policy loans, surrender payments, and commissions rose so high that the company's cash outflow on loans and commissions virtually equaled the $800 million in premiums received during the year.[20] In 1981 loans rose to more than 30 percent of assets. Many insurance companies employed a variety of techniques to delay the issuing of policy loans as long as possible. There is a clause in Northwestern Mutual's policies that permits the firm to take up to six months to issue policy loans. However, in practice the company adopted a policy of processing loan applications on a top-priority basis within three days from receipt. It also allowed a practice by which a loan of up to $1,000 could be obtained without any delay directly from the company's local agencies upon presentation of the policy.

What type of person did Northwestern Mutual grow up to be? Our impression is of a company quiet and reliable—everyone spoke very softly, yet seemed unaware that they were doing so and denied it was according to any policy—consistent and conservative, yet very hardworking and surprisingly dynamic, honest and fair, friendly and cheerful, proud and responsible, accomplished yet ambitious, "with an almost religious devotion to excellence." There is a harmony at Northwestern Mutual between the company's employees, its field agents, and its policy owners—the harmony of a close-knit family that believes that what it is doing is good. Like any real family, Northwestern Mutual's family of policy owners is difficult to enter; but once you are inside, the commitment is total.

The most impressive thing about Northwestern Mutual is the way it translates its highest ideals into daily practice. We have already looked at companies that implement values through a strictly enforced policy, rigorous training, carefully monitored systems, and detailed operating procedures. Northwestern Mutual has all of these things, and it uses them to express several of its core values like cost control, speed and skill of service, and cooperation between office and field staff. But when it comes to the company's single most important value, which is the basis of its mission, the primary means for its implementation is none of these. Rather, it is expressed through the personal attitudes of the employees and the agents. Service at Northwestern Mutual is not—at least it is no longer—merely a policy or program established by top management and implemented through the company's operating systems. It is an attitude that saturates the entire personality and atmosphere of the company and has become institutionalized as a self-perpetuating custom or culture of the organization. That attitude influences the way all employees in the company think about their work and act in executing it, without anyone else's reminding them or instructing them to do it. It is not even the force of peer pressure that perpetuates it. It is a pressure from within each person, not from outside. Northwestern Mutual is the most mature example of value implementation that we have come across, a place where the value is actually internalized by the employees as a personal belief and commitment in their own lives. As Jere Whiteley, assistant regional director of agencies, put it: "I think the company would run without anyone sitting at the top, because everyone has their job, and I think it would run just as well."

The Ever Present Challenge

The three questions we raised in the beginning of this chapter are directly relevant to every company in every field of business, regardless of its age. First, why do companies adopt idealistic values? "The goals of a business give the people who work in it the direction they need to increase their vigor and their strength," wrote Kappel of AT&T. "Goals that excite people's imagination, and rouse them to strive toward accomplishment presently out of reach, are a powerful energizing force."[21] When we speak of a goal, we usually mean a particular destination to be reached in a specific period of time—that is, an objective. But values like honesty, safety, service are also goals. They are permanent goals that can never be fully attained or maintained but serve as a standard of perfection to strive for at every moment in every activity. For this reason they appear more vague than specific objectives but are actually far more powerful. The constant effort of an organization to realize high values in action is a powerful lever for releasing latent energies and converting them into intensity.

In Chapter 1 we looked at several different ways in which intensity is generated in a company—in reaction to a crisis, in response to an opportunity, or by a self-imposed challenge to achieve a higher goal. The highest levels of corporate intensity are achieved when a company accepts the greatest challenge of them all—the pursuit of an ideal, the striving toward a high value, the quest for excellence. The goal may vary from company to company. It may be an ideal like service to society, as at AT&T. It may be a value such as the welfare and well-being of employees, as at Delta. It may be excellence in quality, as at Coca-Cola, or in customer service, as at Marriott. Whatever the goal, the higher it is and the more seriously it is pursued and the more thoroughly it influences the day-to-day activities of the company, the greater is the intensity it generates. A genuine commitment to a higher goal is akin to constantly holding a set of barbells over one's head. It requires an ongoing, unwavering effort. It demands a tremendous expenditure of energy. It generates a steady, ever present upward tension. Yet with each step forward, the personality grows stronger. Greater energies flow in and are put to work. Corporate intensity is the result.

All of the companies we referred to emphatically insist that pursuit of higher values is a key to their success. Public confidence in Johnson & Johnson made possible the dramatic recovery of Tylenol. As Chairman James Burke put it, "We learned that the reputation of the corporation . . . provided a reservoir of goodwill among the public, the people in the regulatory agencies, and the media, which was of incalculable value in helping to restore the brand."[22] Sears' policy of providing reliable products backed by an ironclad guarantee won the trust of American farmers, many of whom later migrated to the cities and formed a loyal core of customers for the company's retail store business. Merck's insistence on factual, objective product presentations and fair balance has earned it the respect of the medical community and the No. 1 position in the industry. Du Pont's obsession with safety for two centuries has saved the company hundreds of millions of dollars, won the loyalty of its employees, and earned it the best reputation in the chemicals industry. And Northwestern Mutual? Well, the point does not require repetition; it is first in everything (except, of course, size).

In support of this, we can cite a little informal research relating to one particular corporate value—public service. The research was carried out by Johnson & Johnson in collaboration with The Business Roundtable's Task Force on Corporate Responsibility and The Ethics Resource Center in Washington, D.C. A list was compiled of those major corporations that had "a codified set of principles stating the philosophy that serving the public was central to their being" and for which there was solid evidence that these ideas had been promulgated and practiced for at least a generation by their organizations. The performance of these companies over the last three decades was then examined. The findings were impressive. On an average, these companies had an annual compound growth rate in profits of 11 percent, which works out to a 23-fold increase in profits over 30 years. This is compared to only a 2.5-fold increase in GNP during the same period and only a 5.3-fold increase in profits for all *Fortune* 500 companies.[23]

The Most Important Person

Who determines the guiding values of a company? At the heart of the corporate personality is a deeper psychic center, consisting of the company's most cherished beliefs, values, and true mission, which give lifelong direction to the activities of the corporation. As in the development of personality in the individual, the process by which the corporate personality acquires a specific set of beliefs and values is influenced by several factors—the personality of its founders, external social conditions at the time of its birth, and geography, as well as experiences and important persons that enter its life later on.

When a company is born, it acquires from its founder or founders many of their dominant beliefs, values, attitudes, opinions, and objectives in life, in much the same way as a child inherits its early value system from its parents. Marriott Corporation inherited a tradition of hard work and an insistence on quality from Bill, Sr. Delta inherited the thrifty ways and personal kindness of C. E. Woolman. External factors also influence the values a company acquires. Like many middle-aged people today, both Delta and Marriott Corporation were children of the Great Depression. Geography had a significant impact on all the companies we visited—California informality at Apple and Intel, midwestern hard work at Northwestern Mutual, and southern gentility at Coca-Cola. In addition, the experiences of the company during its formative and later years are influential. Deregulation has profoundly affected the values and objectives of commercial airlines in the United States. Divestiture has imposed new priorities and new demands on AT&T. The succession of CEOs that come after the founder leave a mark on the corporate personality as well, in proportion to the strength of their own character and the length of their stay at the helm of affairs. Rosenwald and Wood at Sears, Woodruff at Coca-Cola, and Palmer at Northwestern Mutual were far more influential than the companies' founders in shaping corporate values.

As a result of all these influences, the company acquires a core of central beliefs, values, attitudes, a mission, and objectives—the psychic center of the corporate personality—that gives direction to all the firm's activities. The ideas that constitute the psychic center are of several types, and the words used to designate them are frequently interchanged or used as synonyms; therefore, it is better to briefly define the most important of them here.

Beliefs: Beliefs are ideas or principles that are accepted by an individual or an institution as true and serve as a basis for its actions. Johnson & Johnson believes that service to the public helps a business to prosper. Merck believes that "good ethics makes good sense." IBM believes that "if we respect our people and help them to respect themselves, the company will make the most profit."

Values. Values are the operational qualities that companies seek to achieve or maintain in their performance. We do not use the word in a strictly moral sense, although ethical values may be included. There are many functional corporate values. Here are some of the most important physical, organizational, and psychological values:

Physical	*Organizational*	*Psychological*
Cleanliness	Discipline	Respect for the individual
Orderliness	Freedom	Pleasing the customer
Punctuality, regularity	Motivation	Harmony (family feeling)
Efficient use of money and materials	Standardization	Decisiveness
Maintenance of equipment	Systemization	Integrity
Quality of product, service, or work	Coordination	Loyalty, trust
Maximum utilization of time	Integration	Commitment
Optimum utilization of space	Communication	Personal growth
Safety	Cooperation (teamwork)	Service to society

Mission. A mission is the guiding purpose for which an organization exists. The mission is not a statement of beliefs or values, but rather a statement of broad intention. General Motors Corporation's mission, as formulated by its founder, William Durant, was to produce "a car for every purse and purpose." Ford Motor Company's original mission was to build an inexpensive car for the masses. AT&T's was to provide service to all telephone users throughout the United States under a standardized policy and a single, unified system.

Objectives. Objectives are the specific goals that a company seeks to fulfill in carrying out its mission in accordance with the beliefs and values it has accepted. Objectives range from broad and general to narrow and specific. IBM has a broad objective "to serve our customers as efficiently and as effectively as we can." General Mills has a specific objective to achieve a 20 percent return on equity every year. Coca-Cola's present objectives include doubling its revenues between 1984 and 1990.

Corporate attitudes. Corporate beliefs and values are the ideas that guide the decisions of top management, the choice of its mission and objectives, the formulation of its policies and plans. In addition to these central beliefs and values, an organization, like an individual, possesses a variety of fixed attitudes relating to particular issues. When the psychic center is well developed, these attitudes tend to be in harmony with the central beliefs and values of the organization. The helpful attitude of the Northwestern Mutual agent reflects a mature psychic center. The company's mission to serve the policy owners has become a personal attitude of the agent. On the other hand, in companies where the psychic center is not yet developed—where beliefs, values, and mission are poorly defined or poorly translated into action—the common corporate attitudes expressed at lower levels of the organization tend to be at variance with or in opposition to the company's stated convictions. We all know countless instances of companies that proclaim good customer service as a top priority but where the attitudes of customer-service personnel do not seem to reflect that stated goal.

The Psychic Center

In mature corporations the psychic center becomes organized around a few fundamental beliefs and core values that determine its mission, fix its long-term goals and short-term objectives, and influence a wide range of attitudes expressed at different levels of the company. Figure 1 depicts the constitution of the mature psychic center.

From Ideas to Action

Thus far we have spoken about the internal composition of the psychic center and the interrelationship between its constituent elements. We return now to the third question. How, then, does the psychic center interact with the rest of the corporate personality and impose its direction on the company's activities? How does it implement its ideas?

The psychic center provides two types of guidance to the organization. It establishes the basic character and orientation, and it determines its particular initiatives and actions. We can liken these two functions to those of the autonomic and voluntary nervous systems in the human being. The autonomic nervous system controls the functioning of the organs and systems that support and maintain life without the need of any conscious awareness or volition by the individual.

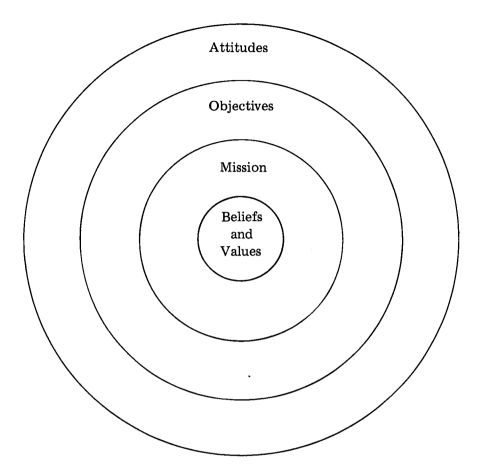

Figure 1. The mature psychic center.

This life-supporting role is akin to that of the psychic center's beliefs, values, and attitudes. They underlie and influence all the activities of the corporation but usually function unnoticed and unthought of. The voluntary nervous system in the individual controls conscious initiatives and the movements of the muscles that govern outward behavior and actions. The parallel function in the company is the formulation and execution of work according to the priorities set by the company during the planning process, based on its mission and objectives. Thus, there are two distinct but interacting pathways for translating ideas into action:

Value Implementation	*Plan Implementation*
(Autonomic system)	(Voluntary system)
Beliefs and values	Mission
Structure	Objectives
Standards and regulations	Plans
Systems	Policies
Skills	Strategies
Attitudes	Programs

The process of plan implementation is well known, but the process of value implementation has received relatively little attention and requires further elaboration.

The Process of Value Implementation

In the entrepreneurial stage of a company's growth, the founder or CEO makes a *decision* about which values are most important and ensures that they are implemented by his or her own personal effort and attention. Bill Marriott, Sr., insisted on quality in his first seven Hot Shoppes by personally visiting each facility every day to inspect the operations. At a later stage of growth, the organization institutionalizes the attention to values by the creation of separate departments to assume responsibility for each of the most important values. A controller's office is established to enforce the values of thrift and efficiency. A research division is created to foster the value of innovation. A human resources department is set up to give proper attention to employees. A customer service desk is opened; perhaps even a safety department, as at Du Pont; and so on. Each value has been institutionalized as a *structure*.

At the next level, performance *standards* are set with respect to each value, *rules* are established, and *systems* are designed to enforce the rules and achieve the standards. At first, there are many separate systems operating somewhat independently of each other—some for quality control, some for cost control, some for innovation, some for customer service, and so forth. Gradually the systems become more and more *coordinated* with each other to eliminate duplicate and conflicting activities and improve efficiency. Later, systems at different levels of the organization are *integrated* with one another to function in a harmonious manner.

Achieving values requires a variety of specialized *skills* for their effective expression. Product innovation and quality control require technical skills. Customer service and good communication with employees require interpersonal skills. Coordination and integration require organizational skills. Discipline and motivation require managerial skills. Companies *recruit* people with the essential personality traits and *train* them to impart the skills needed to achieve the values they consider most important. Merck recruits professional representatives "with a good impact, a high energy level, and an elevator that goes all the way to the top" and then trains them in the necessary skills for presenting drugs to doctors. In hiring customer-service representatives, Hertz Corporation looks for people with energy and a sensitivity toward people and then teaches them how to handle customers pleasantly, even when a customer may be angry or upset for some reason.

The highest level of organized value implementation is achieved through an appropriate structure, standards and rules, systems that are coordinated and integrated, and people recruited and trained to possess the right skills and traits. But it is possible to raise the quality of value implementation to an even higher level by creating an institutional milieu or culture. This usually occurs naturally, after a formal system as described above has been in operation for many years. The values gradually become so deeply ingrained in the people and the organization that external systems of enforcement are no longer necessary. An atmosphere of peer pressure develops that acts to uphold the value and discourage deviation. At Merck we were told that if a copywriter of promotional material ever got a little too exuberant in praising the virtues of a drug, peer pressure would immediately force him or her to retract the idea. In many mature companies the most important values have become part of the *institutional milieu*. The Hewlett-Packard Company was able to do away with time clocks and removed the locks on the laboratory storerooms because an atmosphere of peer pressure "enforces" responsible behavior from employees.

At a still more advanced stage, the individuals in the company come to accept the importance of living up to the company's values, even in the absence of external pressure from peers. They feel that it is part of doing the job right. Hard work at Marriott, satisfying the customer at Sears, safety at Du Pont have become *customs* in these organizations. Finally a stage is reached when the individuals in the company internalize the value and make it a personal conviction in their own lives. They come to feel, like the Delta flight attendants, that making the customer happy is not just a part of the job but is also a means to their own happiness. Many Northwestern Mutual agents come to believe that benefiting the policy owner is a way to make their

10. *Identification:* Relate the value to the personal growth and fulfillment of each individual, so the individual comes to identify with the value and strives to realize it personally in his or her own life.

The Role of the CEO in Value Implementation

Ideas are the starting point; intensity is the goal. Intensity is the direct result of a company's commitment to a higher belief or higher value to an extent far beyond the level achieved by ordinary companies. What is the role of the CEO in this process? The decision to adopt a higher belief or value requires a tremendous mental effort on the part of a CEO. The very thought of maintaining a commitment to full employment during the 1930s when markets were crumbling would have been enough to send most executives into a permanent "depression." Tom Watson, Sr., not only thought about it but actually decided to do it as an expression of commitment to one of IBM's cardinal beliefs. You can be sure that decision was hard work!

But this was only the beginning. Once such a decision has been made, it must travel a very long, ever widening path to be fully put into practice by the company. This path consists of simultaneous movements in two directions. On the one hand, the decision of the CEO or the board of directors must be communicated to all the other levels of the organization and accepted by them with the right attitude and commensurate enthusiasm. On the other hand, the decision must be translated into corporate policy; converted into programs for execution by top-, middle-, and lower-level management; and reduced to action plans for implementation on the plant floor or in the field.

Watson's work did not end with his decision. He had to carry conviction with the board of directors and top executives and, through them, with all the levels below. It was not only acceptance of his decision that was required but a wholehearted commitment at all levels to carrying it out. In practice, this meant that IBM would have to multiply its sales effort during the depression in order to maintain production volume. It also meant that every possible effort had to be made to improve productivity and reduce operating costs in order to compensate for the possibility of falling revenues that could not be offset by reducing labor costs, since full employment was to be maintained. When other companies in the 1930s were feeling that labor was a dispensable and disposable resource, IBM introduced programs to improve its workers' skills and output.

Watson had to inspire confidence throughout the entire organization. He had to enthuse managers and workers for a far greater effort, and he had to conceive of programs for translating his belief into action without endangering the corporation's very existence. These two movements—communication of the decision throughout the organization with an enthusiasm for implementing it and translation of the decision at the top into programs at the bottom—require an enormous expenditure of energy, a total effort, and a constant strain to keep up their momentum.

In order to fully accomplish these movements throughout the entire corporation, the chief executive must continuously increase the quantity of his or her effort. At the same time, the quality of the CEO's energy must change. Mental energy, which has converted the ideal into a policy, must be augmented by buoyant vital energy to communicate the right attitude to others and release their enthusiasm, and these must be supported by physical energy for translation of the policy into action. The entire energy of the leader's personality must pour forth and sustain the movement until the whole company endorses the idea, is enthused with the right attitude, and implements the program. The energy that is expressed as thoughts, will, emotions, enthusiasm, commitment, determination, and eagerness builds up into a pure energy of personality and turns into a simple intensity that radiates from his or her being.

The same process of release, accumulation, and conversion takes place at all levels of the organization as the movement spreads vertically and horizontally. It is communicated from one level to the next, from one department to the next, and one person to the next, until the whole company is saturated with mental, nervous, and physical energy that accumulates as a pure energy of the corporate personality and radiates as corporate intensity throughout the company.

In IBM's case, the impact of Watson's decision cannot be overstated. As one IBM executive explained it:

> It is not correct to say that we managed to maintain employment during the depression because we grew. We grew because we had committed ourselves to the maintenance of employment. This forced us to find new users and uses for our existing products. It forced us to find unsatisfied wants in the market and to develop new products to satisfy them. It forced us to develop foreign markets and to push export sales. I am convinced that we would not today be one of the world's leading producers and exporters of office machinery but for our commitment to maintain employment during the

depression years. Indeed, I sometimes wonder whether we wouldn't be well advised to commit ourselves to increasing employment constantly.[24]

That is the power of translating a higher value into action.

A Luxury for the Rich

Serving the public, maintaining a good corporate reputation, formulating a high-sounding credo and idealistic mission statement may be fine for AT&T, Johnson & Johnson, Merck, Northwestern Mutual, and Sears, but what about the little outfit? Aren't high values really a luxury that only rich, successful companies can afford? The answer is that all these companies adopted high values when they *were* little outfits, and it is these values that enabled them to grow to their present stature. When Tom Watson insisted on the value of job security for employees during the Great Depression, IBM's annual revenues were less than $20 million. Today they are 2,000 times greater. When Rosenwald introduced the money-back guarantee at Sears, the company had only $750,000 in sales. Last year Sears' sales were 44,000 times higher. When C. E. Woolman began treating his employees like members of the family, Delta's entire fleet consisted of 12 airplanes with a total value of about $25,000. Today its property and equipment are valued at 100,000 times that amount. Striving for high values is not a luxury for the rich; it is a way to become rich.

CHAPTER 4

The Living Organization

Take away everything else but leave me my organization
and in ten years I'll be back on top.

—Andrew Carnegie[1]

There are two common misconceptions about the dramatic recovery of
Chrysler in the early 1980s. First, the magnitude of Lee Iacocca's
achievement has been grossly underestimated. Those who refer to the
record $3.3 billion in profits that Chrysler earned between 1982 and
1984 are 50 percent short of the mark. In actual fact, Chrysler earned
$6.6 billion during this period. This error arises because people forget
that during the years 1979 to 1981, the company was generating a
record $3 million a day (in losses, that is)—a total of $3.3 billion over
three years. Iacocca not only overcame a $3.3 billion deficit but capped
it with another $3.3 billion profit between 1982 and 1984. That rep-
resents a net gain of $6.6 billion, or an average increase in earnings
of $6 million per day over the previous period.

Coming to the second misconception, there is an important unsung
hero in the Chrysler story. While no one can overstate Iacocca's remarkable achievement, there is another person at least equally de-
serving of our attention. In 1979 the financial experts were unanimous
in their diagnosis that Chrysler was all but dead. Has anyone ever
actually explained how they could have been so wrong? What the experts failed to perceive was the huge reservoir of vitality trapped
within the organization and waiting for an opportunity to pour forth.
One of Iacocca's greatest acts was to peel away the encrusting layers
of dead habits, vested interests, outmoded strategies, and inertia and
remove the lid on an enormous reservoir of productive energies. He

did it by firing 33 of the company's 35 vice-presidents and allowing long-suppressed ideas, energies, and talents to rise to the surface.

Where did all that vitality come from? It came from within the organization itself. It had been there all the time as an untapped potential. In the process of housecleaning and reorganization, Iacocca stumbled upon an unsung hero—the enormous hidden powers of organization.

Accounts of great human inventions usually begin with the pot or the wheel and work their way up to the transistor and the silicon chip. Most of them omit one of the greatest discoveries of all time—organization. A discovery usually brings into use hidden potentials that were previously unknown, or it creates new possibilities that were hitherto unimagined. Organization does both. Organization makes possible the productive and efficient utilization of ideas, resources, energies, and opportunities.

The Great Discovery

The organization was discovered when a leader first had the idea that far more could be accomplished if he or she could collect a group of people and have them execute work according to the leader's designs and instructions. This was humanity's first glimpse of the power of organization. In 1931 a young businessman was on the verge of making this discovery for himself. In the previous four years, he had built up a chain of five drive-in restaurants in the Washington, D.C., area and was just making plans to open a sixth. He approached a top business lawyer to close the deal on a property for the new restaurant. The lawyer hesitated. He had seen too many restaurant owners do exactly what the young entrepreneur was doing and end up bankrupt. "My advice to you, young man, is to get out of this restaurant business. Quick," the lawyer said. "I've got a lot of clients in this business, and they're all going broke. . . . Your trouble is, you want to expand. . . . But you'll never get anywhere by expanding, because then you can't control it. You can't control the root beer in eight or ten different shops at the same time. You can't control all these people who make your sandwiches and be sure that they're all up to your standards. The bigger you get, the less control you have."[2]

Had the young man accepted his lawyer's advice, the story would have ended there; but J. Willard Marriott did not. His story was only just beginning. Marriott believed what the lawyer said about control, but he felt there must be a solution. Until then the company had consisted of several restaurants run by crews under Marriott's direct supervision. The only real link between his five Hot Shoppes was Bill Marriott himself. In other words, there was no real organization. If he was going to expand further, he could not continue to visit every location every day and personally supervise all important operations. He realized that what he needed was a unifying structure to accomplish two things that up until then had been done by his direct personal supervision and management: It must maintain the quality of the product and service, and it must also encourage and motivate employees at each restaurant as he had done in the past by his friendly personal attention.

Marriott accomplished the first objective by centralization and specialization. He established a carefully supervised central commissary to purchase food and other materials in bulk, process and portion raw food into individual servings, and prepare certain standard items like soup and coleslaw for distribution to all the shops. He then hired a professional food consultant to develop tested and standardized recipes for each dish on the Hot Shoppes menu, and he printed detailed cooking instructions in a small book so that dishes could be prepared in exactly the same way each time they were cooked, regardless of which shop they were prepared in. He also developed systems to reduce the work of each shop to a set of standard operating procedures, which covered every aspect of the shops' functioning.

To accomplish the second objective, motivating restaurant staff, Marriott introduced a policy of promotion from within and performance-based bonuses, and he lavished attention on his employees. He learned to delegate authority and decision-making responsibility at the restaurants to experienced managers who had started as busboys and worked their way up in the shops. He followed the practice of never opening a new shop until he had an experienced person to run it. He recruited his employees carefully—only "good, clean-cut, decent people" who were willing to work hard—treated them in a friendly and fair manner, won their loyalty, and then entrusted the work to them. Shop managers and staff were paid annual bonuses based on the profitability of their shops.

In 1937 a crew member from an Eastern Air Transport flight stopped at Hot Shoppe No. 8 for a quart of coffee to take on the flight to New York. Soon passengers started to come by before their flights to purchase sandwiches and drinks. Before long the Hot Shoppe was supplying box lunches to the airline for service during its flights, and within a year it was servicing all 22 daily flights from the Washington airport. The in-flight catering business had been born utilizing the same structure and systems developed for service in the restaurants.

There was nothing unique or original about the organization Bill Marriott developed. It combined centralization to ensure quality control and decentralization to encourage entrepreneurship and individual initiative. Yet to Marriott, who had begun as a sole proprietor doing everything for himself, there must have been a little bit of magic in the idea that something as intangible as an organization could produce such tangible results.

In 1929 Marriott employed 80 people in three Hot Shoppes and had revenues of about $500,000. A year after Bill Marriott met with his lawyer, gross sales approached the $1 million mark. During the next 20 years, Marriott grew to include 45 restaurants, 3,000 employees, and an in-flight catering service for a dozen airlines. Gross sales in 1952 were just under $20 million. Five years later there were 75 locations, 6,000 employees, and revenues of $36 million a year. This 76-fold expansion had all been based on the simple structure and systems introduced for the opening of Hot Shoppe No. 6.

It was not money that made possible Marriott's phenomenal growth. Though Bill Marriott borrowed $1,500 to start the first root beer stand, thereafter for 25 years he very seldom borrowed a dollar more. It was not any new technology that brought this success, either. Marriott identified a need in the market for fast, clean, convenient roadside service and devised an efficient way to meet it. His success was based on the values of hard work, quality control, cost efficiency, and friendly service; but these ideas could not have achieved anything by themselves. They needed a structure and a system to deliver them to the market. That is the power of an organization.

From Hot Shoppes to Hotels

By 1957 Marriott had reached the pinnacle of success and was already grooming his eldest son to succeed him. But the organization he created had only just begun to reveal its power. In that year the company acquired its first hotel, in Arlington, Virginia. The rest is history. In the following 27 years, Marriott grew to become the eighth largest U.S.-based hotel chain in the world, with more than 60,000 rooms; the third largest server of food in the United States, with food service management operations, Roy Rogers, Bob's Big Boy, and airport restaurants; and the largest airline caterer in the world, with 37 percent of the U.S. market and 12 percent worldwide.

Something, of course, has changed at Marriott. Bill, Jr., took over from his father and has managed the company through its second phase of expansion. But the basics remain the same. Gary Wilson, executive vice-president and chief financial officer at Marriott, says: "The common thread we see running through the whole business is the origin we had as a small restaurant company and the centralized systems that Mr. Marriott, Sr., put into his first restaurants, which we really developed as we grew into a larger chain. And as we moved into the hotel business, the same type of systems were used. We have a very strong centralized management system."

The organization still serves the same two basic functions—to control quality and motivate people. Quality is controlled through centralization and systemization. In most hotel chains each hotel is run by a general manager in the style of an independent entrepreneur with little control from above. But at Marriott there are regional multidisciplinary management teams, each of which controls the operations of about ten hotels from a central office. The hotel managers work under the team, which visits each hotel frequently and possesses expert knowledge in all specialized areas of hotel operations—food and beverage, marketing, controller, engineering, personnel, and so on. This concept of centralization and specialization had its origin in the company's original commissary. The first specialist was a food consultant. Today the company has specialists in almost every relevant field. "Management has expert resources," explained John Dixon, general manager of the company's flagship hotel in downtown Washington. "It has three people studying everything."

As in the old days, quality is controlled through a set of finely tuned systems and standard operating procedures (SOPs). Cliff Erhlich, senior vice-president for human resources, summed it up well: "We are the biggest SOP company in the universe. SOPs have been our absolute survival during the period of rapid growth."

Marriott has SOPs for literally everything—even friendliness. For years we have been impressed by the friendly, informative limousine drivers who take you from the airports to Marriott hotels. It is an SOP. When the bellhop explains the buttons on the elevator as he or she escorts you to your room, it's an SOP. When the lifeguard at the hotel pool removes the "Pool Closed" signs in the morning, it is only one of 14 SOPs for opening the pool, which is only one of his or her nine major daily responsibilities. When the lifeguard replies to your question about the nearest movie theater or the best place to dine, that is an SOP, too. One hotel manager who had previously worked for another major hotel group remarked, while gesturing with his hands to show one pile two feet high and another one inch thick, "SOPs here are like a mountain compared with other hotels."

It is the same in food service. There are now over 6,000 recipe cards in the Marriott collection, each containing such clearly detailed instructions that senior executives periodically try their hand at preparing dishes in one of the company's kitchens. The card system precisely indicates the quantity of each ingredient and the size of each portion down to the detail of where the parsley is to be placed on the plate. Marriott runs its airline catering kitchens like factories. Every meal must look exactly like the others. Why? On your next flight, catch yourself glancing over to see what is on your neighbor's plate and you will know why.

The company's systems are equally effective in managing costs. Centralized systems and centralized food procurement have enabled Marriott to achieve substantially higher profit margins on food service than its hotel competitors. A very tight system of financial reporting enables management to control costs and to diagnose problems anywhere in the company at an early stage. "We make more money in the hotel business because we're able to squeeze more profit out of the dollars that we get than any other company," explained Wilson. "We are able to get more on the bottom line because of our centralized systems."

We usually associate tight discipline, systems, and controls with a rigorous military atmosphere. Yet Marriott has also succeeded in maintaining a high level of employee morale, motivation, and job satisfaction. Employees are trained to regard the systems as a way to help them do their jobs better, which is the key to upward mobility in this company, where about a third of all managers were originally recruited as hourly workers. Marriott believes in discipline, but not force. "You cannot order anything from anybody," says Bill Marriott, Jr. "They've got to do it because they want to do it. They've got to do it because they see that it's important. A lot of these people are really entrepreneurs, particularly the waiters and waitresses. They realize that they can make more money for themselves if they follow the procedures. The name of the game is to convince them that it is in their own interests to do that."

The key to the high morale and motivation is the personal attention given to employees. Fred Malek, executive vice-president and head of the hotel division, believes: "The major thing is making them feel good about themselves and what they are doing, giving them opportunities for recognition and promotion, by recognizing their good work, by giving them some attention, by not just treating them as workers, but as colleagues, treating them with respect, with dignity, treating them as partners in the enterprise." This is the way Bill, Sr., related to his staff of 80 when there were only three Hot Shoppes. The same attitude has been passed down to his sons and institutionalized through personal example. When Bill, Jr., visits a Marriott hotel, his most important work is to shake hands with as many employees as possible. He says: "We have to be friendly with our people. Then they'll be friendly with the customers."

Marriott employs a highly centralized, specialized, and systematized organizational structure to maintain uniform quality standards, keep costs to a minimum, and provide what many people consider the friendliest service in the industry. It is now extending the same approach to provide lodging and food, recreational facilities, and health care to senior citizens at its life-care communities. Marriott's revenues in 1984 reached $3.4 billion, nearly 175 times the 1952 level, and the company's goal is to triple its size over the next six years in order to reach $10 billion by the end of the decade. Fred Malek makes it sound easy. "Everybody can do it. It just takes a will and a systematic effort." That is the power of an organization.

The Power of Organization

There is a power generated by the proper combination of unrelated things. When salt, glucose, and water are mixed together in the right proportions, they constitute a very simple but highly effective cure for the dehydration caused by diarrhea. Hailed as "potentially the most important medical advance in this century," oral rehydration offers an inexpensive, readily available remedy for an ailment that kills some 5 million to 8 million children every year in developing countries. Since this formula was popularized in India a few years ago, the mortality rate due to diarrhea has dropped by 40 percent. The proper combination of three very ordinary substances generates a power that none of them possesses in isolation. The combination of the foot soldier and the work horse to produce a mounted cavalry enabled the ancient Scythians to sweep like a terror over Greece and other countries that did not know the technique of riding. The highly mobile horse soldier transformed the art of warfare and the organization of battle. The combination of the horse carriage and the motor to create the first automobiles had a similar impact. When two or more forces are combined in the proper fashion, they possess a power that is far greater than the sum of their parts. The discovery of techniques for preserving food in bottles gave

Napoleon's army great mobility and a strategic advantage over opponents who were constantly dependent on provisions supplied from behind the lines. Gunpowder plus the sailing ship enabled Europe to dominate the entire globe. The linking of the television screen, typewriter, and silicon chip in computers has produced an enormous power for administration, research, and production—a power that none of these things possesses in isolation. When they are combined with the telephone, their power is multiplied a thousandfold, and their reach extends around the world.

The same is true of people. There are some things that two people can do that a single person could never accomplish alone, no matter how long or hard the effort. Many a great kingdom was founded on the strength of a warrior king combined with the wisdom of a minister or priest. Many of today's great companies are the product of the fortuitous combination of a skilled inventor and a clever financier. As the number of people involved increases, the available talents, and therefore the potential power, increase exponentially rather than arithmetically.

The combination of Richard Sears and Julius Rosenwald was the perfect blend for commercial success. Sears was a freewheeling promotional genius with a flair for writing advertising copy—untarnished by reality—that appealed to rural, small-town America and with a knack for making deals on closeout merchandise on especially favorable terms. But otherwise he was a poor businessman and an inept manager, with little knowledge of business finance and systematic operations. Rosenwald, on the other hand, was a person with high ethical standards and a keen insight into the needs and untapped potentials of the market. He brought to Sears the money-back guarantee and a more systematic marketing strategy. Together their abilities spurred a 13-fold growth of the fledgling mail-order business between 1895 and 1900. They were soon joined by Otto Doering, a master at operating systems. The happy confluence of these three bright stars was the alchemy that propelled a 23-fold growth of the company over the next 20 years.

Alfred P. Sloan, the proverbial "organization man" and architect of GM's modern structure, once declared: "After all, what any one individual can accomplish is not great, but through the power, of organization the effect of a few may be multiplied almost indefinitely."[3] When an individual works alone, that individual has to be everything and can succeed only to the extent that he or she possesses all the technical, administrative, managerial, and financial capacities required for the work. If the person lacks one or more of these, his or her talents will remain unutilized or wasted. But when an organization undertakes any activity, it can utilize whatever talents a single person may possess and draw on other people for the additional skills required. In every company at least 20 percent of the people will have untapped abilities that, if properly harnessed, can help it grow exponentially. Organization complements and completes the incomplete inspiration of an inventive mind or the one-sided capacities of a talented businessperson. Thus, an organization makes possible the maximum utilization of human resources.

Materials, energy, technology, money, people—when combined with each other—generate a power that none of them possesses by itself. The same is true of ideas, systems, and skills. An organization combines all of these resources in new ways to generate a virtually limitless creative power—a power that far exceeds the sum total of all its inputs.

According to scientific reports, the solar energy falling on the earth's atmosphere is sufficient to meet the entire world's energy needs 2,000 times over for the next few million years. The task of science is to discover a way to effectively harness that energy. The power of organization holds equally great potentials for humanity that are barely even glimpsed today, as the power of the atom was undreamt of until less than a century ago. When even a little of this power is released, an organization comes alive and begins to take off.

What makes an organization take off? Consider the airplane. What is the secret of its capacity for flight? Like the car or the train, its engine has a capacity for creating thrust in only one direction. Yet it is able to use this thrust to lift itself off the ground against the powerful opposition of gravity. It does this by means of wings, which convert the force resisting its forward movement into a lifting power to raise it off the ground. A slight shift in the angle of the wing makes all the difference in the world.

Organizations are similar. But whereas airplanes travel in only one direction at a time, organizations are multidimensional. They move in many directions simultaneously. As the wings of an airplane can be tilted to exactly the best angle for flight, there are countless points in an organization that can be adjusted to convert a problem, or resistance, into an opportunity, or uplifting force. When these points are touched and properly tuned, the organization comes alive and takes off. The challenge before us is to identify these points and discover how they can be made into so many wings for the company's ascent.

Organization is the sum total of many powers, a treasure house of creative potential, a vibrant organism with an existence, life, and personality of its own. As the secrets of the human mind and heart and soul have remained unseen and concealed from the searching eye of science, mysteries as great today as ever they were in the past, humanity remains blind to another great mystery, unknown though seen by all—the unveiled enigma of the living organization. Even its founders do not know what they create. Even its leaders do not know the power they wield. Even the society it serves does not know its infinite capacity for service.

From Cottage Handicraft to Multinational Corporation

When Tomas Bata returned from the conference of Czech industrialists in 1922, he carried back with him a value and a goal. The value was a commitment to job security for his employees during a severe recession. The goal was to reduce the price of his shoes by 50 percent. The only way he could achieve either was to bring down his cost of production to less than half its present level. Like Marriott, Bata discovered the enormous hidden powers of organization. But the structure Bata adopted was quite different from Marriott's, because his values and objectives were different. For Marriott the central value was quality control, and the primary objective was growth. For Bata the values were employment security and cost control, and the primary objective was survival. Bata had first of all to *save* a business, not to build one. Despite the differences in structure, their results were remarkably similar.

Bata introduced a highly decentralized structure that he termed industrial autonomy, just about the same time Alfred Sloan was introducing a decentralized structure at GM. He divided his workforce into several profit centers, each consisting of about 50 shoemakers headed by a manager, to whom authority and responsibility were delegated. He drew up a profit-sharing plan whereby each group received premiums equal to as much as 25 percent of base salary for producing more efficiently. Bata believed that maximum profitability could not be achieved by strong central controls from above. It required full motivation and the intelligent participation of every worker in the organization. He wanted every employee to feel an intense interest in producing efficiently. "I want every worker to be the first book-keeper in the factory," he said. "I want him to know in figures all there is to know about his job, and I want all the workers to know in figures how they fared each week. It is no use for these figures to be known by the managers alone, or to know them only once a year."[4] Way back in the 1920s, Bata worked out a system of *daily* production plans for each workshop and a rapid reporting system that fed back *hourly* figures on the output of shoes from each stage of production. He introduced a sophisticated costing system that enabled every worker in the leather-cutting department to monitor his or her group's performance and a *daily* financial statement that gave immediate feedback on profitability. Unlike most proprietors, he posted all these figures so everyone would be fully aware of the company's results.

Anthony Cekota, who joined the company in 1920, described Tomas as a man with "an absolute faith in the potential power of common human effort and of unified force generated by voluntary individual resolution."[5] Half a century before quality circles, Bata wanted to turn each worker in the factory into an entrepreneur and a businessperson, who would constantly contribute new ideas on how to improve production. "The autonomy of the workshops is not only less costly, but also more efficient. No one knows the obstacles to his work better than the man doing it."[6] He decentralized quality control so that every worker was responsible for inspecting the work of the previous operation. This system eliminated repetition of errors, since they were caught as soon as they were made; and it created an atmosphere of peer pressure, which discouraged shoddy work by any operator.

Through this organization, Bata succeeded in enlisting the interest and releasing the energies of his employees. Between 1922, when he introduced it, and 1932, when he died in an airplane crash, his company expanded from 2,200 employees producing about 8,000 pairs of shoes a day to 18,200 employees producing 144,000 pairs. A 9-fold increase in workforce generated an 18-fold increase in production. Productivity had doubled. At the same time, the average weekly wages of Bata's workers rose more than 3-fold, while Bata's sale prices dropped to one-sixth their 1922 level. Even during the worst years of the Great Depression, Bata continued to expand. By 1932 the company was manufacturing shoes in 28 countries. That was the power of Bata's organization.

Bata had said, "I wanted something which functions as naturally and automatically as sunrise and sunset,"[7] and his organization did, even after his death. It not only functioned; it grew right through the 1930s. When protectionist pressures increased, making it more difficult to export shoes from Czechoslovakia, the company concentrated on development of its overseas branches in England, Germany, Canada, India, and many other countries.

A Perpetual-Motion Machine

The real test of the Bata Shoe organization was yet to come. In the fall of 1938, Czechoslovakia was first dismembered at the Munich Conference and the rest of it invaded by Germany in March 1939. All communications with the outside world were cut off. Young Thomas Bata was in Western Europe at the time and then proceeded to Canada, where he managed to gather round him a few other Bata Shoe Company executives who had been able to leave Czechoslovakia before the Nazi invasion. During the course of the war, no civilian communication was possible between this group and the parent company or most of the overseas companies. When the war ended, the Communists seized power in Czechoslovakia and appropriated all the assets of the Bata Shoe Company. Almost the entire Bata staff was trapped forever within the country.

In 1945 Thomas Bata called a meeting in Canada of his country managers from all over the world to find out what remained of what had once been the world's largest shoe company. To his surprise, he discovered that in most of the countries where it had manufacturing facilities, the firm was thriving. Tomas Bata's goal of an organization that would function automatically had been achieved. The autonomy of local profit centers had evolved into a decentralized structure of autonomous country operations, which functioned efficiently without any direction from the head office. Although the company's production had fallen to 40 percent of the prewar level—from 55 million to 20 million pairs—within five years Bata was once again the largest manufacturer of footwear in the world.

Since the end of the war, the company has extended its operations to 93 countries, where it now produces 300 million pairs of shoes annually; but it still retains the decentralized structure developed 60 years ago. As Chairman Thomas Bata says, "The thing is being held together by local dynamism rather than by any constant edicts from a center."

With such a highly decentralized operation, how does the parent company maintain any semblance of a unified organization at all? Despite the local autonomy, there is an extraordinary degree of similarity between the operations in different plants and different countries. There is also a strong sense of discipline throughout the company. This consistency and discipline are maintained by a uniform set of systems, procedures, and forms used by every Bata operation worldwide. A supervisor from Bata's plant at Calcutta will feel completely at home with the systems employed in the Bata plants in Casablanca; Kampala; Bangkok; Panama; Lima; or Belcamp, Maryland. A store manager from Khartoum will recognize the form used for inventory by a store in Mexico, even if he or she cannot read Spanish, because except for the language, it is exactly the same. Uniformity is reinforced by the system of rotating country managers every few years, so that any new idea developed in one country quickly spreads to others. Sitting with a group of country managers from Australia, Kenya, and Sudan, we were surprised by the similarity of their remarks on issues like cleanliness, punctuality, and inventory control. Today, if an employee in any Bata company is late to work, he or she will be reprimanded. The chairman's assistant told us of the scolding he received for being one minute late on several occasions. There is no written rule or system to enforce punctuality. In fact, few people even know exactly how it became so important. Actually, time-consciousness was one of Tomas Bata's highest priorities, and the value has been transmitted through the decades. "You cannot fly an airplane slowly," he used to say. "The worst kind of waste and most costly waste is time waste, because it is invisible."[8] Punctuality at Bata no longer requires the support of rules, procedures, and systems. It has become a custom of the company.

The original profit centers still exist in Bata factories all over the world—even the employee cafeterias are run as separate profit centers within each plant. The system of hourly and daily financial reporting introduced by the founder continues as well. Every morning Bata executives in Toronto meet to discuss production and sales figures coming in from around the world. The reporting system has been an important tool for staying in touch with overseas operations and for exercising control, wherever necessary.

In spite of their marked differences, the organizations created by the Marriotts and the Batas have several things in common. Both combine centralization in some areas with decentralization in others. Both employ well-developed systems to maintain uniformity and consistency. Both impose strict discipline in some areas to maintain control. Both allow wide freedom in other areas to encourage entrepreneurship and individual initiative. Marriott's highly centralized organization and Bata's highly decentralized one appear at closer range as variations on a single model. The power they have both discovered issues more from organization itself than from the particular form that that organization takes in one company or another.

It was not the market that fueled the expansion of these two companies; it was the release of forces from within themselves. They were not driven by the potentials of the market, but by the limitless potentials of organization, to which the market responded. They did not have to seek out opportunities in life. They discovered opportunities within the organization, and life unfolded more rich potentials than either of them ever dreamed of.

Corporate Character

What is this thing that we call organization? It is actually the organizing and executing will of the corporate personality. It is the *character* of the corporation. In the individual, character collects, harnesses, and directs all the energies and capacities of the personality to fulfill its quest for self-actualization. Corporate character works the same way. It gathers together, mobilizes, and directs all the resources of the company to fulfill the values, mission, and objectives of the psychic center. It is the link between idea and action.

The character of an organization has two aspects, one structural and the other functional. The structural aspect determines the form of the organization, the hierarchy of levels. It is like the skeletal system in the human body, which determines the size and shape of the body and provides a structure to which the muscles are attached and in which the organs rest. The structure of an organization—with its various departments, divisions, and levels of hierarchy—plays a similar role. In another sense, the structure of an organization is like the circulatory system in the body, consisting of a matrix of interconnecting vessels of various diameters. These vessels are the channels or pathways through which energy, information, money, and materials are transported within the company. The size of each vessel determines how much it can carry. Its connections with other vessels determine the destination of the things it transports.

But this structure constitutes only the passive and external component of corporate character, the one depicted in organization charts. Character also has an active functional aspect. It exercises authority. This functional aspect is like the field general who is in charge of directing an army during battle. The broad aims and objectives of the war, as well as the strategy to be pursued in the battle, are established by the chief of staff. The field general's task is to execute the battle plan according to the plans and strategies received from above. That task involves coordinating the actions of armored divisions, artillery, air support, and infantry to ensure that they act in unison and not at cross-purposes; without the field general, the movements of these various forces might not coincide properly, and there is even the possibility of aerial or artillery bombardment's endangering the general's own army, a thing quite common in war and not unheard of in business.

In this sense, character is the organizing and executing will of the corporate personality that releases all its energies, mobilizes all its resources, and coordinates all its actions to fulfill its mission and objectives in accordance with its central beliefs and values. It does not fix the goals—that is done by the psychic center—but it directs all the company's capacities to realize them. People, ideas, skills, systems, money, technology, machinery, and materials are like the armed forces that the field general commands. In the absence of a central authority, they tend to act on their own, independently of the rest and often in conflict with one another.

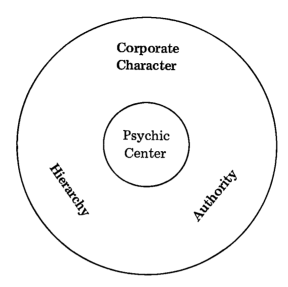

Figure 2.   The role of the corporate character
                in the corporate personality.

The corporate character establishes a hierarchy of levels and exercises authority for the execution of work. It imposes common rules, regulations, standards, and strategies on the various departments and divisions. It coordinates the activity of all the company's resources and integrates activities at different levels of the company to ensure smooth and harmonious operations. It is the central will or authority for the execution of work. (Figure 2 depicts the role of the corporate character in the corporate personality.) In the absence of a strong corporate character, top management decisions are not properly executed, employee discipline and morale are low, departments and divisions are in frequent conflict and work at cross-purposes, human talents and physical resources are not fully utilized, systems function poorly or in isolation from each other, and market potentials remain untapped.

Hierarchy and Authority

What is the source of an organization's incredible power? There is not one source, but many. When Bill Marriott, Sr., ran Hot Shoppe No. 1

with the help of his wife, Allie, and a few employees, he was all things to his business—a worker, a supervisor of others' work, and a decision-making manager. When Hot Shoppe No. 2 was added, he and Allie could station themselves simultaneously or successively in one shop or the other carrying out the same functions as before. But when Nos. 3, 4, and 5 were added, Bill's job changed in character. It was no longer possible for him to personally oversee all the work going on in all the shops all the time. Therefore, Bill had to select one from among the group of employees at each shop to act as an extension of his senses and watch over things in his absence. Bill ceased to be a worker or even a supervisor. He now had to devote most of his time to making decisions and leave supervision to someone permanently located at each shop. Gradually, he found it possible to delegate decision-making authority on routine items of work to his shop supervisors, thereby freeing himself from most of the repetitive, ordinary operational decisions so that he could concentrate his attention on general management issues like finding locations for additional shops or thinking up some new advertising strategy. In the process, his supervisors were upgraded into managers. Bill's evolution from worker to supervisor to manager to general manager coincided with the establishment of a multitiered hierarchy in his company and the delegation of authority to personnel at lower levels of the organization. The net result was an enormous increase in his personal productivity and a fivefold expansion of the business. The creation of a hierarchical structure and the delegation of authority are two of the primary powers of organization.

Specialization and Systems

When Tomas Bata started his business, shoemaking in Czechoslovakia was still a cottage handicraft in which each cobbler performed all of the tasks involved in making shoes, usually in the family kitchen. Inspired by the idea of mass production, Bata took a group of people and divided their work into specialized tasks along a production line. This division of labor made them each far more productive and efficient than any individual cobbler. It enabled Tomas and his father to start their business in 1894 with 50 employees instead of one cobbler and to expand to 120 by 1900. Specialization is another primary power of organization.

Although technology was gradually changing shoemaking from a manual into a machine-driven trade, the organization of production still followed the old pattern of the cobbler's shop. Bata introduced new machinery and developed a lot of his own, but his real innovation was the Bata system. He introduced automated production conveyors as Ford did for cars. Then he developed innumerable systems for procurement of raw materials, inventory control, planning, production, distribution, and marketing. These systems enabled him to produce far more efficiently than the machine-driven factories based on the traditional pattern. He also introduced various types of records and reports, which enabled him to supervise, monitor, and control a far larger operation. Systems and reporting are also fundamental powers of organization. They enabled Bata to expand his daily production another tenfold between 1900 and 1910.

Coordination and Integration

As Bata's business expanded, it came to encompass a whole series of related activities, which no individual cobbler minus an organization could undertake. Bata sent out purchasing officers to scour the country—and, later, foreign countries—in search of good-quality, low-priced leather. He established tanneries so that he could process the leather himself. He set up machine shops to build and repair his equipment. He developed more efficient means of transporting his shoes to the market. He created new channels of wholesale and retail distribution within the country and overseas. All these activities had to be closely coordinated in order to ensure a smooth flow of work.

Bata's organization also expanded vertically to include several more layers between the proprietor and his executives at the top and the thousands of purchasing agents, production workers, technicians, salespeople, and clerks at the bottom. It became essential to integrate activities at each level with those above and below, to ensure that what the planners decided was carried out at all the lower levels in all departments within the country and overseas and to ensure that all significant events at lower levels were reported and acted upon by management.

Coordination ensures that the hand and mouth work in unison. Integration ensures that the mouth eats what the mind approves, the taste enjoys, and the body can digest. Coordination and integration are higher powers of the organization that unfolded for Bata a rich creative potential for growth. Daily production in 1932 was nearly 50 times greater than it was in 1910 and 3,000 times greater than it was in 1894. Productivity per worker had grown from an average of one pair of shoes per day to an average of eight pairs per day.

Harmony

Marriott underwent a similar line of horizontal expansion and vertical development. It gradually expanded its activities from root beer to Mexican food, from drive-in restaurants to in-flight service, from hotels to life-care communities. As it grew, it also developed a much deeper hierarchy than the three-tiered structure that ran the first Hot Shoppes. This growth was made possible by the close coordination of related activities and the integration of different levels of the organization through a sophisticated matrix of systems for reporting, monitoring, controlling, and executing work.

Coordination and integration enable Marriott to operate a wide range of businesses and expand rapidly while maintaining high standards of service. For instance, the hotel division has opened between 10 and 20 major hotels every year for the last five years and had them operating up to Marriott standards almost immediately.

When structure and systems are coordinated and integrated, as at Marriott, the organization begins to function like a well-tuned Mercedes engine or a precisely made Rolex watch. Movements become smooth and swift. Interactions are frictionless and trouble-free. Productivity increases enormously. Frustration, irritation, conflict, and confrontation are minimized. People become relaxed, even-tempered, cooperative, and cheerful. An atmosphere of harmony is established.

One of the things that impressed us about Marriott was that the firm's friendly, personalized service is delivered through a highly complex system of procedures and controls. The smooth-running systems make everyone's job clearer and easier. They reduce friction and confusion. As one vice-president explained, "We try to develop systems that help make an experience pleasant instead of detracting from it."

Harmony depends on recruiting the right kind of people, imparting the right kind of training, and communicating the right values and attitudes to all employees. Harmony, too, is a power of organization—potentially more powerful than all those that come before it and make it possible—because when harmony is present, employees will go to great lengths to serve, and customers will go to great lengths to seek out that service.

The Greater Powers

Hierarchy, delegation of authority, specialization, systems, coordination, integration, and harmony are some of the powers of organization that have been discovered and harnessed by modern corporations to accomplish incredible feats of growth and productivity. But these are still the lesser powers. There are greater ones as well—powers that come from people. What, after all, is an organization other than people? "People are the key to everything," says Thomas Bata. "The key to success is . . . people. Management is nothing more than motivating people," wrote Iacocca.[9] Money, technology, raw materials, products, and systems come to life and generate power only because of the people who wield them. Walt LeSueur, director of sales administration at General Mills, summed it up best: "All we've got here is flour and water and people."

For thousands of years great leaders have searched for the key to the infinite power of people. The pharaohs resorted to force and fear of death to mobilize people to work. But all they obtained was the merest physical labor in return for a minimum level of sustenance. Napoleon succeeded for a while in winning the hearts of his young, ill-trained recruits with the glorious battle cry "Vive la France." Gandhi awakened an entire nation and made it rise up unarmed against the might of the British Empire with the inspiring call for the liberation of Mother India. But these were only brief moments in history, when a leader or an ambition or an event released the powers latent in people, more often for destruction than for creation. The real challenge is to release those powers for continuous production.

Discipline

How do organizations harness the power of people? They do it through an effort of will, through the exercise of authority. The real character of a corporation is expressed in the way it exercises authority, the manner in which it exerts its will to influence people. Every organization must exercise authority in order to survive. There was a time when this was done almost entirely through negative means, through discipline and threat of punishment. Today discipline is not a very popular concept; yet no organization can exist without it.

When Lee Iacocca arrived at Chrysler for his very first day on the job, he observed several clear signs that the organization was in deep trouble.

> . . . the office of the president . . . was being used as a thoroughfare to get from one office to another. I watched in amazement as executives with coffee cups in their hands kept opening the door and walking right through the president's office. Right away I knew the place was in a state of anarchy. Chrysler needed a dose of order and discipline—and quick[10]

Without discipline, the energies and talents of an organization cannot be fully harnessed and put to work.

Every company, even the most people-oriented, has areas where it insists on obedience and discipline. Wherever high performance levels are considered absolutely critical, negative forms of authority are employed. At Du Pont the surest way to get fired is to ignore safety regulations. At Merck it is to give erroneous or exaggerated information to a physician. At Bata, if any inventory is found missing from a company-owned store, the store manager is personally responsible for compensating the company for the loss. Sears really means business about the way customers are to be handled. Mistreating a customer is a quick way out the door.

IBM has been known for its Marinelike discipline since the days when Tom Watson, Sr., forbade his employees to drink alcohol on or off the job—even prior to national Prohibition—discouraged smoking among his employees, and insisted that salespeople wear dark business suits and white shirts. Although the Watsons are gone, the codes of behavior remain, and most of them are still in force. The old dress code is no longer a strict regulation, but most IBM sales reps stick to it. Drinking off the job is a personal matter now, but those who drink at lunch are expected to take the rest of the day off.

When it comes to business ethics, there is no compromise allowed at IBM. The company has a 32-page code of business ethics, which employees must strictly adhere to. As IBM's director of management development commented: "If anybody does anything that is the least bit shady, the heavens descend on them. . . . People see we have a basic set of beliefs and we adhere to them."[11] The strength of this commitment "elevates the whole company," says Frederick W. Zuckerman, who worked 12 years at IBM before joining Lee Iacocca's management team at Chrysler.

At IBM the commitment to after-sale service is taken so seriously that the company considers it a grave lapse if any one of its customers give up IBM equipment in favor of another brand. IBM has a policy to ensure that account representatives fully understand the importance of follow-up customer service and act on it. If an IBM customer switches to another brand, the present account representative for the customer's territory has to refund to the company out of his or her salary and bonus the full amount of the commission paid on that customer's original order, even if that commission had been paid to a previous representative who is no longer covering the same territory.

Soon after taking over as president of a middle-sized corporation, a former IBM vice-president launched a program to cut overheads. During one of the executive meetings, he asked for a copy of the individual records maintained by all executives for long-distance calls from company phones. The executives looked at the new president in surprise and bewilderment, and one of them asked, "Do they keep such records at IBM?" The president replied, "Of course, they do. Don't you do it here?" To which another executive responded, "We are trying to follow the latest practices here. We never thought that companies like IBM still did such things."

Intel

Companies vary enormously in the degree to which they resort to discipline as well as the manner of discipline. When IBM acquired 12 percent of Intel's stock in 1983, some considered it a strange match—straitlaced IBM and informal Intel, where executive attire consists of sport shirts and no ties. But IBM and Intel do have one thing very much in common—discipline. Discipline at Intel is a serious matter. The workday starts at 8 A.M. If any employee comes in after 8:05, he or she has to sign in on the "late list" in order to get by the guard—even if the employee happens to be the president. Repeated tardiness is grounds for dismissal. Cofounder Robert Noyce once remarked: "Intel is the only place I have ever worked where an 8:00 A.M. meeting starts at 8:00 A.M."[12] Part of the rationale for this discipline is that when one person is late, other people's work may be affected. At most Intel meetings over 90 percent of the people will be there at the appointed hour, and the rest will usually be less than five minutes late. Intel is in an industry where you just cannot wait.

Intel is also in an industry in which you have to be clean, at least in the plants where the chips are made. In Intel's plants cleanliness is an absolute must; chips are manufactured in an environment where the air is a hundred times cleaner than the air in a hospital operating room. So far, it all makes sense. But cleanliness at Intel does not stop there. It spills over into the administrative environment, too. About twice a month, teams of three or four people in each building inspect every work station and rank it in terms of cleanliness. Composite scores are calculated for each building. "Mr. Clean," as the teams are called, is quite effective. Financial and administrative officers at most companies are known for their cluttered desks, but Intel's Larry Hootnick keeps his office so neat and orderly that we actually could not find a single piece of paper in sight.

There is also a corrective action program at Intel. Any employee who does not perform up to expectations is called in for a discussion, and a specific program is drawn up to solve the problem. Ninety days later performance is reviewed to determine whether the program has been successful. If it has not, the employee better look for a new job, either inside or outside the company.

There are also semiannual reviews of hourly employees and annual reviews of salaried personnel, in which the individual is rated on a scale ranging from "superior" to "does not meet requirements." Even superior performers will have areas where they can improve, and individual programs will be charted out for that purpose.

This does not mean that there is always someone looking over your shoulder at Intel. Discipline has become institutionalized as a custom. Although there are rules and peer pressure, to a great extent discipline has been internalized as a self-critical attitude in people. Rebecca Wallo, of the company's public information department, explained: "The people are very self-critical here. If you talk to people who have been here awhile, they would say they are as critical of themselves as they would expect others to be."

Financial control is an area that is strictly enforced at almost all the companies we visited. Travel expenses must be precisely accounted for. Bills for long-distance calls are monitored to eliminate unnecessary or unsanctioned use of the phone. At Intel nobody, including the chairman, flies first class. The same is true at Marriott, where even Bill Marriott, Jr., flies economy class.

Delta

We have already referred to the strict cost control at Delta, but in nonfinancial matters Delta is not exactly the sort of company you would associate with strict discipline. Then, again, companies are not quite so stereotyped as we often portray them. When it comes to Delta's core values, the company does not compromise.

The personal appearance of flight attendants is governed by fairly strict regulations. Being overweight is grounds for dismissal, because good service depends so much on an attendant's agility in narrow, crowded aisles. For men, whether or not to wear a tie "isn't one of the things you can decide on. You wear it."

Punctuality is also an important value at Delta, because it is a critical factor in providing on-time customer service. Delta has the lowest delayed-flight rates in the industry. There is no late list, but if an employee comes in late five times, his or her manager will sit down with the employee to find out what the problem is. About 95 percent of the people arrive before the 8:00 A.M. opening time and return from lunch promptly by 1:00 P.M. There is a strong atmosphere of peer pressure at Delta. Even if the boss is not around, other employees are. "If the boss doesn't know, the troops know," remarked Dennis Schmidt, general manager for methods and training. "If people have not held up their end of the deal and they are looking for support, they won't find it."

Managers deal with individual problems like punctuality on a one-to-one basis with the individual rather than by an impersonal memo or a 90-day written contract for improvement. Delta practices what it calls "progressive discipline"—in which the individual and his or her manager work together to clearly understand what the problem is and devise ways to remove it. We asked President Ron Allen what is the best way for an employee to get in trouble at Delta. "Acts of dishonesty," he replied. "That's something that we don't tolerate." Although discipline is enforced in many areas, sometimes Delta's own employees feel the company is not being tough enough. One executive commented, "Our people tell us we go too far in giving employees a second, third, and fourth chance to change."

Delta tries to enforce discipline less through the threat of punishment than through what it calls "an atmosphere of approval." There is a positive milieu in which everybody knows what is expected and is motivated to live up to the standard. Allen says: "We don't want people to be afraid that if they don't come to work on time or don't do this or that, then they will really get in trouble. Instead we want them to feel good about doing things correctly and giving of their best. That doesn't mean that people don't get in trouble at Delta, but we want our managers to manage people through this environment of approval. It is the value of the person. Our managers recognize the value of the individual." One past president of Delta summed up the company's policy this way: "You can do anything around here that you don't think you'll get fired for."

Freedom Versus Laxity

Recently a lot of attention has been paid in management circles to the value of using positive reinforcement through rewards and attention to motivate people and get work done rather than negative reinforcement through fear and punishment. But this should not obscure the critical importance of maintaining discipline. As a rule, the more developed the corporate personality becomes, the more clearly defined are the policies, rules, and procedures for monitoring and enforcing authority in areas of central importance. The form of authority and the manner of enforcing it may vary with the character of the corporation, as Intel differs from Delta, but the critical commitment to discipline will be there. Companies that feel it is "unprogressive" to insist on punctuality and accurate travel accounts, or look the other way when staff members bypass traditional lines of authority, mistakenly confuse laxity and indiscipline with the freedom necessary to achieve enduring success. The two are vastly different concepts. Even when a company gets away with lax discipline in a few instances or for a short while, it tends to undermine the whole edifice of organizational character. A breath of fresh air may seep in through a crack in the hull of a surfaced submarine, bringing relief to the crew in a stuffy engine room; but when the ship is submerged, water will pour in through the same crack.

The Dividing Line

How, then, should we understand all the talk about positive reinforcement, freedom, autonomy, individual initiative, open doors, informal communications, flexible working hours, visible management, and the like, which are practiced with apparent success by many of the most respected corporations? Discipline and freedom are the two ways in which the corporate character exercises its will to accomplish work—one by restricting employees' freedom of action, the other by asking employees to practice self-restraint.

Discipline and freedom are both essential, and in mature corporations they complement each other. Discipline, which is authority physically imposed from above, is insisted on in areas central to the organization's existence, where employees cannot be relied upon to always function in the prescribed manner on their own initiative. Freedom, which is self-imposed authority exercised by the individual over himself or herself, is extended in areas where employees are obedient and cooperative and have already accepted the need to act with self-control and a sense of responsibility in conformity with the higher values and goals of the corporation. Peters and Waterman found that America's best-run companies "are on the one hand rigidly controlled, yet at the same time allow (indeed, insist on) autonomy, entrepreneurship, and innovation from the rank and file."[13]

The proper dividing line between discipline and freedom, between negative and positive forms of authority, depends on social custom, geographic location, the laws governing employment, the extent of the employees' economic dependence on the firm, and alternative job opportunities; but most especially it depends on the strength of the corporate character. If every American company abolished time clocks and fixed working hours and removed the locks on their laboratory storerooms as Hewlett-Packard has down, a good number would find their factories empty, except on pay day, and their storerooms permanently vacant.

Positive forms of authority are successful in proportion to the general level of education of employees, their technical capabilities and job satisfaction, and the extent to which a supportive milieu of teamwork, peer pressure, loyalty, and commitment to the company has developed among the employees. There is no clear dividing line for one and all. It depends on the company, and it depends on the stage of the company's development. Forty-five years ago General Wood addressed a conference of Sears store managers on this subject. He said that in order for a decentralized structure based on freedom for individual initiative to work, "there must be self-imposed discipline. You as Managers must discipline yourselves, otherwise discipline has to be applied from above."[14] Wood had learned this lesson well from his predecessor, Julius Rosenwald. During the prosperous years of World War I, when Rosenwald was away assisting with the war effort, lax discipline set in at Sears. Then came the postwar recession, and the company almost went bankrupt. Insisting on discipline where freedom is effective cancels opportunities and retards growth; but relying on freedom where discipline is required can destroy the company altogether.

In a well-balanced organization, the foundations and structure are established by discipline and control, while expansion and development are based on self-discipline and freedom. Survival and preservation are imposed from above; growth and dynamism are released from below. The company that fully establishes discipline in all core sectors and fully enlists the cooperation and self-restraint of its employees for expansion functions successfully at the peak of performance. Its opportunities for growth are endless.

A Perpetual Youth

For years America's leading business schools have been teaching their MBA candidates about the theory of product life cycles. Products, like people, are born, grow, become old, and die. It is certainly true that many products have behaved according to this theory. The Model T lived a long life; the Edsel, a very short one. But at General Mills it is the theory that has died, not the products. "There is no such thing as a product life-cycle," insists the firm's vice-president and general manager, Ned Bixby.[15] General Mills is still pushing Cheerios, Bisquick, and Gold Medal flour—all of which are as old as or older than Betty Crocker herself and look nearly as young. Like the face of Betty Crocker, these products are continually updated to keep in step with the times. Fifty years after its birth, Cheerios is America's leading breakfast cereal in dollar volume.

What is the secret of this perpetual renewal that has made General Mills the most profitable and admired company in its industry? General Mills has learned how to harness the creative power of people through positive authority. It all began in 1928, when James Bell, the president of a 60-year-old flour mill, consolidated five independent companies to create the largest flour-milling company in the world, General Mills. The mills were all well-established operations spread throughout the country, so there was no need to centralize their management and little advantage in doing so. After the merger, the mills continued to operate very much as before, like independent entrepreneurial businesses.

Bell believed that a corporation's most important asset was its people rather than the figures set down in its balance sheet. He valued intelligence, enthusiasm, and aggressiveness more than money. His goal was to preserve the local autonomy of the mills while giving them the support of a centralized national organization with research, production, training, packaging, and merchandising expertise. "Our aim," he said, "is to give the maximum of help to our associates with the minimum of interference."[16]

As General Mills grew over the years, Bell applied the same philosophy not only to the proprietors of the previously independent mills but to all employees in the organization. His objective was to release enthusiasm, initiative, and enterprise as far down the line as possible, to foster a process of perpetual self-renewal in the company. Bell said: "New and young blood must flow steadily through the veins of any successful company. It is the spirit of our organization to keep the way to the top open and to keep the young men alert to opportunity by developing their sense of responsibility."[17]

In 1965 General Ed Rawlings closed 9 of the company's remaining 17 flour mills, thereby surrendering the title "world's largest." Although the mills went, the company's basic character remained. Rawlings stayed with the decentralized structure and the entrepreneurial atmosphere, but he added new systems for planning and control in order to increase coordination throughout the company. His aim was to combine individual initiative with teamwork, two organizational powers that rarely are found together. "The full effect of our system is yet to be felt," he once claimed. He was certainly right.[18] During the following two decades, General Mills set a course that was defined in terms of "continuity and change." This meant steadfast adherence to principles of conduct combined with a willingness to initiate change as dictated by the external marketplace and by internal strategic goals. The result was tenfold growth to a $5.6 billion enterprise, focusing on three business areas—consumer foods, restaurants, and specialty retailing.

A Free Spirit and Incorrigible Entrepreneur

When you enter the home of Betty Crocker, you somehow expect to find an atmosphere as old as the name—traditional, conservative, and more than a little stodgy. But that image hardly fits General Mills today, any more than the first portrait of Betty Crocker in 1936 resembles her latest remodeling. The company may be old in years, but it is very young in spirit. The atmosphere is intense, alive, saturated with a wholesome vitality and dynamism. It feels more like a gymnasium than a kitchen. Its employees are reminiscent of John Wooden's fast-break, full-court-press basketball teams at UCLA during the 1960s—competitive team players with high morale.

The most visible expression of the company's exuberant atmosphere is the brand manager system. Every year the company recruits about 40 graduates of the nation's top business schools. In the first year the new recruits may be assigned to one of those products that the theorists say should not exist anymore. Old-timers like Wheaties (introduced in 1924), Cheerios, and Kix (circa 1940) are reinvigorated and rejuvenated by the energy, enthusiasm, ambition, and ideas of a youthful MBA. The product may be half a century old, but for the fledgling marketing assistant it is brand new. The advertising budget may be well structured and controlled, but for someone right out of graduate school, helping to manage it is a big responsibility and a big challenge. The marketing assistants also realize that experienced marketing professionals with General Mills can earn a performance bonus of 20 percent or more on what is already a handsome base salary. Couple these factors with the knowledge that a significant percent of the new marketing assistant's "classmates" will not be with the company a year or two later—either because some could not make the grade or stand the speed or because they were lured away by one of the many companies that prize General Mills' "graduates"—and you have a formula for dynamic action.

A recent issue of the company's employee publication carries a cartoon of a young marketing assistant with briefcase in hand flying through the office. The cartoon is entitled "General Milieu." That pretty well captures the atmosphere. Maybe the brand managers do not have very much real authority. Perhaps often they do not really do anything very different from the way their predecessors operated—just a little change in the package here or in the advertisement there. But that little bit of alchemy is often enough to transmute an aging product into a rising star, and so the process of renewal is repeated year after year.

The system often fails, with old products and new ones, but failure is not something that is frowned on too much at General Mills. As one executive put it, "We fail more than others, because we try more new things." The positive atmosphere does result in more than an equal number of success stories. The company still makes acquisitions, but usually small ones that it builds up. Over $1.5 billion of General Mills' revenues in 1984, and about one-third of its profits, came from eight operations that had average sales of only $8 million in their first year with the company. In 1977 a little cottage cheese factory in Michigan with a French recipe for yogurt was purchased for $3 million. It is now a $150 million product called Yoplait.

One thing that struck us about the company was the apparent invisibility of top management, which was expressed as an enormous latitude of freedom for personal growth at lower levels. After listening for a while to Chris Steiner, a marketing director in the foods division who joined the company as a marketing assistant eight years ago, we began to wonder who actually runs this place or if anyone really does. Steiner constantly referred to "I" and "we" but never once mentioned any "they" who sit above her and tell her and her colleagues what to do. "There is nobody looking down over your head and asking you if you did this or that," she explained. The same view of management was expressed by John Machuzick, a sales operations manager in Grocery Products Sales. "They let people run their own businesses. They get involved in the major decisions, but for the everyday business going on, we are allowed to make the decisions. Young managers have a lot of authority in this company." It requires an enormous self-restraint and confidence to give freedom for others to make decisions and act. That is the corporate character of General Mills and one of the keys to its continuing momentum and enduring success.

The entrepreneurial spirit at General Mills is not confined to consumer foods or even the marketing end of that organization. Innovation and entrepreneurship pervade the entire organization. In manufacturing, innovation is encouraged at the very lowest level. Small teams study problems that individually may not involve more than $1,000 in operating costs, in an effort to improve efficiency. In the process, people get involved and enthused, and they begin to think creatively. In another striking example of the entrepreneurial spirit, the company was one of the first to employ a whole series of new investment techniques. Treasurer Jim Weaver proudly explains how he earned excellent returns on arbitrage transactions involving zero-coupon bonds popular in the Eurobond market.

Discipline by Objectives

Discipline is a word you do not hear much at General Mills. Authority is felt as a constant pressure to excel. "The company makes great demands on us," Chris Steiner explained. "They demand excellence in terms of the product and the profit. So there is always that kind of demand. You've got to do it better." The company relies more on an atmosphere of expectation than on rules and regulations to enforce appropriate conduct. Executive Vice-President Paul Parker confirmed: "We are loose and relaxed. Peer pressure will force people into a proper behavior pattern."

A lot of the pressure at General Mills issues from the commitment to the company's financial objectives—a return on equity of 19 percent or more and an annual growth rate at least 6 percent above the rate of inflation. The company has maintained a five-year compound growth rate of 11.3 percent in earnings per share. In a slow-growing field, this performance has made it what *Fortune* called "the toast of the industry."

The company is very serious about meeting its financial goals. Separate profit and loss statements are maintained for each product, retail store, and restaurant. "The object is to make running a General Mills company as much like running a free-standing business as possible," according to the company's chairman, Bruce Atwater.[19] "Profit responsibility is fundamental. If a product manager has it, it pushes him into manufacturing efficiencies, productivity gains, ingredient substitutions, and anticipating commodity fluctuations."[20]

The systems and controls for financial reporting constitute one area where discipline is rigorously enforced. "We do insist on very stringent rules in the accounting and control function," Parker said. "There is no deviation. You have to have figures you can trust." When we asked Steiner how people get in trouble at General Mills, she echoed the same view. "If you aren't honest with someone, if you try to hide something or misrepresent information, that is the only thing I can think of that leads to real serious trouble."

Despite the go-go pace of the brand manager system, the people are surprisingly warm, relaxed, informal, and friendly at General Mills. They really seem to enjoy their work and feel excited about it rather than feeling the stress and strain of a highly competitive race. Freedom, individual involvement, and enormous opportunities for personal growth mitigate the pressures of the fast pace.

Material Incentives

The key to General Mills' youthful exuberance is its ability to release the energies of its employees through positive rather than negative means. The positive forms of authority fall into a gradation ranging from purely material incentives to purely psychological ones. The basis of positive authority is attention to people, recognition of achievement, respect for the individual, and freedom for self-expression. Its most common form is the use of material rewards to motivate people.

For a long time it was commonly believed that monetary incentives were the key to maximizing individual performance. General Mills employs generous monetary incentives; but long before most companies, it recognized that nonmaterial, or psychological, incentives can motivate as nothing else can. Tom Watson, Sr., made the same discovery more than 50 years ago. He converted all factory workers at IBM from piece rate to salaries while expanding the scope and enriching the content of their jobs to the maximum. Many people expected productivity to fall after these changes were introduced, while actually output per worker continued to climb right through the depression and even during the war years, when productivity was declining in most other industries in spite of higher wages.

The major limitation of material incentives is that they relate only to people's performance, not to the people themselves. Like the threat of punishment, which motivates only so long as there is a chance of getting caught, monetary incentives motivate primarily in areas where achievement is measurable and likely to be rewarded. They are also limited by a person's ambition and expectations. Those strange stories we have heard about people in developing countries who work only as hard as is necessary to sustain their present economic level are not so strange or foreign as they may seem. Many people—executives included—are quite satisfied with their present standard of living and beyond that point cannot be easily motivated by financial rewards. In addition, monetary incentives are inherently limited by the economic costs involved in continuous salary increments.

Social Incentives

Attention to people and recognition of achievement are also given through a variety of nonmaterial ways, ranging from a simple pat on the back for a job well done to promotion to a position with greater status, responsibilities, or decision-making authority. These forms of recognition are not limited either by economic constraints on the company or by the ambitions and expectations of the individual. Everyone responds positively to attention and recognition from his or her boss, peers, or subordinates. We all have an unquenchable thirst for social approval.

This is the reason for the success of all the unorthodox and nontraditional techniques now being used to motivate people, such as recognition for heroes and champions and collective rituals like beer busts, award ceremonies, and other forms of hoopla. These methods work because they are all ways of giving positive attention to people, releasing their pride, competitive spirit, sense of community feeling, and willingness to meet challenges. The forms and techniques may differ from company to company, but the principle remains the same.

However, these external forms of attention still belong to the lesser of the greater powers. There are inherent limits to their effectiveness. They tend to become routine, habitual, empty, and flat after a while, like the parting smile of a tired flight attendant who has already said good-bye to a hundred passengers who left the plane before you did.

These methods are successful only so long as and to the extent that they express a real interest, concern, and commitment on the part of management for its employees. When management genuinely feels this way, the form of attention given is less important, or rather, any form will do. It need not even be planned. In fact, the spontaneous expression of attention in the course of work has a greater significance, because it is unexpected and more natural. When management has the right motives and feelings in its relations with employees, employees change their attitude. Their submissiveness changes into loyalty, obedience turns into cooperation, and reluctant or resigned acceptance is converted into enthusiastic agreement. Employees come to identify with the company's beliefs, values, and goals. Work becomes expansive.

Sears' System

Freedom and responsibility are greater incentives than money. When General Robert Wood moved Sears into retail stores in the 1920s, he built up a decentralized, loose-knit retail system that extended a great deal of freedom to store managers and demanded a large measure of self-reliance and personal capacity from them. As James Worthy described the system in *Shaping an American Institution:*

> People were encouraged, even pushed, to reach to the limit
> of their capabilities, and sometimes to develop capabilities
> they never knew they had. . . . It was built around dynamic
> forces which fostered the processes of growth and matura-
> tion. It left ample room for growth to occur within the in-
> dividual, recognizing that while growth could be encouraged
> or inhibited by external conditions, it was the individual who
> had to do the growing.[21]

Wood's system is still in force today. Entrepreneurship in Sears' 798 retail stores is encouraged not only at the level of the general manager but all the way down. The Wayne, New Jersey, store is divided into 15 divisions, each headed by a separate manager. Each division maintains its own profit-and-loss accounts. The divisional managers are given greater freedom and responsibility than many store managers running other retail shops. The store manager, Bill Collett, explains:

> By responsibility, I mean the magnitude of the job, the abil-
> ity to merchandise, to schedule our people, to set up and
> control inventories—it's far beyond what most retailers give
> their employees. Our people have more involvement. . . .
> The autonomy that you have is one of the areas that is most
> exciting. The company gives you freedom. There are param-
> eters, obviously, that you have to stay within, but within
> that you do have a broad range of decision making. I don't

look over the managers' shoulders and breathe down their necks. I explain what I want from them and give them enough rope to do their jobs. I think people respond very positively to it. I know that I do myself.

Psychological Incentives

The most powerful incentives for motivating people are neither the lure of material rewards for high performance nor recognition and approval for surpassing one's peers. The greatest potentials of organization are revealed when the psychological energies of the individuals are released in pursuit of their own personal growth. When people grow through their work, they require no material incentives or social recognition. Their work becomes self-rewarding, self-motivating, and filled with joy. Employees at Delta derive a sense of personal satisfaction from making the customer happy. Delta flight attendant Chris Hendrix said: "We don't smile at the passengers because we feel we have to do it for the company. We do it because the company is there for us. We want to do it for the company. I'm proud of this company. This company has done a lot for me, personally." When an organization provides individuals with opportunities of this type, it becomes a living organization.

The Living Organization

What makes an organization come alive? Let us start with the individual. When does an individual become interested, vivacious, overflowing with energy? Recollect the most exciting moments in your own life, and the answer will be clear. When the outer circumstances or activities of our life appeal to our own inner seeking, we become actively involved and enthusiastic. When our work becomes an avenue or occasion for personal growth, we feel energetic and take joy in what we do.

People have two ways of existence—surviving and growing. When they are just surviving, life is routine, habitual, dull, flat, boring. The only satisfaction comes from physical pleasures and comfort. When they are growing, life becomes fresh, exciting, challenging, thrilling, and enjoyable. The child grows physically for 18 years or so, but people can continue to grow in knowledge, maturity, life experience, emotions, and skills throughout their whole life. Surviving requires a minimum of energy; growth requires a maximum. During times of growth our physical, nervous, and mental energies are at their peak, flowing and overflowing on all sides. When our inner motives or outer circumstances release our maximum energies, we grow psychologically.

When an organization genuinely commits itself to the personal growth of its people, it can help create the right inner motives and external conditions for their development. When the company grows, the people grow with it. When the people grow, the company grows, too. Each can stimulate the other. The individuals come to identify their personal seeking more and more with the company's progress and find personal fulfillment by giving themselves to it through service. When this happens, the psychological energies of the individual are constantly being released in work and flowing out to animate the life of the organization. The organization becomes alive and charged with a vivifying energy.

Ten Steps for Establishing Positive Authority

A natural, progressive development of authority takes place in organizations: personal enforcement of discipline by the proprietor or founder; impersonal discipline enforced through rules and systems; self-discipline by employees and peer pressure based on an attitude of loyalty and commitment to the success of the organization; and finally, self-motivating and self-rewarding dedication by each individual worker in an atmosphere of freedom.

The stages of this progression can be reduced to ten basic steps:

1. *Decision:* Decide which areas and values of the company are absolutely vital to its very existence.
2. *Standards:* Establish clear and precise lines of authority, decision-making powers, and guidelines for behavior in these core areas.
3. *Regulations:* Develop well-defined rules and regulaltions for enforcement of proper conduct in the core areas.
4. *Systems:* Create systems to monitor and evaluate performance and to enforce discipline in the core areas wherever necessary.
5. *Training:* Educate new recruits and present employees to fully understand and appreciate the importance of conforming to the standards.

6. *Communication:* Constantly re-emphasize the importance of these standards through various forms of communication and by example.

7. *Reward:* Introduce incentives for outstanding performance by individuals or groups with respect to core values.

8. *Recognition and award:* Offer personal recognition either publicly or privately to those who perform exceptionally well.

9. *Corporate milieu:* When the values are fully accepted and adhered to without the need for rigorous systems and strict discipline, relax the external forms of enforcement, extend greater freedom, and gradually allow self-discipline and peer pressure to take the place of external authority.

10. *Identification:* In each individual try to build up a personal understanding of, commitment to, and identification with these values, so that the person's adherence to them becomes an expression of his or her own personal growth and a self-rewarding experience.

CHAPTER 5

System, System, System!

In the fall of 1542 Humayun, the second Mogul emperor of India, was on a military campaign, while his wife lay in bed at home expecting the birth of their first child. Humayun longed for a son to inherit and expand his empire, and he was anxious to receive news of the child's birth the moment it occurred. So he called all the ministers of the court to advise him on how the news could be sent from the city where the empress lay to his camp 100 miles away in the shortest possible time. One minister suggested sending word by the emperor's best rider on his fastest horse. But over rough terrain in the scorching heat, a journey of 100 miles would take an entire day or more. Another minister improved on this idea by suggesting a relay of horses, with each rider traveling at top speed for 5 or 10 miles and passing on the message to the next one. The emperor was not satisfied with these suggestions. The ministers were stumped.

Finally a wise old minister announced, to the amazement of the assembly, that he had found a solution and would arrange for the message to travel faster than the fastest horse, faster even than the wind. The emperor was intrigued by the minister's boast and ordered him to execute it. The minister issued instructions for tall towers to be erected every few miles between the city and the emperor's camp. On top of each tower, someone was stationed with a drum. As soon as the child was born, a drum message was relayed across the 100-mile span in less than five minutes, announcing the birth of a son, who later became known as Akbar, the greatest of all the Mogul emperors of India. A simple system made possible a feat that seemed unimaginable at the time. That is the power of a system.

Talk about systems has become so very commonplace that there hardly seems any point in discussing them further. But though the word has been severely overworked, systems themselves still remain a vastly underutilized resource. Almost everyone who wears eyeglasses has, on at least one occasion, looked everywhere for the glasses, only to discover he or she was wearing them. Our search for the secrets of the living organization is not very different. As a rule, people never understand the value of the things they enjoy. Systems are no exception. They are so pervasive, fundamental, and essential to the routine workings of business and society that we take them completely for granted—unless, of course, they break down.

The Corporate Impersonality

Let us begin with a definition and description of what systems are all about. Individual acts are the basic units of any work. Several acts occurring in succession for a particular purpose constitute an activity. In an organization there are many activities like recruitment, purchasing, sales, planning, accounting, shipping goods, receiving customers, and distribution of mail that are repeated over and over again in the same way. Every type of repetitive activity can be reduced to a system. A system is an arrangement of acts or activities into a standardized, fixed sequence consisting of a series of step-by-step procedures. Systems link activities in an orderly manner to ensure greater efficiency and a smoother flow of work.

Earlier we likened systems to the temperamental traits of an individual's personality. Each person has certain characteristic and predictable ways of behaving that tend to recur under particular circumstances. So do corporations. Systems are an organization's fixed patterns of response to recurring situations. When a handbag is lost or a child is separated from his or her parents at Disneyland, there is a system to handle the problem and set it right with a smile. When an employee at Eastman Kodak Company has an innovative idea, there is a system for receiving, evaluating, and rewarding the suggestion.

Systems are like the nerve channels of a corporation. When we accidentally place our hand on a very hot object, the hand is quickly withdrawn by an automatic nervous response, which does not require or await a conscious decision on our part. Companies have similar automatic or habitual responses to most types of recurring situations. When orders come in, they are automatically processed without requiring fresh instructions each time from the CEO. When stocks are depleted, they are automatically reordered. When sales are made, they are immediately recorded and reported to the accounting department on a regular basis. When products are manufactured, they are routinely subjected to rigorous quality-control checks. All these routine, habitual expressions of corporate behavior are made possible by systems.

Modern commercial organizations are distinguished from those of earlier times primarily by the presence of sophisticated, impersonal systems to replace functioning through personal management. This has enabled these organizations to grow to a much larger size, to function over longer distances, and to maintain greater uniformity and coordination than could ever be attained otherwise. All systems, regardless of their purpose, share several common attributes:

1. A system is a mechanism that completes a full cycle of activity. It is not uncommon to find "fragments" of systems operative in modern organizations, such as inventory records that are never examined to analyze discrepancies and errors, or personnel evaluation forms that are never utilized to improve performance or distribute rewards.

2. A system can function effectively only when it is based on a set of accepted standards and clear policy directives to handle exceptions. A mechanism that works most of the time but is often circumvented is a habit, not a system. The fixing of salaries is not governed by a system if the decision is made by different people at different times following different guidelines.

3. Systems make possible evaluation of individual or group performance against an established standard, thereby providing a work incentive for the individual and a means of monitoring and control by management. Without this element of evaluation, no system is complete.

4. Systems constitute the central nervous system of an organization. They must be fully integrated with each other and supported by subsystems that extend into all "limbs" of the organization's functioning. The health of the organization as a whole can be assessed by monitoring the performance of its peripheral subsystems. It is in the execution of small, routine matters that organizational efficiency is most easily measured.

5. Systems are creative in the sense that they make creativity possible. When appropriate systems are introduced or existing ones are perfected, the organization is able to convert underutilized and untapped resources into new growth and expansion.

People constitute the personal side of organizational life. Systems constitute the impersonal dimension of a company. Creativity, expansiveness, enthusiasm, inspiration, leadership, and human satisfaction are expressions of the personal side. Organization, productivity, order, efficiency, harmony, consistency, and stability are expressions of the impersonal side. This impersonality is embodied in the rules, procedures, and systems that an organization adopts for its functioning.

The Thinking Manager's Capital

At the turn of the century, 60 percent of the American people lived in rural areas, many of them isolated by vast distances from life in the cities, where retail merchandising was almost exclusively concentrated. With mechanization, the farming community was becoming more productive and more prosperous, yet farmers still depended almost exclusively on traveling sales reps and ill-provisioned general stores to meet their growing appetite for modern conveniences and luxuries.

Julius Rosenwald saw the growing opportunities of the rural market. When he joined Richard Sears, he brought to their enterprise an inspiring mission and new values. The mission he conceived was to become a buyer for the American farmer, to sell a broad selection of products that the rural community could not readily obtain through existing sources—clothing, dry goods, patent medicines, bicycles, musical instruments, hunting equipment, kitchenware, tools, and so on. The new values he contributed were embodied in the policy "Satisfaction Guaranteed or Your Money Back." With these basic elements as a psychic center, Sears, Rosenwald, and later Otto Doering created an organization to carry out this mission. The psychic center gave direction to their enterprise, and the organization gave it form; but in order to put their inspiring ideas and prodigious talents into practice, they required one more thing—a system.

Although 45 million Americans were residing out in the countryside at the time, 90 percent of them lived in areas with populations of fewer than 100 people. The average density of the rural population was so low that establishing retail stores to serve even half of this community would have required a prohibitive investment and yielded extremely poor returns. An alternative system was required and was already in existence—the mail-order catalog. In 1872 Montgomery Ward had established a catalog to serve the needs of the rural community, and it had grown to include some 10,000 items.

Rosenwald adopted the mail-order system and the money-back guarantee from Montgomery Ward, but he upgraded the system to reflect his own business values. By insisting on very high ethical standards in advertising and a consistently higher quality of merchandise, he in effect created the first factual mail-order catalog, the "wish book." The combination of these values and the talents of the two proprietors enabled them to surpass the performance of Montgomery Ward & Company within the first five years, using the very system that Ward had developed.

Systems are the channels through which organizations translate their ideas into actions. What a large investment of capital in retail stores could never have achieved, a system could. Systems are the thinking manager's capital. As the mail-order system enabled Sears to sell its products to an inaccessible rural market, the drive-in restaurant and the in-flight catering service enabled Marriott to sell food to mobile American travelers. In each case, a new system spanned the gap between a business and its customers.

The Golden Gap

The catalog-sales system was so successful that it brought more orders than either Sears or Rosenwald ever dreamed of—and more problems, too. The sheer volume of new orders pouring in threatened to drown the young business in a sea of paper. As one executive described it: "The whole operation became chaotic. Long delays in shipments, a rising tide of errors leading to a flood of returned goods which in turn were badly handled, absenteeism, replacement of 'quitting' employees by inexperienced people—all were combining to make the place a shambles."[1]

Otto Doering joined the company in 1903, just in time to save the system by introducing another one—the schedule system. Doering designed and commissioned the Chicago mail-order factory, the first modern mass-production plant, covering an area of over 3 million square feet of floor space and equipped with moving conveyor belts, an assembly line, pneumatic tubes, elevators, and miles of railroad tracks.

The plant actually derived its enormous efficiency from the coordination of two systems: a supply system to handle the purchase, delivery, and storage of tens of thousands of items of merchandise from hundreds of vendors, and a delivery system to handle the processing and dispatch of tens of thousands of customer orders a day. The huge volume of incoming goods had to be sorted out, stocked, and matched with the orders on hand. The quantities of merchandise and paperwork were far beyond anything attempted before. Proper execution demanded strict discipline and precise timing.

When the gap between two related activities is bridged by linking and coordinating two separate systems, an enormous creative potential is unleashed. Doering's invention was so effective that "a company which had been on the verge of having to halt its growth suddenly found itself with a virtually unlimited capacity for continued expansion."[2] The system enabled the company's catalog sales to grow from $50 million in 1907, the first full year of its operation, to $235 million in 1920; and they have multiplied another 20-fold since then, to around $5 billion a year.

Systems are not only the basic building blocks of an organization. They are also the bridges and bonds it uses to connect and bind its various parts into a single whole. There is gold buried in the invisible zone between two uncoordinated systems. How many such gaps are there in every company? There are as many gaps as there are systems—gaps between design, production, distribution, sales, marketing, purchasing, research, accounting, recruiting, training, planning, and countless other systematic functions of a company. Every one of them possesses a rich vein of unmined ore. Sears' example is impressive because its size is impressive. But the principle is equally true of the smallest retail store, corner restaurant, and garage-scale manufacturing firm, thousands of which are multiplying this very moment at much greater rates than Sears ever did, without fully understanding the reason for their own growth.

Systems Magic

When Sears entered the retail store business, its mission was broadened to encompass all American households as its customer base. New systems were required to serve this wider mission. One of the most productive of these has been the Sears credit card.

The aim of most credit-card systems is to attract the higher-middle-income and upper-income families, who buy more and can afford to pay for what they buy. Since Sears' mission is to serve as many American households as possible, the aim of the system is to extend credit to the maximum number of families, including those in the lower income groups, but at the same time to keep its losses from nonpayment as low as possible. These two objectives are in direct conflict with each other, yet Sears has successfully reconciled them through a system.

Today Sears' credit card is the most widely held in the world. Approximately 40 million American families hold a Sears card. Sears receives roughly 10 million new credit applications every year and approves 4 million of them. The volume alone requires a fairly remarkable system. Sears provides credit to more households with incomes above $30,000 than does the American Express Company and more credit to lower-income households, too—about 14 percent of all households in low-income urban areas. More remarkable yet, Sears' losses from nonpayment amount to only 1 percent of credit sales, which is less than all the major bank credit cards and less than half the level of Sears' major competitors. Unbelievable as it may seem, Sears does not even have a minimum income standard for approval of credit.

How does Sears do it? That is the magic of a system. Over many years of experience, the company has developed a very sophisticated credit-approval system, which consists of 700 models, a different model for almost every geographic region in which it sells. By carefully refining the system, the company has identified the characteristics of creditworthy customers at different levels of income and in different parts of the country. The system enables it to extend more credit—$12 billion worth—to more households than any other credit-card system. Largely because of this system, Americans buy 40 percent of all washers and dryers, 40 percent of automobile replacement batteries, and an incredible 75 percent of all bench power tools from Sears. A system makes it possible for the company to achieve its mission as supplier to the mass American market.

The Technology of Organization

A common misconception of small entrepreneurial companies is the belief that today's giant corporations achieved their present status on the strength of some unique personal endowments of their founders, a brilliant idea or new technology, or a large reserve of capital it tapped for investment. In most cases, the only unique endowment of the founder was a willingness to work hard; the only brilliant idea was a commitment to quality or service; the only new technology was a knowledge of how to motivate people; and the only reserve the firm tapped was one of the many powers of organization.

In assessing the productive strength of a corporation, we naturally focus our attention on its financial, technical, and human resources—assets, cash flow, product quality, managerial abilities, technical skills, proven capacity for innovation, market position, and so on. In so doing, we tend to overlook the enormous productive power of other organizational resources. It is well known in industry that a good technology is as important to success as capital and can sometimes achieve what money alone never can. Many a poor inventor has died extremely rich. It is less commonly recognized that inventing the right system can be even more profitable than inventing the right product. As technology is the engineer's capital, systems are the businessperson's technology.

Whatever a company's financial or technological resources may be, systems possess the power to increase their productivity thousands of times. When Ford was founded in 1903, the American automobile industry consisted of several hundred small-scale assembly units, each manufacturing a few hundred or a few thousand cars a year. The cars ranged in price from $1,000 to $2,000, placing them beyond the reach of the vast majority of Americans.

Henry Ford was one among the many. His company sold 1,745 cars in its first year of operation at a little less than $1,000 each and increased the number to 9,000 in 1906. But his dream was to produce an affordable car for the masses. The two major constraints were the slow speed of existing production techniques and the high costs involved in the process. He overcame both with a system.

Five years after Doering commissioned the Chicago mail-order plant, Ford's new Highland Park factory for mass production of the Model T came into full use. There was nothing new or original about the plant, except that the proven system of a moving assembly line was employed for the first time to manufacture automobiles.

Ford's gigantic "Crystal Palace," covering some 50,000 square feet, consisted of three main assembly lines supported by an endless number of conveyors, chutes, tubes, bins, and hoists supplying components to fixed work positions along the lines in a steady stream to ensure nonstop production. These physical systems were supported by a host of administrative systems for inventory control, job routing, purchasing, shipping, and accounting. After visiting the plant, a reporter from the *Detroit Journal* described the operation in three words: "System, System, System!"[3]

Ford's systems reduced the work required for assembling a chassis from 728 minutes of one worker's time to 93 minutes and brought down the price of the Model T from $950 to $290, well within the reach of the common person. From 1906 to 1916 the company's car production increased 80-fold. Between 1908 and 1927 over 15 million Model Ts were built by these systems. During World War II, Ford employed a similar integrated production system at its Willow Run plant to produce new B-24 bombers at the rate of one an hour.

These systems not only produced cars, they produced capital, too—lots of it. In 1903 Ford started with a cash base of $28,000. By 1913, without any subsequent investment, the company had accumulated assets valued at more than $22.5 million and had paid out $15 million in dividends. By 1927 the company's cash surplus alone was nearly $700 million—a 25,000-fold increase in 24 years!

Ford applied a known organizational technology to a new field with phenomenal results. The introduction of these systems transformed the industry from a group of a few hundred small-scale units into a handful of large-scale manufacturers. In the process, he demonstrated once and for all the incredible productive power of coordinated systems.

A Distant Traveler

While many companies are alive to the potential for applying proven technologies such as the computer to new fields, how many see the far greater potential for applying proven systems to new fields as Ford has done? One example of a system that has been going places is the one developed by Coca-Cola for distribution of its soft drinks.

Until 1899 Coke was sold only through soda fountains. In that year two men from Chattanooga attending a baseball game came across a soft drink that was sold in a bottle. They approached Asa Candler, who owned Coca-Cola at the time, to suggest that he sell Coke in bottles. Candler was not interested but agreed to give the two men a perpetual franchise to sell bottled Coke throughout practically the whole United States. The franchise was awarded for $1. Legend has it that even that dollar was never paid. If so, it was the best dollar Coca-Cola never made—"a master-stroke" as *Fortune* called it.[4] For this was the beginning of the company's franchise bottling system— the granddaddy of franchising—consisting of independent bottlers, whose entrepreneurial spirit has carried Coke to the four corners of the world. Today the system includes 1,500 bottling companies in 155 countries.

Just as people respond to personal attention by performing better, so do systems. In recent years Coca-Cola has been giving a lot of attention to its franchise bottling system to raise its performance to the highest possible level. Many of the bottlers had become so successful and so wealthy that they felt little incentive to expand further. In 1979 Coca-Cola began a major program to upgrade the system by bringing in a new generation of entrepreneurs who are raring to grow and willing to invest. Since then more than 120 franchises covering over 50 percent of Coca-Cola's business in the United States have changed hands in transactions valued at more than $2 billion. Coca-Cola's attention to the system paid off. Between 1979 and 1983 the company's operating revenues grew by 50 percent, and its share of the U.S. soft drink market exceeded 38 percent. As the president of one large independent Coca-Cola bottling company described the systems update: "Coca-Cola USA has energized the system. . . . The sleeping giant is wide awake."[5]

Following its acquisition of Columbia Pictures in 1982, Coca-Cola is in the process of taking its franchise system into an entirely new field—entertainment. It has begun test distribution of movies on videocassettes through the bottling companies to retail stores. Whatever the outcome, it demonstrates the tremendous potential for adapting systems for new applications.

A System Diversifies

The franchise system adopted by Coca-Cola in 1899 has formed the basis for many entirely new industries. In 1955, at age 66, Colonel Harland Sanders founded the business for which he has become famous. At the time the only things he had going for him were a good idea, a great system, and a $105 Social Security check. The idea and the system long outlasted the check. His idea was a recipe for frying chicken in a special high-temperature cooker. His system was to sell franchises to restaurants—leasing them the cookers, supplying napkins and buckets carrying the Kentucky Fried Chicken name along with his image, and charging $0.05 for every chicken the restaurants sold. By 1964 Colonel Sanders had granted more than 500 franchises and sold the business for $2 million. Today there are over 6,000 units in 54 countries with total sales of more than $2 billion. That is the productive power of a system!

The fast-food business actually began way back in 1921, when White Castle opened its first hamburger stand. The company had the right idea, but not the system. White Castle never sold a franchise. Sixty years later it still had only 175 units. If it had not been for the franchise system, there might only be 175 McDonald's restaurants today, too, instead of 7,500. Ray Kroc, the founder of the McDonald's Corporation, opened his first McDonald's franchise in 1955, and within five years he surpassed the level reached by White Castle over the period of a half-century. By 1982 there were McDonald's franchises all over the world, with sales of $7.8 billion.

The power of the franchise system results from combining the entrepreneurial initiative of private owners with the name, expertise, and experience of the parent company. Franchising is a system that is transforming the way retail business is done in the United States. Today there are nearly half a million franchise outlets selling goods and services for around $500 billion a year, which represents more than a third of the nation's total retail sales. The system has accommodated itself to an incredible variety of businesses, including franchise mail and package delivery, film sales and processing, dry cleaning, printing, photocopying, health clubs, home security, computers, and home renovation.

How many hundreds or thousands of systems are now being employed in other companies and other industries that could be adopted or upgraded to enrich the life of any organization? Adopting a system that is already prevalent in the field enables a company to compete with the leaders of the industry. Adapting a system to a new field enables a company to become leader of the industry.

The Values of Systems

Bill Marriott, Sr., and Tomas Bata utilized systems for more effective implementation of corporate values. Values can also be utilized to give greater effective force to systems. There is virtually an infinite scope for increasing the power of systems by a commitment to higher values in their implementation. This is what Julius Rosenwald did when he insisted on honesty and reliability in the operation of Sears' mail-order system. Merck enhanced the effectiveness of its marketing system by insisting on truthfulness with the medical community. Du Pont increased the efficiency of its operating systems by striving hard to protect its workers.

The Federal Express Corporation created a new business out of an old system based on two values: reliability and punctuality. Recognizing the tremendous importance that Americans place on time, Frederick Smith devised a system to save it. He adopted the basic elements of the system from the U.S. Postal Service and United Parcel Service, Inc.—a squadron of airplanes and a fleet of delivery vans— but brought down delivery times for a parcel from three days or more to less than 24 hours. The idea itself was not new, but the quality and reliability of service were—99 percent of packages delivered on time. Virtually overnight, Federal Express has grown into a $1.4 billion company, and the overnight-delivery business as a whole has exploded into a $5 billion industry.

There is an unlimited scope for upgrading the values of systems— quality, cleanliness, punctuality, reliability, friendliness of service, safety, job satisfaction, efficiency, productivity, and integrity— whether they are systems for serving a customer, serving food in an employee cafeteria, monitoring travel expenses or individual job performance, or delivering goods and services on time or at the lowest possible cost.

A Productive Marriage

In the case of Sears, we saw that the proper combination of two personalities or two systems generates a much greater power than the sum of the parts when they operate in isolation. The same golden gap exists for every organizational resource (such as skills, capital, technology, or machinery) and for every combination of two different resources (such as capital and technology or skills and machinery). Each enhances and multiplies the effectiveness of the other. This potential also exists when any other resource is combined with a system.

One of the most obvious present-day examples of this principle is the impact of computer technology on business systems. The marriage of systems with computers has increased the productive powers of the organization many times. Yet most companies have only just begun to explore the enormous opportunities in this area.

What would you do if you had 50,000 cars that you were trying to rent to the public from 1,000 locations around the United States and your highest priority was good customer service, which means always having a car available to the customer when he or she has reserved one? Most companies would probably go out of business. The fact that Hertz has twice that many cars, a reputation for reliable service, and a profitable business as well is primarily due to a computerized management system.

It all sounds so logical that it is easy to assume things were always this way, but they were not. When the rent-a-car business began to take off in the 1960s, computers were being used by companies almost exclusively for standard accounting purposes. Hertz and the other rent-a-car firms kept track of the supply and demand for their cars around the country on manual worksheets. In the mid-1970s Hertz introduced one of the first computer-based decision-support systems used in business.

The supply and demand for cars is influenced by such factors as day of the week, season of the year, special events, conventions, transfer of cars from other locations, impact of weather on incoming flights, and availability of cars from competitor companies. The new system takes into account these variables and enables each city manager to project the demand and availability of cars at each location on an hour-to-hour basis with 95 percent to 98 percent accuracy.

After introduction of the system, there has been a 10 percent improvement in the utilization of Hertz's fleet of cars, which represents a saving for the company of between $25 million and $40 million a year. More important, the system has enabled the company to double its size, which would have been extremely difficult under the old manual system. The quality of customer service is also significantly better.

Five years ago the operating system was integrated into an overall business planning system that enables managers to quickly evaluate the impact of any major decision concerning things like pricing, level of investment, or expenditure on advertising on overall performance and profitability. The rent-a-car business has become so competitive and complex and the margins of profit so marginal that, according to Vice-President Marty Edelstein, without the system "we probably couldn't even run the business."

There are countless other types of systems, both simple and sophisticated, that can be linked to the computer with similar results. The increased productivity arising from linking systems to a higher order of technology can be obtained by linking systems with other organizational resources as well. The introduction of higher-order skills, for instance, can raise the efficiency of a system manyfold. The opportunities are all around us.

Too Much or Too Little?

Despite the widely shared impression that American business is organized to the core and is suffering from an overdose of bureaucracy, even the best of American companies tap only 50 percent or 60 percent efficiency from their systems. On August 5, 1984, *The New York Times* carried an article reporting an unusual event that occurred a few months prior to the breakup of the Bell System:

The American Telephone and Telegraph Company dispatched a cadre of white-collar soldiers to its warehouses to find out why shipments of small office switchboards were running behind schedule. At one Manhatten warehouse, a group of crates that had sat ignored for no one knew how long turned out to contain 200 of the phone switchboards for which customers had been clamoring.

The *Times* article goes on to quote a former AT&T salesman:

Here's the largest company in the world, a company that's supposed to be so sophisticated and computerized, opening boxes to find out what it had in inventory.[6]

The purchasing department of another large telephone-equipment manufacturer called up one of its suppliers urgently requesting a particular component to meet a production run in one of its plants. Since the supplier did not have the item in stock, it scanned its files to see if any other customer might have some extra pieces available. After a while it called back the manufacturer to report it had located a very large stock of the component just a few miles away—at another plant belonging to the same manufacturer! How is it that the purchasing department had no record of the extra inventory? It happened because each of the plants has its own inventory coding system for components, and the code numbers used by the two plants for the item were different. According to Ed Devine, who has managed the American Management Association's Purchasing Division for many years, such incidents are quite common, and the larger the company, the more common they are.

When Iacocca joined Chrysler, he discovered to his "horror" that there was no overall system for financial control or effective financial planning and projecting. Some of the bankers who reluctantly agreed to go along with the U.S. government's loan guarantees for Chrysler were not much better. One bank in Minnesota had a filing system that was so effective that Chrysler's loan agreements were put through the shredder by a cleaning lady before they could be signed. Another bank in Alaska had a dispatch system that was so well perfected that loan agreements required in Detroit to meet a government deadline were put in the postal system instead of being returned by express courier.

Until recently the accounts payable section of one of America's five largest insurance companies was run very efficiently by two women. The filing system they employed was excellent, except that no one but the two women could figure out how to use it. It is fortunate that the system was changed, because just two weeks later, the two women were involved in a traffic accident and hospitalized.

Are these examples all rare flukes or exceptions to the American rule? It is more likely that they represent standard operating procedure in many companies. Every company, even the most excellent, has dozens of experiences like these that it wishes had never happened but that always do because systems do not receive the constant and continuous attention they deserve. "Systems?" says the executive. "We've got all we need." The real issue is not how many systems a company has, but how well and appropriately it uses them. Systems do some things very well and other things quite poorly. Systems stimulate growth in some areas and prevent it in others. Systems are merely an instrument. They function productively only when guided by the right psychic direction and controlled by a strong corporate character.

Systems Review

Almost every problem can be solved in more than one way. A cash-flow problem, for instance, can be resolved by obtaining a loan, firing staff, or selling assets. It can also be solved by an organizational innovation that raises productivity, speeds up deliveries, accelerates collection of receivables, or attracts additional business by improving the quality of a product or service. All the other solutions cost money. The organizational solution may cost nothing. Perhaps that is why it is often neglected or underestimated. Imitation of another country, like Japan, even when possible, is difficult. Why go to the trouble when there are hundreds of organizational innovations that we can make based on our own cultural heritage that will yield equal or greater results?

Have you ever noticed the impact that a small improvement in a system can make on efficiency, quality, speed, or ease of functioning? Much time and money can be saved, much irritation and confusion can be eliminated by making simple refinements in the systems we use. It has become standard practice in many companies to periodically or continuously review long-term goals, short-term objectives, plans, budget allocations, job performance, salary scales, and many other aspects of their business in order to assess the adequacy of their functioning. Adjustments are then made because of changes within the company or in its external environment. Systems are one organizational resource that is not frequently subjected to close scrutiny and review in order to update them or improve their performance. Yet the benefits that can result from regular reviews of all systems are quite substantial. Otto Doering recognized this and set up a methods department in 1906 to continuously refine and improve systems at Sears' mail-order plant.

Merck regularly reviews its system for introduction of new products to shorten the period required for research, development, clinical testing, FDA approval, training, and marketing. Every day's delay in getting a new product on the market represents not only a lost sale but also a shorter period before the expiry of patent rights on the drug or the development of a better one by competitors. For this reason, Eugene McCabe, vice-president of marketing at MSD, says, "We are constantly changing that system and constantly modifying and upgrading and improving it."

The policy-owners' services department of Northwestern Mutual is continuously reviewing its procedures for receiving and replying to customer inquiries. In 1969 a major systems update was undertaken, which brought down the time required to open a new insurance service account from six days to one. The ratio of policy-owner letters answered within five days rose from 11 percent in 1969 to 80 percent in 1970.[7] Although there is a lot of research involved in responding to inquiries from customers about their policies, Northwestern Mutual is still not satisfied with its system and is continuously trying to improve it. Where payments are involved, the response time has been reduced to two days; for transactions, three days; and for all other correspondence the goal is to respond within six days. Three times a week the service representatives report their oldest pending case, and twice a month an accurate measurement is made of their response time. The representatives themselves are constantly suggesting ways to improve the system. In the new business department the face amount of new policies issued has increased by 50 percent over the last two years, but staff has increased by only 7 percent. Systems reviews are one of the reasons why Northwestern Mutual has the highest productivity in its industry. The company's operating expenses are 20 percent to 30 percent lower than those of its competitors.

Every company has recurring types of problems that crop up now and then under certain circumstances. These problems become characteristic traits of the company, just as its systems are. But at Coca-Cola, every time a problem arises, the firm not only tries to solve it, but also tries to remove its cause at the source. Coca-Cola's senior vice-president for finance remarked that confidence in the proper working of its systems is very important to the company. "We spend a lot of time when something doesn't go right, not so much to analyze the mistake but to analyze the systematic failure that caused the mistake. I'm liable to call six people together and say: 'OK, we are all part of a system. Where didn't the system work?'"

General Mills is continuously striving to improve its systems. In the Grocery Products Sales Division, constant modification of the sales representatives' routing system has enabled the company to raise its sales volume by 60 percent without any increase in personnel. The Package Foods Operations Division encourages employees to suggest even minor improvements involving less than $1,000. It creates an atmosphere of participation and an urge for perfection, which has spawned a 10 percent increase in cases produced per worker-hour over the last two years, and productivity is still rising. Constant improvements in the distribution system have held costs per case to a 1 percent increase since 1979, despite a 15 percent increase in salaries. The quality of service has also improved, so that the company has moved up from No. 5 to No. 1 in customer surveys. At General Mills, systems reviews have become a regular activity. Gene Sailer, director of manufacturing, Package Foods Operations Division, says:

> We've done a lot of looking at our organization. We're using outside resources to keep ourselves abreast. We're permitting employees to visit from one plant to another, so they can share ideas. To be successful in the long term, we have to *institutionalize* these things. It's not a program. It's a process. . . . And we're still not where we want to be. It's a continuing effort to get better.

Senior Vice-President and Technical Director John Luck says that in general a company can "improve its operations up to 40 percent when threatened—we try to tap that resource *before* being threatened."[8]

Have you ever wondered why telephone operators are not quite so talkative as they used to be? The reason is very simple. From about 1970 until the breakup of AT&T, the Bell System was continuously trying to improve the efficiency of its operator systems in order to keep phone rates down. Before 1970 the average time required by an operator to handle a single call was 60 seconds. By a combination of improved technology, better operator training, and constant monitoring, the average time was gradually brought down to 30 seconds, then 20, and finally 15.9. Today's operator handles nearly four calls per minute instead of one. Who ever said Ma Bell is getting old?

A periodic review of all systems can give fresh momentum to the activity of any department. Each system can be broken down into its step-by-step procedures and carefully analyzed. Then the links between systems can be studied to determine to what extent they are properly coordinated. Another proven technique is the one followed by Coca-Cola. List all problems and try to trace each one back to a defective system, or at least try to find a way to solve the problem by upgrading systems. This strategy focuses attention on the golden gaps in the existing fabric of interacting systems and highlights the points where the system itself or its coordination and integration with other systems are not adequate. As Herb Dean, a systems consultant and former director of office operations at Kodak, expressed it: "You should review everything you are doing. Systems are really the key to success."

Maximum Utilization of Systems

Systems are an invaluable resource. Like other resources, they should be fully and properly utilized. Systems are the lifelines of an organization, and the organization's efficiency is measured by the effectiveness with which it utilizes them. The most successful companies are not only the most value-driven, innovative, and enthusiastic. They are also the best organized and most systematic. Every company can profit by asking itself five simple questions.

1. *Are all our systems functioning properly?* If a system is occasionally inadequate to keep up with its workload or if it is sometimes necessary for a manager to interfere with a system to set things right or if unforeseen problems arise in routine areas of work, something is wrong with either the design of the system or the way in which it is being used.

2. *At the points of intersection between different systems, is there harmonious coordination and integration?* Managers spend a lot of time acting as informal and personal links between two or more systems that have not been properly joined. Most problems a manager is confronted with arise from systems that are poorly designed or inadequately coordinated. Both problems can be eliminated.

3. *Are we fully utilizing all the systems we have introduced?* Companies frequently introduce a system and then bypass it during normal operations. If a system is no good, change it or scrap it. Otherwise, use it without exception. Half-hearted implementation is a sign to the employees that management is not very serious about systematic functioning.

4. *Are there any systems successfully employed by other companies that we could introduce here?* Of course there are—probably dozens. Imagine how long a company could compete in today's world if it re-

fused to employ the latest technological developments introduced by its competitors. It wouldn't last very long. That is a quick recipe for technological obsolescence. A company that fails to introduce new systems that have proved successful elsewhere is heading for organizational obsolescence or worse.

5. *Can we innovate any new systems that will further improve our performance?* When Hal Geneen took over as CEO of ITT in 1959, he devised a system to counteract the rigidity and compartmentalization common to large corporations. The system consisted of a team of headquarters staff specialized in different fields, whose job it was to move throughout the company in search of new ideas and unresolved problems. The system created a supportive atmosphere for change and contributed to ITT's phenomenal growth through the 1960s.

The Acid Test

Many companies pride themselves on the efficiency of their systems for low-cost production, effective marketing, and good customer service. But the truest measure of the extent to which a company effectively utilizes systems is not in these key areas where the company focuses the bulk of its energy and attention. The acid test of efficiency is the speed and manner in which the most insignificant, routine work is accomplished.

Filing: How many executives feel lost the moment their secretary calls in sick, because they cannot find the papers they need in the filing cabinet? When files are arranged systematically, anyone who knows the system should be able to find any document with ease. This may frequently be the case for central files. But most company files maintained by individuals are kept as though they really were "personal" property and no one else's business. Trivial and unimportant, you say? There are presidents of multi-billion-dollar companies who squirm in embarrassment because their office cannot locate a letter or report sent to them. If that is the situation at the top of the organization, it should come as no surprise to learn that raw materials, products, and customer needs are misplaced or overlooked down the line. Filing papers promptly is also a difficult task for most companies. Every secretary seems to have a catchall drawer that never empties. Retrieving things quickly when they are needed is often even more difficult. When all individual files conform to a general filing system intelligible to every staff member, and when materials are filed promptly and are easily retrievable, the company passes a key test for systems utilization.

Customer inquiries: Many companies do not have a formal system for accurately determining where incoming calls should be routed. The caller gets bounced around until he or she is connected to the right party. Our personal experience with IBM indicates that it has a customer inquiry system capable of handling even unconventional inquiries smoothly and swiftly. The time required to reply to a routine letter is another index of systematic functioning. Many companies do not even have established standards for answering letters promptly. Some reply only to certain categories of letters. Those that answer all letters promptly are likely to be leaders in their field.

Accounts: A multinational company that sends out invoices 15 days after shipping orders may sound like an anachronism. So does one whose accounts are perpetually 30 days behind. Apart from the loss of interest due to delayed collection of receivables, these delays are symptoms of a deeper malady. Have you ever noticed that organizations that run into financial trouble inevitably have trouble keeping their accounts up to date, too? New York City in the 1970s was a classic example. It took months for the auditors to figure out what was really going on. Argentina, which reneged on its international financial obligations in 1984, was in a very similar position. The government did not know either how much money it had or how much it owed. Up-to-the-minute accounting systems may sound fairly easy, but they are extremely difficult to maintain—as difficult, perhaps, as enduring corporate success. Our feeling is that the two are very closely related achievements.

Test Your Systems

There is a simple technique that any manager can use to evaluate the efficiency of his or her department. Once a month, circulate a questionnaire to all department personnel to be filled in anonymously and returned. The questionnaire should contain items like the following:

- What is the oldest letter on your desk awaiting a reply?
- How many telephone calls have been received but not yet replied to?
- How many files, books, and other articles have you finished using but not returned to their proper place?
- How many minutes late have you been today reaching the office,

attending meetings, returning from lunch, meeting deadlines, and so on?
- How many routine items of work like preparing a proposal, a plan, or a quotation are behind schedule or overdue at this moment?
- How many bills due for payment remain unpaid, and how many invoices are there for which collection is overdue?

A constant improvement in results on the test over three to six months will be highly correlated with improvements in other objective measures of the department's performance, such as sales or productivity.

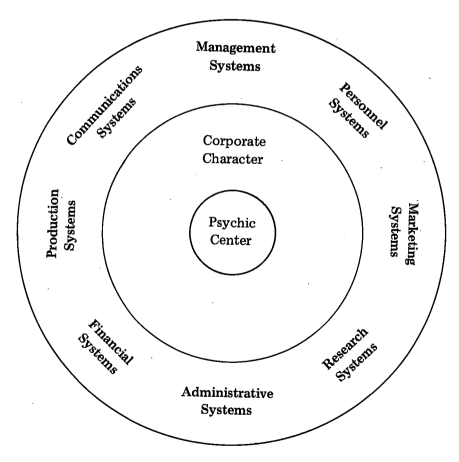

Figure 3. The role of systems in the corporate personality.

A Trusted Servant

Systems are an essential component of the corporate personality. Through them the organization exercises its will to realize values and achieve goals. Without systems the corporate personality lacks a means of effective, coordinated self-expression. But however great their importance and their power, systems are at best only obedient subordinates, as illustrated in Figure 3. Their effectiveness depends on the direction set by the psychic center and the willpower of corporate character.

It is ironic that the man who did the most to demonstrate the value of systems also demonstrated most graphically their limitations. In spite of Henry Ford's keen insight into the power of systems, he was blind to the greater power of which they form a part. He failed to understand that systems are only one component of the organization, and not the organization itself. During the 1930s he ran Ford in the same way he had when it was a tiny proprietary concern. He refused to delegate authority, develop managers, or permit anyone else to make decisions. Those executives who tried to manage either left the company or were fired.

Ford failed to discover the very first principle of organization—creation of an impersonal hierarchy and authority independent of the proprietor. As a result, the company's share of the automobile market, which had reached about 65 percent in the early 1920s, fell to 20 percent in the late 1930s. As Alfred Chandler, Jr., wrote, "The incredibly bad management of his enormous industrial empire, which was so clearly reflected by the lack of any systematic organizational structure, . . . helped cause the rapid drop in Ford's profits and share of the market."[9] Half a century ago Alfred Sloan, the organization man, beat Henry Ford, the engineer. GM won the battle for supremacy. That Ford Motor Company survived its founder at all is a great tribute to the staying power of systems.

CHAPTER 6

Making a Habit
of Success

Skill in works is yoga.

—The Bhagavad Gita[1]

March 4, 1933, was a turning point in American history. It was a dark, cloudy day, and the country was in an equally sullen mood. Over 13 million workers had lost their jobs. More than 10,000 banks had failed in the last four years, and $5 billion had been lost. In the preceding month, 120 million people had rushed to the banks to withdraw their deposits before they, too, were lost. On March 3, in a single day, people had withdrawn more than $300 million from the system in a state of panic. It was clear that the nation's banking system was on the verge of collapse. This was the day on which Franklin Delano Roosevelt was inaugurated as the thirty-second president of the United States of America.

 Roosevelt had a plan to save the banks. His strategy was so simple that it almost defies belief. He would appeal directly to the people. A day after assuming office, he declared a national banking holiday, and a week later he addressed the nation on radio in the first of his famous "fireside chats." What did he say to the people? He explained in clear, simple language what the banking crisis was all about. It was a crisis of confidence, not of substance, and the root cause was fear. What did he tell these countless frightened millions, who had withdrawn billions of dollars from the banks? He told them there was nothing to fear, and he asked them to turn right around and return their hard-earned savings to the banks. And miracle of miracles, they did! When the banks reopened the next day, the lines of people waiting to withdraw their money did not form. The panic was stopped by a man's voice.

Politically, Roosevelt was in a strong position. He had an election mandate and the full support of Congress to back him up. But what he needed most was the confidence and cooperation of the people. He won them both with a brief radio address to the nation and a winning smile. Walter Lippmann wrote at the time, "In one week the nation which had lost confidence in everything and everybody has regained confidence in the government and in itself."[2]

Most of the New Deal ideas were not actually new. Many had been aired before, some even tried by Hoover. Congress had supported Hoover, too, but he lacked the charm and spirit and homely way of speaking that FDR had perfected as an art. Roosevelt had a warm and vibrant personality, which inspired hope and trust, and he possessed consummate skill in communicating his ideas to the people. Without these two attributes—personality and skill—all his bright ideas, good intentions, and political backing could not have moved the people and saved the system.

A proper blend of personality and skill is a key attribute of corporate success as well. Personality expresses the basic qualities of people—their values, character, and temperament. It tells us whether the basic material is a piece of quartz, a ruby, or a diamond. Skill expresses the degree to which the basic human material has been shaped, refined, and polished into a fine gem. Without skills, even the finest personality is an uncut stone, rich in content but poor in form. Without personality, skills are empty, lifeless gestures.

Recruiting a Whole Person

In recruiting new employees, most companies focus on technical qualifications, educational background, and job experience. But very often the most critical factor is none of these. These are only the attributes of something more basic and more central—the person. Once Benjamin Franklin was looking for an editor to help run his newspaper. One man applied for the job, and Franklin invited him out to lunch. After lunch Franklin politely informed his guest that the job was not for him. The bewildered applicant asked why he had been rejected. Franklin replied that it was because the man salted his steak before tasting it. The job required an individual who would verify every fact before accepting it and never jump to a hasty conclusion. The man's action revealed that he was a creature of habit, who could act without prudence; therefore, he was not suited to be an editor. Franklin's technique may be a little too subtle and intuitive for most companies, but the incident does illustrate a point. Personality is important.

When we visited Delta for the first time, the taxi driver who drove us from the airport casually mentioned that he often brings over young women to be interviewed for flight attendants' jobs with the company. He said: "I can always tell in advance which ones they are going to hire. I know a Delta person when I see one." Intrigued by his remark, we eagerly asked: "Who is a Delta person?" He replied, "She is a good person, wholesome—the kind of girl that any guy would be proud to bring home to meet his parents."

Thanks to the cabdriver, we were alerted to an interesting phenomenon. Wherever we went, we began to inquire more seriously about the type of people each company is looking for. Not surprisingly, a discernible pattern emerged. Companies look for people with personalities like their own.

When we visited Apple, we asked several people, "What is an Apple person?" They replied: "An Apple person is self-starting, very entrepreneurial, flexible, bright and open to new ideas, not hung up in bureaucracy and politics, not status-conscious, people who are basically themselves, and perhaps just a little arrogant."

Apple considers recruitment so important that it hires nearly half of its new people through recommendations of existing employees rather than agency referrals. It is everybody's responsibility to find the right people. Candidates go through anywhere from 10 to 20 interviews, not only with the manager they will be working under but with their peers as well. Any employee can exercise a veto power if the employee feels the person is someone he or she cannot work with. If people have to be terminated, it is almost always for "cultural" reasons rather than for lack of technical competence.

Apple does not mind if its people are a bit arrogant. After all, you need a little spunk to keep up the fire with Big Blue hovering above your head. By contrast, at Coca-Cola arrogance is considered the deadliest of all sins. Coca-Cola looks for people who are extremely bright, articulate, with integrity and a sense of style—not those who take themselves too seriously (after all, it is not a very serious product), and definitely not those who are arrogant. "A symptom of arrogance is a serious problem," says Don Keough, the president, who is constantly looking at the character of the executives as much as or more than their professional competence.

Why knock arrogance? When you control 40 percent of the world market for anything, the worst enemy you face is your own sense of importance, satisfaction, and complacency. Coca-Cola fears that more than it fears Pepsico. Keough explains, "Woodruff said that the world belonged to the discontented, and it does. The one thing that we fight is that thumb-sucking attitude that we have arrived. The joy of this business is the joy of trying to improve on what you are doing, because success is a journey, not a destination."

The people we met at Merck seemed to be cast in the image of the company itself—intelligent, dynamic, aggressive, and articulate. How do you know Merck people when you see them? Elliot Margolis, executive director of field administration, replied:

> When you look at them, there's somebody home. There's a light behind the eyes, and you can see all the circuits clicking at a million miles an hour. The individual has a certain presence. We are looking for people who have a high energy level, very high impact. We want them to have initiative, to be highly motivated, to have good presentation skills, and to be good communicators and good problem solvers. We want creativity and tenacity. Now I'm not talking about somebody who walks on water, . . . but we'll take that, too!

Contrast the emphasis on independence and entrepreneurship at Coca-Cola and Merck with this description. "We're looking for someone that is going to be compatible with this environment—a caring person, a quality person, a positive person. Someone who is too independent and ambitious, with little regard for others, is not going to work out here. If they are not willing to play as a team member, they are not going to fit in," says James Ehrenstrom, vice-president of personnel at Northwestern Mutual. At Northwestern Mutual the team comes first, individual ambition only afterward.

Aside from what the companies told us, our own impression was that you simply could not shuffle people around between them without coming up with some striking mismatches. The difference in the personality of the people was as great as the contrast between the personalities of the companies themselves.

What the Taxi Driver Did Not Tell Us

All of these corporations recognized that intelligence, education, technical training, skills, and experience are not enough to qualify a person for a particular job. But no place we visited took the task of hiring the right kind of people as seriously as Delta.

Delta has about 36,000 employees. Every six months the company receives about 150,000 new or updated job applications without even advertising; that is, 4 or 5 applications for every single position in the company. About 50,000 applications are for one of the company's 6,500 flight attendant jobs. From all these flight attendant applicants, Delta selects a total of 500 to 700 new employees a year.

You would certainly think that with so many people trying to get into the company and the high priority Delta places on thrift, it might regard recruiting as a casual affair and simply select a few from the cream of the applications on file. But that is not the Delta way. For a new class of 50 flight attendants, the company interviews about 500 applicants. Even temporary hires are sent to Atlanta from elsewhere in the country for a final round of interviews before being selected.

What is Delta looking for? Delta personnel we interviewed say that education is not a very important consideration; it just so happens that most Delta employees have a lot of it. A large number of flight attendants have MBAs or other graduate degrees. Basically, Delta is looking for members of the family. That does not mean members of their existing employees' families. That is strictly prohibited in order to avoid the possibility of hurting anyone's feelings by turning down a relative. The company is looking for people who belong, and a person's family background is one important indicator. A person's background tells a great deal that would otherwise be difficult to learn. A person's traits and talents are determined by family background, upbringing, and self-motivation. The values, beliefs, education, and occupation of the parents can be very revealing clues to a person's character.

"We're looking for someone that has wholesomeness," says Marvin Johnson, assistant vice-president for employment, "people who can express themselves, who can relate to their peers, service-oriented individuals. They don't have to be the richest, nor the best educated, because we hire them based on how they fit in and how they will grow with Delta. There is a thread of that Delta person. The fiber of the individual doesn't differ as much as it appears on their outward expressions." Delta is quite successful in discovering people with that thread. Of those that join the company, only 3 percent leave of their own accord every year. When you consider that many of those that do leave are young flight attendants interrupting their careers to become mothers, you begin to understand just how much a family Delta really is.

The Knack

On April 1, 1980, Chrysler called a meeting that was attended by representatives from 400 American and foreign lending institutions to which the company owed $4.75 billion. The meeting was a last desperate effort to persuade the banks to approve $655 million in financial concessions so that Chrysler could become eligible for the $1.5 billion in loan guarantees granted by the U.S. government.

According to provisions of the government guarantees, every single one of the 400 banks and insurance companies had to agree to the concessions. They all stood to lose 90 percent of their loans to the company if it failed. Yet Chrysler found them far more difficult to persuade than the entire U.S. Congress. The bankers were constantly squabbling among themselves, and some seemed more inclined to write off their loans than to approve the package of concessions. Chrysler was making one final attempt to push the package through before it ran out of cash.

When the meeting began, Chrysler's chief financial officer, Steve Miller, rose to address the group:

> Gentlemen, last night Chrysler's board of directors held an emergency meeting. In view of the terrible economy, the declining fortunes of the company, and skyrocketing interest rates—not to mention the lack of support that we've had from our lenders—at nine-thirty this morning we decided to file for bankruptcy.

The room was silent. It suddenly dawned on all the people present what the consequences would be if they failed to come to an agreement. Miller paused for a few moments to let the reality of the situation sink in and then added, "I should probably remind you all that today is the first of April."[3] Miller's ploy worked. During the meeting, the concession plan was accepted by all the banks. Chrysler was saved.

As Iacocca has remarked, "Miller had the perfect personality for the job. He was tough and well-organized. . . ."[4] But in this case, personality strength, motivation, and intelligence were not enough. By themselves they could never have persuaded the bankers to give in. Miller also relied on his consummate skills in negotiating. It was his skill that enabled him to express his other capacities effectively and accomplish the unenviable mission he had accepted.

Skills are the instruments through which personality translates intention into accomplished action. Our values and goals give us a direction; our character and will provide the energy and strength to pursue it; our skills are the precision tools through which we direct our energy to achieve the desired result.

Skills are habits of our personality that we have consciously acquired for effective execution of work. Every action requires an expenditure of energy. When an action is done with skill, the energy expended is less, and the act is more perfect. A skill is the capacity to carefully control the energy that is expressed in movements, making them more precise and refined, like the graceful, easy movements of a dancer or a gymnast. An action done with skill is more effective in achieving its purpose and more efficient in its utilization of energy, time, and materials.

Corporate Habits

We think of structure, systems, and values as characteristics of organizations. We usually think of skills as characteristics of individuals. It is true that a company's skills are expressed through its people, but companies do acquire characteristic skills of their own, which are not merely the sum total of skills possessed by their employees. Different companies acquire a high level of skill in certain areas, which they come to possess independently of the particular people who presently happen to be working for them. These corporate skills characterize a company's behavior and distinguish it from other companies. The courtesy and efficiency of a Marriott hotel receptionist are not just qualities of an individual. They reflect attitudes and skills that are imparted by the company to receptionists in all its hotels. The selling skills and service orientation of IBM representatives have become something of a legend in the marketplace. A combination of careful recruitment and comprehensive training is required to create such a consistently high level of behavior by thousands of employees. Even if most of the present employees at Disneyland left the company, next year you would find the new staff behaving in the same cheerful, friendly manner as the old, because at Disneyland pleasant, courteous behavior.is a corporate skill.

Skills are corporate habits. They are the instruments through which an organization expresses its personality. No matter how high a company's values, how strong its character, how coordinated and integrated its systems, the practical results of corporate action depend to a very great extent on the quality of the skills it possesses. Skills are the final link in the chain connecting intentions with actions. The decisions of top management determine a company's direction; the will of the organization determines its strength; systems determine its efficiency; and skills determine the quality of its performance.

Why Talk of Skills?

You may be wondering why we should be going back to such a basic subject as skills when every company on earth recognized their importance decades ago. Admittedly, systems is an area where every company can improve—but skills? In our view, skills is, too.

Our reasons are twofold. First, there are many types of skills, and traditionally companies recruit and train only for some of them. Every company recognizes the productive value of physical and technical skills. But there are others that are even more essential to corporate success—interpersonal, organizational, and managerial skills—that get much less attention than they deserve. And there are still others— what might be termed psychological skills—that possess an enormous productive power yet are almost completely neglected. Second, there is wide variation in the level or quality of skills companies possess. When we say that an individual is skilled, we imply that the individual possesses both the necessary types of skills for his or her work and a high level of competence in them. The phrase *skilled driver* does not distinguish the housewife who has been driving her children to school safely for ten years from the professional test-car driver who has survived ten years of high-speed competition without a major accident. The difference is in the level of skill. Here, too, there is an enormous scope for improvement. Let us begin by enumerating the important types of skills required by modern corporations.

Physical Skills

A physical skill is one that involves fine control and coordination of physical movements. Typing neatly without errors, balancing dishes on your arm, flipping pancakes without dropping them, counting dollar bills quickly, serving drinks on a bouncing airplane, cleaning glass without leaving streaks on it, packing a suitcase so that clothes do not get wrinkled, keeping one's desk and drawers clean and orderly are basic physical skills required in business.

How many companies actually enumerate all of the physical skills required to do each job perfectly and recruit or train people accordingly? When hiring a typist, companies usually look for one or two skills and very often get only what they looked for. At least one middle-sized company we know did not even do that. It hired several secretaries who did not know how to type! Typing quickly without errors is only part of the job. There are secretaries who can do that but cannot fold a letter into three equal parts or file papers systematically or answer the telephone in a friendly manner or report a message *accurately* to the boss or remember the work that has been assigned to them. Has your secretary ever come in with a letter you drafted three weeks ago and gave for typing but that was misplaced and never went out? These are not all physical skills, but they are all essential skills for doing the job well. How sweet and easy life becomes when you have a secretary who places papers on your desk in a neat and orderly fashion with each sheet in its right, logical sequence and nothing missing. But for many executives, that is just a dream.

Technical Skills

A technical skill is one that requires mental knowledge of a mechanical apparatus or process. Technical skills have been an essential part of production, maintenance, research, and product development for a long time. But with the extension of sophisticated automated equipment to the office, the need for technical skills has dramatically increased, even for nonproduction jobs. Many people are struggling to cope with all these newfangled gadgets. Have you ever noticed cashiers taking longer to ring up a sale on an electronic register than on the old manual machines? Probably the staff received a half-hour demonstration and a few minutes of training. They learn the skill while the customer waits.

Most companies certainly do acquire technical skills in many, if not all, of the areas where they are required. Our point is that very often the level of competence attained is barely the minimum that is necessary to function and only rarely the maximum that is required for high performance. Frequently, complete training is given to only one or two persons in a department, and the others are expected to pick it up from them. IBM learned the value of maximum-level technical skills 40 years ago. Semiskilled machine operators used to sit idle for several hours a week waiting for the set-up person to come around. Then Tom Watson suggested that the operators be taught to set the machines themselves. All that was needed was a few days of additional training. As a result, output and quality of production both increased, and so did job satisfaction. When the company made the jobs bigger, workers were more interested and more enthused about their work. Enlarging the scope of each job and expanding the skills of each worker became corporate policy at IBM.

Organizational Skills

As an engineer must have the ability to make machines work properly, an executive must be skilled in making systems run smoothly. Organizational skill is the ability to execute work in a methodical and systematic manner. Orderliness and punctuality—the capacity to arrange tasks in the most efficient sequence and to execute them at the appropriate time—are the hallmarks of organizational skill. Of this capacity Lawrence Appley, former president of the American Management Association, said:

> Human beings are, by nature, unorganized and they resist orderliness. Organizing one's work is a matter of discipline and concentration. . . . If you want to know what to expect to see in a plant, in the way of maintenance and housekeeping, visit first the superintendent's office. The chances are pretty good that if he and his work are orderly and neat, the plant will reflect it. If he is sloppy and disorganized himself, you are quite likely to find that reflected also. . . . Organizing one's own work is a management skill, and when it is exercised to a high degree, it is reflected throughout an entire organization.[5]

It is easy to recognize the presence or absence of organizational skills in a company as a whole. Long lines at the service counters, late departure of shipments, sending the wrong product to the wrong customer or the right product at the wrong time, delays of all types, waste of every description and variety, disorderly stockrooms and missing inventory, misplaced correspondence, lost orders or money, and general confusion are a few of the symptoms that organizational skills are lacking.

Some companies excel in the strength of their organizational skills. Marriott's capacity to open up 15 to 20 major hotels a year while maintaining high-quality service in all its older ones is a premier example of corporate organizational skills.

Social Skill

A social, or interpersonal, skill is the capacity to carry out a task involving other people effectively in a socially acceptable or pleasing manner. Giving a helpful suggestion to a colleague, correcting the errors of a subordinate, revealing a fatal flaw in the boss's pet scheme, selling anything, replying to a letter politely, displaying tact in handling problems and complaints, negotiating a contract, motivating others to work harder, and clearly communicating your ideas and intentions are just a few of the areas in which social skills become important. John Huck, of Merck, says: "Most very good people who don't succeed, don't succeed because they do not relate well with people. Interpersonal skill [when it is absent] is the skill that most frequently is the reason for failure."

Social skills are required at every level and in every department of a company, because interpersonal relationships are an activity in which every employee is engaged almost all of the time. Some companies have recognized the importance of these skills and actively recruit or train for them, particularly in the areas of customer service, negotiations, communications, and sales.

At Delta social skills are of vital importance for expressing one of the company's core values—warm southern hospitality in customer service. Delta wants its flight attendants to treat every passenger as they would a guest in their own home, with natural courtesy and pleasantness. That requires selecting people with friendly and cheerful dispositions and instilling a positive attitude toward the people they serve.

Teamwork and cooperation are near to the heart of Northwestern Mutual's personality, and the company recognizes that interpersonal skills are essential for fostering these values. At Northwestern Mutual, as in many companies we visited, the most common reason for a manager's not getting along is lack of skill in working as part of a team rather than lack of technical competence.

Social skills for communicating can be of critical importance. As Ron Allen, of Delta, put it: "Generally, when we have a problem in the company, it is not a problem in policy or procedure; it is a problem in communication. We managers have not done a good enough job in communicating. We haven't been good listeners, or we haven't been clear enough or taken enough time to communicate the real intent of what we are trying to do." Since good communications are critical for maintaining a family atmosphere, Delta has institutionalized this skill through periodic meetings between top management and personnel all over the country, in which the executives discuss the company's objectives and suggestions from employees.

Communication skills are required at the lowest as well as the highest levels of a company. Anyone can answer a telephone, but not everyone can handle a call from an irate customer who just spent five days trying to make a new computer work properly, only to discover that the machine is defective. That requires calm nerves, a soft voice, plenty of patience and humility, and a genuine capacity to please other people.

Coca-Cola's recent negotiations with 250 independent bottlers illustrate the importance of social skills for negotiating. Under the perpetual-franchise contract Coca-Cola signed in 1899, its U.S. bottlers have a fair amount of leverage over the company. Yet Coca-Cola succeeded in reorganizing and revitalizing the entire distribution system through the negotiation process. As one executive expressed it: "This is a company that has to use persuasion almost above every other business ability. Every ounce that we can pull out of this bottler system is done to a great degree by persuasion."

Social skills are indispensable for IBM to fulfill its mission of being the best sales organization and giving the best customer service of any company in the world. IBM was not the first to market a commercial computer. Remington Rand did that in 1951 with its Univac computer. Although Univac was considered technically superior as a product, IBM was far more successful in dispelling customer resistance to the new technology. By 1956 the race was over. When the dust cleared, IBM had won 85 percent of the U.S. computer market, and it has never looked back since. As *Time* put it, IBM's "salesmen were so knowledgeable and thoroughly trained that their very presence inspired confidence. . . . More than anything else, it was IBM's awesome sales skills that enabled the company to capture the computer market."[6]

Managerial Skills

Physical, technical, organizational, and social skills are capacities that can be possessed by an individual and expressed in his or her work without reference to the work of other people or an organization. But there are also higher-order skills that are broader in their scope and that influence a wider field of activity. These are managerial skills.

An organization consists of many individual resources—people, ideas, time, energy, money, materials, and so forth. It also consists of many physical, technical, social, and organizational skills—orderliness, punctuality, technical know-how, social poise, the ability to communicate, the capacity to organize, and so on. Managerial skills have the ability to combine, coordinate, and integrate the utilization of all these resources and the expression of all these skills in order to accomplish the goals of the organization. Managerial skills have the power to unite all these things for a common purpose. Managerial skills involve the capacity to conceive of a work in its entirety, seeing all the relationships between its component parts, to plan out all the necessary steps for its accomplishment, and to direct execution in order to complete the task with the resources available for the purpose.

Managerial skills are possessed not only by individuals. They can become institutionalized by a company as part of its capacity to execute work. In other words, companies as well as individuals can be characterized by their managerial skills. These skills are of several types.

1. *Conceptual skills.* Managers should have the ability to understand their work in its totality and conceive of its place in the wider organizational framework. In the absence of this skill, each person, activity, or department functions in isolation or opposition to others. The organization is fragmented, inefficient, and chaotic. You have a situation like Geneen described—everyone "thinking of his own terrain, his own people, his own duties and responsibilities, and no one thinking of the company as a whole."[7] General Mills tries to actively foster this wider perspective among its managers in order to preserve the integrity of a highly decentralized organization of semiautonomous divisions.

2. *Planning and decision-making skills.* Thinking work out in advance, planning, and making decisions are crucial management skills. Planning identifies objectives. Decision making provides the will to achieve them. Unfortunately, these two skills are often exercised in isolation from each other. Planning without deciding is like a Barmecide feast—sheer speculation. Deciding before planning is to act before you think—impulsiveness.

Many companies draw up estimates of future performance over a quarter, a year, or a decade based on current trends and then watch to see how close their projections were to their actual performance. They use planning as a tool for prediction, like the weather forecaster, without ever linking it to the decision-making process. These companies possess only half of the skill. Planning becomes a meaningful management skill only when it forms the basis for decisions. Companies that decide what their performance should be and set the plan projection as a goal to be realized combine the conceptual powers of the mind with the executive powers of the will. ITT under Geneen was a classic example of this type. Geneen understood the power of an idea, a goal, when it is supported by a decision. "Decide what it is you want to do and then start doing it," he said.[8] Planning supported by a commitment to act links the objective of the psychic center to the will of the organization. The decision is critical. As Iacocca said, "If I had to sum up in one word the qualities that make a good manager, I'd say it all comes down to decisiveness."[9]

3. *Skill in exercising authority.* The exercise of authority involves controlling people through discipline and motivating them positively through freedom and delegation of responsibility. The strength for exercising authority comes from the will, but the expression is basically

a skill. A great deal of skill is required by a manager or an organization to exercise authority in the right form and measure to suit every situation. When the skill is absent, the organization is either threatened by anarchy as Chrysler was before Iacocca or stifled by authoritarianism as Ford was during the 1930s.

The manager's authority is derived from functional position and role within the organization, not from personality. Yet many managers behave as though the power they wield is their very own and they should be implicitly obeyed, just because they demand it. When authority is exercised as a form of personal power, it rubs people the wrong way and offends them. They become aggressive, defensive, resistant, or resentful.

It requires skill to exercise authority as the job requires it in order to get work done properly without asserting one's ego. It requires skill to know when to explain and when to instruct. Often an instruction cannot be executed properly unless it is preceded by a lengthy explanation to clarify the intention. But when a lengthy explanation is given to justify a disagreeable decision, it erodes the manager's authority. It requires skill to correct the shortcomings of subordinates without creating offense or bitterness. Perhaps the greatest skill of all is required for a manager to relate to subordinates in a friendly manner without undermining his or her authority or relinquishing power by becoming one of the group.

4. *Time-management skills.* Management of time is a complex skill that involves planning, decision making, organization, and delegation of work. Most managers are continuously involved in work, but that does not mean they maximize the utilization of time. Managing time effectively means to always be doing the most important work to be done and delegating other responsibilities to subordinates. Most managers plan out their schedule for the week or the month. How about planning for tomorrow morning?

The clearer the mind and the more detailed the planning, the better the management of time. But time management also depends on strength of will. The stronger the will, the faster the work is accomplished. When we are tired or indecisive or weak, discussions drag on, decisions get postponed, and work gets delayed.

Utilizing time to the maximum requires quickness but not hurrying. Hurrying is a nervous trait connoting agitation, stress, impatience, and anxiety. An efficient manager or company learns to think, decide, and act at high speed without agitation or disturbance. For Tomas Bata, "If anything had to be done, it had to be done on time. . . . All the planning techniques and administrative organization were nothing but instruments helping the human will and resolution to do things on time."[10]

5. *Skill in developing people.* The most important managerial skill for the long-term growth of the organization is the ability to identify and develop human potentials, to recognize unexpressed talents in individuals, to help them acquire new or greater skills, and to delegate responsibilities that will bring out and fully utilize all their latent capacities. The greatest power a manager or an organization can wield is not the power of money or technology. It is the power of people. The ultimate art of management is to foster the growth of the organization by fostering the personal growth of the individuals within it. When a corporation has as its highest value the development and fulfillment of the individual, and when it possesses the knowledge and the will to strive toward this goal, it releases power for endless expansion and a self-generating momentum for enduring success.

Psychological Skills

Finally, there is a whole range of abilities that are basic psychological skills of living. They are extremely useful for managing a wide range of situations in life and become more and more indispensable as one rises to higher levels of human interaction.

1. *Factual reporting.* Learning to distinguish a factual from a false report is not easy. People tend to report their thoughts, opinions, and interpretations instead of the facts. Managers who fall prey to inaccuracies, exaggerations, rumors, gossip, and unfounded criticism of other staff members invariably land in trouble. "The highest art of professional management," according to Geneen, "requires the literal ability to 'smell' a 'real fact' from all others." A manager must become "a connoisseur of . . . unshakeable facts."[11]

2. *Listening.* Listening is a skill and an art. Most people are anxious to talk and express their ideas. The person who knows how to let the other person speak has the skill and self-control needed for growth. As Delta's Hollis Harris said: "The most important skill for a manager is being able to deal with people. A good people person knows how to listen, has to train himself how to listen. You have to work on it. You have to have the capacity to relate to people at their level." Bill Marriott, Jr., remarked: "Managers get in trouble when they stop listening to their staff. If you stop listening to your people, you're in big trouble."

3. *Empathy.* Once when Churchill visited the United States to

meet President Roosevelt, FDR gave instructions that no one in his party should mention the name of Jawaharlal Nehru, who was then leading India's campaign for total independence from Britain. At the mention of Nehru's name, Churchill had been known to fly into a rage, and FDR wanted to avoid any embarrassing situation. Despite the president's instructions, while he and Churchill were chatting at a reception, one of the guests asked Churchill a question about Nehru. FDR quickly intervened with a blank expression on his face, "Which Nehru?" Churchill was pleased beyond measure by Roosevelt's feigned ignorance and kept his composure.

The capacity to know how another person thinks and feels and to honor his or her thoughts and sentiments is a consummate skill in human relations. One of the keys to Delta's high quality of service is C. E. Woolman's constant admonition to his employees that they "put themselves on the other side of the counter," identify with the needs of the customer. This skill is central to Coca-Cola's management philosophy, too. "You have to be able to see things from the other person's point of view," one executive explained.

4. *Judging people.* Perhaps the greatest skill a manager can possess is the capacity to judge people's character, motives, and abilities objectively and perceptively. Contrary to common belief, it is a capacity that can be acquired through training. Woodruff, who was notable for his lack of other talents, possessed this one in good measure. "He has an ability for finding good men," as one Coca-Cola executive said. Iacocca acquired this skill from the psychology courses he took during college. He says, "As a result of this training I learned to figure people out pretty quickly. . . . That's an important skill to have."[12]

5. *Self-awareness.* Have you ever seen someone repeating the same old folly for the umpteenth time as if it were the very first and being shocked or outraged when it once again leads to trouble? Just about everyone does it. Our lives consist of many patterns that tend to repeat over and over. The capacity to observe these patterns in the lives of other people and of organizations gives a great and very useful knowledge. Observe, for instance, the recurring pattern of crisis that overtakes Chrysler once every decade, getting a little worse each time. The capacity to observe the same patterns in our own lives brings wisdom and power for enduring success.

6. *Silent will.* Speaking pleasantly carries a power. "There is a force hidden in a sweet command," so goes the proverb. Speaking sparingly carries an even greater power. "A great man is sparing in words but prodigal in deeds," said Confucius.[13] And silence creates the greatest power of all. "Nothing," wrote de Gaulle, "more enhances authority than silence."[14] The English writer Thomas Carlyle once commented

that "silence is the element in which great things fashion themselves together; that at length they may emerge, full formed and majestic, into the daylight of Life, which they are thenceforth to rule."[15] The two types of speakers that are most effective are the ones who speak in a loud voice, projecting their energies into the audience, and the ones who speak very softly, so that the audience must strain to hear. Of the two, the first is more dramatic but the second can be infinitely more powerful.

Controlling the volume and intensity of speech to a soft or moderate level is far more difficult than it sounds. It requires self-restraint. When an idea or question enters the mind, it creates a powerful urge for expression that can be hard to contain. When you are able to master that urge by postponing expression until the proper moment and then speaking in a soft tone, using only the minimum number of words necessary, your words carry a far greater power for effecting results.

One of the most important applications of this skill is in meetings. Each person present in a group has his or her own ideas, opinions, preferences, and suggestions about what should or should not be done. The moment you express your idea, there is a good chance of raising opposition and counterarguments from others, which neutralize or cancel your suggestion, no matter how good the idea may be. But if you restrain the urge for expression, very often the same idea will be expressed by others or your very silence will evoke a more favorable atmosphere and an invitation to speak.

When people speak softly, they think more clearly, work more efficiently, feel calmer and fresher than otherwise. When an organization practices soft speech, it becomes charged with a tremendous power. If the effort starts with top management and works its way down, two things will become apparent. Speaking softly is one of the most effective means of improving performance, and it is also one of the most difficult! All right, if you cannot follow it completely, at least reduce the volume of voice by 10 percent. Efficiency will double.

The Ultimate Skill

Each person develops one or two skills to a higher level than the average. This is the individual's strong point, which he or she likes to display as often as possible. If the person is a good mechanic, she takes every opportunity to inspect or comment on the operation of a machine. If the person is a good communicator, he is always looking for somebody to communicate something to. Whether the person's skill is in settling quarrels, judging people, making people happy, designing systems, or cutting costs, he or she constantly seeks opportunities to express it.

So far, so good. The problem comes when someone insists on extending a skill to areas where it is ineffective or inappropriate. "To a hammer," says an old proverb, "everything looks like a nail." The car mechanic starts tinkering with a computer. The communicator communicates confidential information. The cost cutter tries to hold down expenditure in a new experimental R&D project. The manager who makes people happy tries to please customers by reducing prices to below cost or tries to please his or her staff when they disobey legitimate authority.

The skill of skills is to know what is the proper time and place for exercising—and refraining from exercising—each skill. The ultimate skill is the capacity to organize all our other skills, coordinate their expression, and rightly choose which one to express in each particular circumstance.

Levels of Skill

For even the simplest task, there is an almost infinite gradation of levels of skill, ranging from total incompetence to perfection. Perfection may be a difficult goal to achieve and maintain, but it is a wonderful standard by which to evaluate present performance and motivate improvement.

Take a simple physical skill like typing a letter. Speed is only one criterion of perfection. There are many other skills involved in typing: feeding paper into the typewriter straight, keeping proper margins, punctuating and hyphenating at the appropriate places, spelling correctly, spacing, numbering pages in exactly the same place on each page with the right numbers, error-free correspondence, and so on. Trying to type a single page perfectly according to all these criteria is a challenge for most typists. Typing one page perfectly may have very little value indeed, but acquiring the skill required to type every page perfectly gives a tremendous boost to any organization. There are two reasons. First, doing any activity with imperfect skill generates tension, boredom, frustration, and fatigue. Second, doing any activity with perfect skill releases energy, enthusiasm, and joy. This applies not only to typing and other physical skills but to all types of activities and all levels of skills.

Everyone has a long list of hated tasks, like driving in rush-hour traffic, processing administrative paperwork, keeping travel expense accounts, telling subordinates to shape up or ship out, presenting a new budget to the board, and so forth. But there are people who enjoy every one of these tasks and even find them a thrilling challenge. Many of the things we dislike doing are things we lack the skill to do easily and well. Instead of acquiring the necessary skills, we shun the tasks. When skills are perfect, even driving across Manhattan in late afternoon can be an exhilarating experience. Presenting a budget with brief, clean, confident, and precise explanations can be much more so.

Most acts involve many levels of skill. Driving during rush hour requires more than smooth, quick, coordinated movements. You need calm nerves, patience, and preferably a cheerful disposition that does not get angry or irritated every time another car cuts in front of you. An ability to think while you drive makes the time spent productive and reduces the strain. All of these capacities can be cultivated. How much more complex, challenging, and potentially rewarding are the other activities we consider boring, routine, or despicable? Delivering a speech, keeping accurate travel expense accounts, making a sale, interviewing a job candidate, communicating an idea—all involve a multiplicity of skills that can be improved without limit. The scope for growth is infinite.

On the surface of it, the job of a bank teller offers very little challenge or charm. But if all the relevant skills are present, this need not be so. The following scene took place a few years ago at a southern California bank branch in a middle-class, predominantly white neighborhood on the day before Christmas. All the tellers were at their windows to handle the last-minute rush for Christmas shopping. There were 7 or 8 customers waiting in front of most of the windows, and the tellers were going about their business as usual. But in front of one window there were at least 20 customers waiting patiently, many of them carrying gifts in their hands. The teller at this particular window was a tall, ungainly young black woman with rather unattractive facial features but a broad, almost irresistible, smile. The counters around her were piled high with presents that she had received in the course of the morning, and the long line in front of her window consisted of other customers waiting to wish her a Merry Christmas and perhaps give a present, too.

Everyone knew the secret of the woman's popularity. She was a naturally happy person who took pleasure in making other people happy rather than in just satisfying the customers. We satisfy customers when we provide them with a good-quality product or service at a reasonable price while treating them with courtesy and respect.

We please people when we relate to them as individuals with a genuine desire to make them happy. This woman had the physical skills necessary to provide good, prompt service, the social skills required to please people, and the right temperament. Not only were customers pleased but she drew immense personal enjoyment from her work because she was so well suited for it. The right skill and the right personality combined to generate high productivity, the appreciation of customers, and personal fulfillment.

The satisfaction that the bank teller derived from fully exercising her skills on a job for which she was ideally suited can come to any person at any level whose skills are well developed and appropriate for the work. Harold Geneen found "the fun, the enjoyment, the pride, and the sense of self-fulfillment" at the highest level of corporate activity.[16] The bank teller found it at the lowest level. A company that recruits the right people for each job and helps them acquire all of the skills required to attain the highest level of proficiency taps a great productive power that is now only partially utilized. It eliminates a major source of frustration and conflict in work and releases the joy of skilled execution in its people.

Knowledge of a Skill

We usually think of a skill as a physical capacity for a particular type of behavior or action, like repairing a machine, writing a report, or communicating an idea. The behavioral part of the skill is what is usually acquired by training. But there is another component to every skill—the knowledge of how and why the skill is effective. Theoretically, the mechanic can repair a machine even without understanding how it works, as many people use computers without any clear idea of how they actually function. But the knowledge part of each skill is extremely important for upgrading the level of performance beyond the minimum. Merck has recognized that the effectiveness of professional representatives can be immeasurably enhanced by broadening and deepening their technical knowledge of medicine. Many Merck representatives are treated as professional peers by physicians because of the depth of their knowledge. Merck also believes that the representatives must know the importance of factual presentations. The company not only insists on honest behavior; it also imparts a clear knowledge of why credibility is so important.

The capacity to sell at the wholesale level depends on a knowledge of the product, how it is produced, how it is utilized, and how it is repaired or maintained. It also depends on a knowledge of the buyers, their business, and their customers. This capacity can be significantly improved by acquiring a greater knowledge of people and human nature as Iacocca did. The same is true for every skill involved in managing people. There is no end to the opportunities for improvement.

The knowledge of a skill has several levels. The operators of a machine must know how to run it. If they know how to repair it, too, their skill as operators is greater. If they understand how the machine is designed and constructed, it is even higher. If they also know the principle upon which the machine functions, then and then only is their knowledge complete, and the skill can be perfected.

The accountant's skill as a controller depends entirely on his or her knowledge of the smallest details of the business. The greater the accountant's knowledge of production, administration, marketing, and research, the greater the capacity to control expenses effectively with maximum benefit to the company.

Value Implementation Through Skills

The role of skills is so ubiquitous and so vital to the success of a company that it has led many to believe that skills alone are the key to excellence and that high values and organizational structures are only window dressing. There is truth in this observation, but it is a partial truth. A well-developed individual skill is a very powerful tool. A well-coordinated assortment of skills is a formidable weapon. But for enduring achievement, skill must be inspired by the vision of a goal and commanded by the determination of an inner will. The Taj Mahal is a work of awesome beauty and perfect skill, but its graceful lines and fine details were inspired by an emperor's love for his deceased wife and his desire to immortalize that love in white marble. Vision and will as much as skill are needed to build a Taj Mahal, a Great Pyramid, a great nation, or a great corporation.

Nevertheless, the contribution of skill to any high accomplishment is truly enormous and all-pervasive. Whatever a company's values and goals, ultimately they must be expressed in a thousand small details of life through a vast array of well-developed skills. If skills are lacking, the whole process of value implementation comes to naught. It is like building an atomic power plant, sending out electricity through wires across the country, carrying those wires to millions of houses, and then

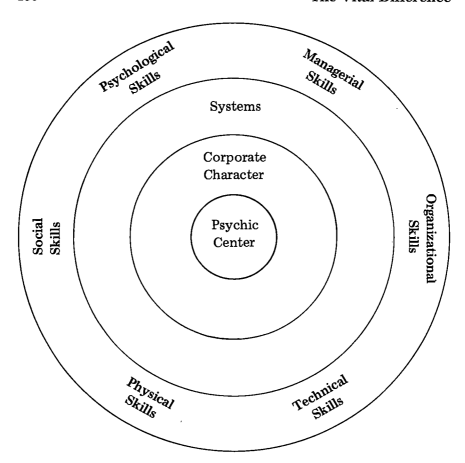

Figure 4.   The role of skills in the corporate personality.

discovering that all your light bulbs have defective filaments. The result—no light! It is not enough that the company accepts certain values, establishes standards of performance, and creates systems for
achieving them. Every employee must possess all the skills required
to make that high ideal a living reality. Figure 4 illustrates the role
of skills in the corporate personality.

It is not just managerial and psychological skills at the top and
physical and technical skills at the bottom that are needed, but all
types of skills at all levels of the organization. The highest psychological skills and the simplest physical ones are necessary for the smooth
running of a board meeting. A spilled pot of coffee, wrongly typed num-

bers, a malfunctioning projector, mixed-up papers, a missing chart, an ill-planned agenda, a poorly chosen word or phrase can all interfere with a billion-dollar decision. So, too, the highest psychological and managerial abilities are necessary for perfect functioning on the factory floor or out in the field. A supervisor who acts on a false piece of information, a manager who moves too closely with his or her team to command their obedience, a sales rep who is late for an appointment, a mishandled machine, a wrongly typed price list, a telephone operator who is cold or rude to an important customer—all can have a serious impact on overall corporate performance. And they do have a serious impact on every company every day.

As the organization develops, each individual and collective skill has to become more and more smoothly coordinated and fully integrated with other skills at the same level and at other levels of the organization. Factual reporting by top executives is fruitless if the same habit is not acquired at all the levels of management below, from which data are constantly being received. The same is true of every other skill.

For an organization to become a single, unified, living whole, all these separate strands of skill have to be carefully woven together. This can be done only when top management recognizes the multiplicity of skills it requires for high performance and methodically cultivates them at all levels of the organization by education, training, and proper recruitment. This knowledge has to be translated into precise performance standards for each skill at each level, and these standards must be supported by systems for imparting, monitoring, and evaluating levels of skill.

A Delta flight attendant related a story about perfect skill. She was on a DC-9 landing at Chicago. The nose gear would not come down, so the captain instructed the crew to prepare the passengers for an emergency landing and quick evacuation in case of fire. She recalled her fright as the pilot brought down the plane. Everyone was braced for a heavy jolt. The captain landed on the rear wheels in such a way that a secondary mechanism locked the nose gear down in place. The plane rolled to a halt. "We had the smoothest landing I have ever had on any airplane!" she said. "He had to have done something which was just right. Now I like to fly with him." High corporate achievement and enduring success require the presence of physical, technical, social, organizational, managerial, and psychological skills in every area of functioning and at all levels of the company. Companies that strive for excellence cannot afford to leave anything to chance.

CHAPTER 7

The Artesian Spring

There is no saturation point in education.
—Thomas J. Watson, Sr.[1]

A famous Indian scholar and statesman once said that it takes centuries of human experience to make a little history, centuries of history to create a little civilization, and centuries of civilization to distill a few drops of culture. Culture is something acquired over millennia; but one man had the ambition to compress all that history into a few months through education.

Everyone knows the story of Eliza Doolittle, the poor, illiterate flower girl who was trained by Professor Higgins, a linguistics expert, to acquire the behavior of an English aristocrat. Through an intensive, rigorous, and painstaking effort, Eliza was taught to dress elegantly, walk gracefully, pronounce words aristocratically, reply to questions appropriately, and otherwise conduct herself with the charm and poise of a highly cultured person. Her training was so complete that at her debut in society, another linguistics expert mistook her for a princess of the Hungarian royal family.

Eliza's father stumbled upon a fortune by good luck, but Eliza discovered something infinitely more valuable through education. She developed some of the latent potentials of her own personality. The same sort of miraculous transformation that Higgins brought about in Eliza education is doing today for millions—helping them expand their mental horizons, develop their talents, and enrich their personalities.

Higgins' formidable accomplishment contains two important lessons for business. The first concerns the power of education; the second, the power of training. What if Eliza had been an educated middle-class girl rather than a "guttersnipe"? Instead of wasting his time teaching

158

her the fundamentals of speech and human conduct, Higgins could have helped Eliza acquire greater intellectual knowledge, sensitivity to other people, or useful and productive skills. As it was, even after the training, Eliza barely knew how to add or subtract. An educated girl would have received the training in much less time and with far greater perfection than Eliza, who was able to maintain her poise only until she got home from her debut in society and then reverted to throwing shoes.

Eliza's training was in the external forms of cultured behavior. Education makes the inner content of personality more cultured. Higgins chose an uneducated girl to teach because he wanted to illustrate dramatically the power of systematic linguistic training. But companies are not after dramatic proof of principles. They are after dramatic results. For that, there is no substitute for education.

The American Revolution

Education is far more than just a process of acquiring useful knowledge. Education makes the ordinary mind more active and alert. It converts physical energy into mental energy. Education trains the mind to consider many possibilities, to see things from a new and wider perspective, to question and challenge the status quo, to think and imagine, to innovate and invent, to make decisions for oneself, and to act on one's own initiative.

In his time Thomas Edison was one in a million. But today education has institutionalized the talents of the genius, so that great inventions and innovations can be made by far more ordinary people. The transistor and computer represent advances at least as great as the light bulb, but how many people even know who invented them?

Education is the foundation and driving force for two of America's greatest assets—entrepreneurship and innovation. Education has probably been the single most important factor in making America the world's leading industrial power. The American people themselves cannot be anything unique, since nearly all of us came from other countries at one time or another. But long before the nations of Europe, our leaders recognized the importance of education and developed a national system that extended education to all levels of the population.

America's postwar success was supported to a great extent by the tremendous expansion in higher education generated by the GI Bill of Rights. The aim of the law was to keep the returning GIs out of the workforce. The result was to provide American commerce and industry with a highly educated pool of personnel to fuel an unprecedented economic boom just at a time when educational systems in other nations had broken down. By 1981, 58 percent of the American youth in the 20- to 24-year age group were enrolled in higher-education courses, compared to 37 percent in Sweden and 20 percent to 30 percent in other West European countries.

Whatever the deficiencies of our system may be, education has widened our horizons and stimulated freedom of thought, a scientific outlook, original thinking, imagination, social tolerance, an experimental temper, technical innovation, and dreams of perpetual progress. It has also been used as a conscious instrument by the nation for absorbing and assimilating immigrants of widely diverse cultural backgrounds, inculcating in all these various peoples the common values of American culture.

The Sun Rises in the East

Education has demonstrated its tremendous power elsewhere, too. When Admiral Perry sailed into Tokyo harbor with the American fleet in 1857, demanding the opening up of Japan to foreign traders, the traditionally isolationist Japanese were rudely awakened to the reality of their backwardness and impotence in the face of Western industrial technology. One of the very first strategies they adopted to correct this imbalance was to introduce a Western system of compulsory education in 1872, long before many countries in Europe. By the 1930s, education had become a craze in Japan and came to assume even greater importance than it had acquired in the United States. The rise of Japan to its pre-eminent position in the world today is not the product of chance or a miracle. It is the natural result of a century-long endeavor to educate its people.

Japan learned its lesson from us very well, and now we are relearning it from the Japanese. In his book *Japan as Number One: Lessons for America*, Ezra Vogel writes, "If any single factor explains Japanese success, it is the group-directed quest of knowledge."[2] The Japanese drive to extend formal education has been as vigorous as the country's efforts to increase its GNP. In 1955 only about one-half of Japanese youth entered high school, and less than 10 percent went on to college. By the late 1970s over 90 percent were completing high school, compared with 80 percent of Americans. Japanese students attend school about one-third more than their American counterparts, for 240 days a year compared to 180 days in the United States; and virtually all Japanese who enter a school complete it. Although the same percentage of college-age youth are attending a university in both the United States and Japan, many more Japanese complete their education. And they do not stop there. In Japan education is an ongoing social activity that continues throughout life—in study groups, educational tours, and educational courses on television. The Japanese have understood the value of education better than their teachers.

The American Higgins

The importance of education in business has been endlessly debated in this country by just about everyone except Thomas J. Watson, who refused to discuss what he considered an obvious fact. The controversy focuses on the relative value of education and job experience. The old-timers in every company who have worked their way up through the ranks without education resent the value placed on a young greenhorn with a piece of parchment from a college or university. Education is not a substitute for experience, but it enriches an individual in a way that experience alone rarely does. It broadens the mind and makes a person more open to new ideas and new ways of life. It expands and develops the whole personality rather than just giving some specialized skills and working knowledge. Work experience can greatly enhance the effectiveness of an educated person, but it cannot develop the potentials of human personality the way education can.

Despite all the controversy, Watson never doubted the truth for a moment. Oddly enough, he first recognized the importance of education for sales and customer service rather than for research. Nearly 60 years ago he hired 140 college graduates as sales reps, selecting them mostly on the basis of personality and character, which he considered the prime requisites for a good leader. He then put them through a three-month orientation course on the company's culture and its products, six months of field training, and another two-month course on selling, before appointing them as junior sales reps. He also recruited graduates from technical and engineering colleges to become customer engineers (that is, to repair equipment) after a five-month course in the shop and classroom. Women with college degrees were hired to teach customers the use of the punch-card machines.

Because IBM's sales reps possessed a high level of general education, they could acquire a high level of technical competence regarding the company's products and a highly professional manner of conduct in marketing. Their education also enabled the sales reps to better understand the needs of the customer and to identify untapped potentials in the market. These three endowments based on education have made IBM a superb marketing organization in whatever field or country it competes.

Watson made education and basic training the foundation for a continuous learning program. In 1932 he established a corporate educational center to provide systematic education to existing employees. As Peter Drucker said: "Watson trained, and trained, and trained. All employees were expected to continue to learn while on the job. But for the men who were considered 'IBM's business'—that is, for salesmen, servicemen, and sales managers—continuous training was a way of life."[3] By 1940 more than 7,000 factory employees had attended educational courses at the company's school. Because of this ongoing program, managers who joined IBM when it was still selling manual punch-card machines were able to adjust to the move into electronic computers during the 1950s. As Drucker wrote, "Having grown up in continuous training, they had learned to learn."[4] Or as Harry Bernhard, IBM's program director for advanced management development, put it: "Education has made change normal." Nor did Watson stop there. In 1936 he established the first training school for customers, which, as *Fortune* commented, "achieves the almost incredible sales feat of luring the quarry into camp and fattening it up before dispatching it."[5]

After World War II, IBM built up a rich reservoir of technically educated people in its research division as well. The company expanded its engineering force by over 400 percent, recruiting mostly new people with M.A.'s and Ph.D.'s. It also promoted a large number of advanced degree holders into high management positions to ensure that management could stay abreast of the rapid changes in technology. When Tom Watson said, "Think," he really meant it and wanted to be sure his people did it. He understood that education is one luxury you can never have too much of. He said, "There is no saturation point in education."

Consciously or subconsciously IBM came to recognize that there is a qualitative as well as a quantitative difference between education and training. *Whatever a person's inherent capacities, training improves the level of skills available for expressing those capacities; but education increases the level of capacity itself.* Training refines the tools of expression; education improves the person. The most intelligent mechanic who has acquired technical skills without a general background of in-depth technical knowledge rarely attains the level of competence achieved by the most mediocre engineer. The mechanic may be very effective in repairing a machine; but when it comes to designing or inventing a better one, the engineer's knowledge will usually prevail over the mechanic's skills. Companies that mistake technical training for a more practical version of technical education introduce built-in limitations and inefficiencies in their work.

IBM continues to invest heavily in its scholastic tradition. There are several thousand people involved in providing over 4 million student-days of training a year to IBM personnel at a cost of more than $100 million. All of IBM's 42,000 managers are required to have at least 40 hours of additional training a year, including 32 hours of training in people-management skills. There are also special outside programs for executives at leading educational institutions. According to Ed Krieg, corporate director of educational programs, "IBM believes that without its intensive educational program, the company would lose maybe 35 percent of its effectiveness." This enormous investment in the education and training of IBM employees lends credence to Watson's claim: "You can take my factories, burn up my buildings, but give me my people and I'll build the business right back again."[6]

An Asset More Valuable than Money

Watson was not the only business leader to discover the value of education. Tomas Bata did, too. But Bata did not have the luxury of recruiting college-educated people for his company because there were virtually none available in Czechoslovakia at the time. Instead, he decided to educate them himself. His son, Thomas Bata, explained: "One of the crucial events and decisions which made it possible for this organization to grow explosively in the thirties and again in the fifties and sixties was really the establishment of a college in 1924."

The college offered a three- or four-year course that involved a full day of work in Bata's factory followed by classes every night. These classes covered general subjects like economics and accounting as well as technical subjects related to the shoe business. The first year, the college received 600 applications for a class of 80. Within a few years the class had grown to 1,000, and the number of applicants was around 35,000. Initially, all the students were from the local area, but by 1930 about 200 students a year were coming from foreign countries. Most of the graduates of the college became managers within the company;

the brighter ones were appointed department heads; and some with unusual abilities were sent overseas in search of raw materials or markets and to establish Bata's foreign subsidiaries.

When the Nazis sealed the Czech borders and later when the Communists expropriated the company's assets, it was this core of managers, who were raised and educated at the college in the Bata tradition, that ran Bata's foreign companies without any control or support from headquarters and then united to rebuild the company after the war. Education proved to be a more valuable asset than all the company's buildings, money, and machines.

The Well

People have a way of believing in possibilities only after they have become actualities. We can understand the skepticism that the Wright brothers aroused when they first announced their intention to fly. But what about after they had already flown? In fact, for a full five years after Wilbur and Orville made their first successful flight at Kitty Hawk, the newspapers and the public were both firmly convinced that flying was not possible!

People also have a way of believing only in things they can see with their own eyes. Geologists tell us that only 3 percent of the earth's fresh water is on the surface in the form of rivers and lakes. The other 97 percent remains as a huge subterranean reservoir down below. During the last century in Artois, France, a hole was dug 2,000 feet into the ground, and from it a fountain of water rose 290 feet into the air, gushing forth 1 million gallons of water per day. The term *artesian* is derived from the name *Artois*.

The potentials of human personality are much the same—only 3 percent on the surface and 97 percent below. Training takes the 3 percent that is on the surface and utilizes it much more efficiently by imparting skills to improve performance. Education digs deep below the surface and taps the infinite reservoir below, so that the concealed potentials of the human personality can overflow onto the surface in rich, creative profusion, like the waters of an artesian spring.

The Challenge

A century ago managing a business was like running in a cross-country race. The most important qualities for success were endurance, persistence, and a willingness to work hard. Fifty years later the race had become a sprint. Life began to change more rapidly, and the speed of response became a major factor. Today managing a business is more like competing in the decathalon. Not one or a few but a very wide range and depth of capacities are needed even to enter the contest. It requires not only speed and endurance but also a multiplicity of skills and an infinite reservoir of energy.

Modern technology is unveiling new discoveries and improved inventions at a lightning pace. Products have become highly sophisticated. The time interval between the day a new technology is discovered and the day it becomes obsolete is shrinking rapidly. Labor is no longer the uneducated, unskilled, and unsophisticated resource measured only in numbers that it used to be. The supervisor and the plant manager are no longer mere assistants who execute the will and whims of the proprietor. The individual has become the single most important factor in the success of a business. The quality of the person counts first. Money is no longer the proprietor's. It comes from banks and bonds, investors and investment groups. It carries with it greater responsibilities and obligations. The public is no longer ignorant and uninformed. It is alert and aware. Companies are projected before the public eye in a hundred ways, and the image they cast determines their future, like the carefully chosen words and gestures of a presidential candidate during a nationally televised debate; only in this case, debate is perpetual, and every one of a company's acts is carefully screened by consumers, investors, employees, the government, and competitors.

Gone forever are the days when a manager could afford to behave like a proprietor running a one-person show. Gone, too, are the days when hard work was sufficient even for survival. No company can meet today's demand for quality, service, speed, and efficiency unless all its systems are faultless, all its activities are smoothly coordinated, all levels of its structure are finely integrated, and all the requisite skills are present in the requisite measure. Gone are the days when a manager could just push or bluff along the path to success with lots of energy and a loud voice. Management today is a very sophisticated activity that requires comprehensive knowledge, superb skills, and precise execution—like a perfect score of 10 on the parallel bars.

In the good old days, people learned a business by working as apprentices under experienced individuals or in established firms. Gradually they acquired whatever knowledge and skills of the trade their boss possessed or cared to teach them and in the course of time were upgraded to managerial positions or set out to establish their own business. For modern corporations the price of learning by experience is very high. Companies can no longer afford a long, slow learning process that provides managers with partial knowlege and incomplete training.

It is no longer enough that the manager be strong, intelligent, and alert. The basic stuff of human personality has to be developed through higher and higher levels of general education, and the multiplicity of essential business skills has to be further refined and upgraded by constant and continuous training.

We have already seen in Chapter 6 that there are a lot more skills and types of skills that contribute to making a business successful than many people and companies realize. Physical and technical skills are essential, but social, organizational, managerial, and psychological skills are equally essential or more so. There is also a great deal more to acquiring a skill than mere physical proficiency. True mastery involves in-depth knowledge of the process, principles, and rationale for each action. When this mastery is present, individual workers are far more interested, enthusiastic, and productive; and the organization is many times more efficient. Highly developed skills are absolutely indispensable for properly translating corporate values and goals into action. A company can be said to possess a high degree of skill only when its lowest-level workers have acquired essential elements of top-level executive skills and its highest-level managers have acquired an essential knowledge of the lowest-level skills for execution. This is the challenge.

It may sound like a good theory of skills, but is it really possible for companies to practice it? The fact is that consciously or unconsciously, companies do practice it, and the most successful companies practice it very successfully. That is why they are so successful.

There may not be much debate about the possibility of imparting a very high level of physical and technical skills, because we have been doing it successfully in schools and in companies for many decades. But what about the higher-order skills—social, organizational, managerial, and psychological?

We refer to Professor Higgins' second important lesson for companies: Any skill can be learned through proper training. The cultured behavior of an aristocrat is an expression of many highly refined skills acquired and developed by the upper classes over hundreds of years. Like any other skills, they can be learned by almost anyone who is willing to make the required effort and who has the proper guidance. It takes centuries to develop an aristocratic culture. Successful corporate cultures are built up in a few decades. If the behavior of an aristocrat can be acquired by training, why can't the behavior of successful companies be learned the same way? If a flower girl can be trained to acquire the social skills of the English nobility, is there any skill that cannot be taught?

Upward Corporate Mobility

The greatest challenge before management is coping with the accelerating pace of changes in the world today. Some companies, like IBM, have accommodated to the pace by increasing the speed of growth within the company through continuous education and training. Another company that has accommodated to rapid change is Merck. A few decades ago the marketing of prescription drugs in the United States was almost as aggressive as any other commercial hard sell. Merck was one of the first to see that times were changing and that a purely commercial approach to marketing drugs would no longer suffice. Twenty years ago the company introduced what was then one of the most sophisticated training programs in the industry. Now it is the standard. The aim of the program was to upgrade drug marketing to the highest level of professional activity. This meant raising the technical competence of the professional representatives until they were on a par with that of the physicians, at least in specialized areas. It also involved refining their presentation and communication skills until the relationship between physician and representative became a free exchange of knowledge rather than a sales pitch. Finally, it required the adoption by the representatives of a standard of objectivity and integrity rarely associated with the art of selling.

Merck's executive director of field administration explained the rationale for the training program this way:

> Every company has access to the same computers. Our competitors all have access to the same textbooks on medicine. We have access to the same market research firms and the same everything. So how do we get a competitive edge? It is the quality of our people.

Recruit the best and continuously train them to be better is Merck's formula for successful marketing in a highly competitive industry.

Every Merck representative starts with a four-year college education as a minimum. Most new entrants have master's or pharmacist's degrees; a few even have Ph.D.'s. New representatives spend 15 weeks in basic training before they make their first call and another 35 weeks under close supervision. After that an additional 50 hours a year of classroom training are mandatory. The company also encourages representatives to continue their formal education, and it pays their tuition fees.

Ralph Goodison came to Merck 20 years ago with a B.Sc. in economics and has since acquired two master's degrees. "They encourage us to continue our education. When we stop learning, we stop growing. There is an atmosphere of growth here. If you take the time to become better, you are not only better for Merck but also for your family, your society. The sky is the limit."

While many drug firms still regard selling medicine as essentially a commercial activity, Merck has moved all the way to the other end of the spectrum—and all the way to the top of the industry, too.

How Much Is Too Much?

Every company believes that training is important. The real questions are: What should we train for? And how much training is enough? The answer to these questions is quite straightforward. *Train for absolutely everything without exception, and keep on training—because there is no such thing as too much.*

In the area of physical skills, Marriott's training covers every aspect of the job with a fine-tooth comb. The training system for a hotel limousine driver includes a study of the hotel property and surrounding area, defensive driving, vehicle maintenance, knowledge of the hotel staff, and guest relations. The drivers are made aware of how their slightest positive or negative action can influence repeat business favorably or unfavorably, so they realize the full importance of their job and feel a sense of responsibility.

In the area of interpersonal skills, Hertz has established a comprehensive training program to ensure that it stays No. 1 by providing the best customer service in the rent-a-car industry. In earlier years the company sometimes had customer-service representatives working at its counters who had not even gone through new-hire training; but not anymore. Hertz has recognized that every employee who comes in contact with the customer is a potential salesperson for the company and must be thoroughly trained. Shirley Gunzer, director of training and communications, says, "Top management really understands the value of training." Front-counter personnel now receive a total of four weeks of orientation and training. Approximately half of it focuses on interpersonal skills. They are taught to project a cheerful, positive image; to listen carefully to the customer; to deal with facts rather than emotions; to understand the customer's point of view; and to meet the customer's unexpressed needs.

The most comprehensive training program that we came across for interpersonal skills was at Northwestern Mutual, where maintaining the highest possible level of teamwork and internal harmony is a core value of the company. For the last 15 years, Northwestern Mutual has periodically conducted confidential surveys of all personnel to determine employees' perceptions and satisfactions concerning their bosses, peers, and work teams; from these perceptions it is possible to identify areas where each manager and work team can improve performance or acquire new skills. The survey results are translated for managers into a "training needs analysis." The training programs emphasize skills in communication, listening, empathy, supportiveness, goal setting, coordination, team building, and resolution of conflicts between managers and subordinates. There are also special training programs, such as the one to help customer-service representatives deal with irate customers on the phone. Wherever a skill is lacking or can be improved, Northwestern Mutual trains to provide it.

Making Mr. Watsons

In earlier centuries people commonly believed that the qualities of a successful leader were entirely innate and unique to the individual. But as we have come to understand the nature of human personality better, we have realized that many attributes of successful individuals—barring the rare genius like Einstein or the leader of superhuman power like Napoleon—are actually skills that they acquired by virtue of their upbringing, training, and experience. We have also recognized that these skills can be learned by almost anyone through proper training.

This is as true in the field of business as it is in war and politics. The aura of mystery and romance that surrounded the builders of the first industrial empires has given way to one of understanding and objective appraisal. There was nothing unique about the ability of individuals like Carnegie, Ford, Rockefeller, Sloan, or Vail—except perhaps their dedication to the goals they pursued, in some cases to the exclusion of all other considerations.

Today there are other individuals, who are virtually unknown to the public, running enterprises far bigger than those commanded by any of the early industrialists. How many Americans even know the names of the CEOs of Exxon Corporation, GM, Mobil Corporation, Ford, and IBM? Of course, none of these individuals was a founder or empire builder. But that is not the only reason for their relative anonymity. The mystique surrounding the earlier leaders of business has been shattered. The veil has been lifted. We have discovered that success in business is very much a matter of skills—skills that can be taught.

This is the rationale for the entire management-development program at IBM, which has produced a series of new leaders from the ranks to direct the fortunes of a $40 billion business. When Frank Cary became president at the time of the retirement of Tom Watson, Jr., in 1971, Cary "seemed the very model of faceless bureaucrat so often found in the executive suites of major bureaucrat firms. . . . He tended to blend in with his background rather than to impress people by force of intellect or imagination." In short, he was what former employees described as "a perfect IBM product,"[7] trained through the system and equipped with all the skills required to direct it. John Opel, who joined IBM in 1949 and succeeded Cary as chairman, considers himself an interchangeable part of the company. "I'm a product of the culture of IBM, of the way we do things."[8] Cary and Opel may be outstanding managers, but they are also outstanding products of a training system.

Looking to the time when Bill Marriott, Jr., steps down as CEO, Marriott has established a management-development program to prepare other executives to take over. The program covers a wide range of organizational, managerial, and leadership skills, including time management; delegation of responsibility; and, most interesting of all, problem solving.

A Critical Skill

The ability to solve problems is one skill that many managers believe cannot be transmitted through training. Actually, there is a process or technique to problem solving that most managers follow unconsciously but that can be made conscious, systematized, and taught to others. In almost all cases, a solution can be found by viewing a problem in its wider context, tracing the problem to its original source, and making a firm commitment to resolve the problem at all costs.

Bill Marriott, Jr., related an incident in which he went into a Marriott hotel restaurant and found the service unsatisfactory. Instead of immediately calling over the manager to demand greater discipline, he called over a waitress to hear about the problem from her point of view. She explained that the hotel received many foreign guests who are used to a system in which tips are included in the bill, so the waiters and waitresses did not earn much on tips and the good ones quickly left. On hearing this explanation, Marriott instructed the manager to raise the salaries of the staff, and the problem was solved. He explained:

> The manager of the hotel had been casting about for several months to get better service, and he never bothered to ask the people that were on the line. I'm sure that this happens a lot.

Marriott's problem at the hotel was a small one. Iacocca's problem at Chrysler was gargantuan. But the process of arriving at a solution was the same. As Iacocca soon discovered, the problem boiled down to the fact that "everybody at Chrysler was doing something he was not trained for."[9] The design engineers, for instance, were telling the production people what to produce and the marketing people what to sell.

The problem could be traced back to the fact that the company's founder, Walter Chrysler, was a talented engineer who gave a greater emphasis to innovative engineering than to marketing. As a result, a bias developed within the corporation in favor of the engineering department, which became the most powerful and dictated policy to the production and marketing people. The company was turned inward and lost contact with the needs of the market. Iacocca took one look at what was going on and saw the cause of the problem. Chrysler was producing what the engineers designed, not what the market desired. The solution followed naturally: Find out what the customer wants and make it.

There was a lot of good common sense in what Iacocca did at Chrysler, but not much genius. Problems are created by ordinary people. They can be solved by ordinary people, too. What Iacocca did at Chrysler can be taught to anyone through proper training.

Whatever Happened to Eliza?

In George Bernard Shaw's original British play *Pygmalion*, Eliza eventually ends up married to Freddy, whose family has fallen from the heights of aristocracy into the depths of poverty. In Lerner and Loewe's

American version, *My Fair Lady*, she decides to stay on with Higgins in the lingering hope of marrying him someday. Shaw was wise enough to know that Higgins—an aristocrat, the son of an affectionate mother, and a confirmed bachelor—would never marry a flower girl, no matter how pretty she looked or how sweetly she spoke. He also knew that no bright girl like Eliza would prefer spinsterhood with a gruff bachelor to marriage with a doting young man.

But Lerner and Loewe understood far better the power of education and training. Eliza had discovered that it was possible to radically transform her appearance and behavior with a little help from a good teacher. Having drunk from the waters of the artesian spring, she undoubtedly hoped that over time the same power could be used to transform a confirmed bachelor into an affectionate husband. Considering the power of the instrument and the intensity of Eliza's commitment to the goal, we tend to think she was right—as America has proved right about education.

CHAPTER 8

Building Up the Corporate Body

It is said that the true greatness of a poet lies in the capacity to express a great inspiration in simple, ordinary language. There is a story about an Englishwoman who attended a literature course in her later life to make up for a complete lack of childhood education. When she read Shakespeare for the first time, she remarked: "This writer takes all the most common English phrases and stuffs them into his books." The woman did not realize that it was Shakespeare who created all those common phrases. Shakespeare possessed the capacity to express his profound insights about human nature and life in vivid phrases that have enriched the everyday English language and come to be taken for granted.

The true greatness of a corporation is measured in the same way—by the capacity to express its highest values in the smallest physical details and most ordinary, routine acts of daily life, which everyone takes for granted. A small, thoughtful innovation on the dashboard of your car, a typewriter that operates silently without vibration or hesitation, a computer instruction manual that is very simple and easy to understand, spotless rest rooms in a crowded public building, a telephone that is answered with a friendly voice on the first ring—these are the finer expressions of the art of corporate excellence.

You can tell a lot about an individual's personality and character from his or her appearance or smallest act, if only you are perceptive enough to observe carefully. When Sherlock Holmes was first introduced to Dr. Watson, he astonished Watson by discerning his profession and his recent tour of military duty in Afghanistan from Watson's speech, clothes, and gestures.

The perceptive person can learn just as much about a company by

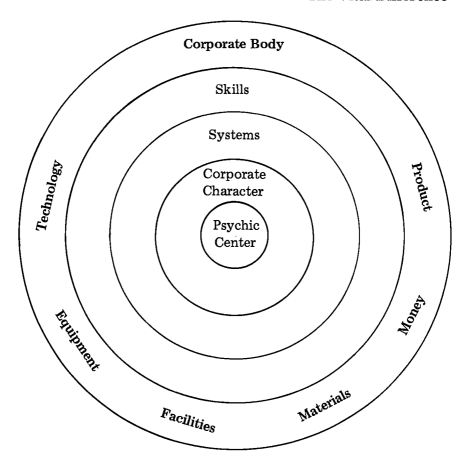

Figure 5.   The role of the corporate body in the
corporate personality.

observing the appearance of its facilities, the quality of its products or
services, and the way it handles materials, money, and machines. Of
course, these material things, which constitute the physical body of a
corporation, represent only a small part of what a company really is.
(See Figure 5.) Behind these things, controlling them and expressing
itself through them, is the personality of a living organization. The
more developed and integrated that personality is, the more fully and
clearly its values will be expressed in the most mundane material
aspects of its existence.

The health and performance of the corporate body—like those of
human body—depend very much on the way they are cultured and

used or neglected and abused. Hygiene is as important to the proper functioning of an office or a factory as it is to the health of a person. Exercise and proper diet are as essential to the performance of equipment and machinery as they are to the organs of the human body. The vitality of both the person and the company depend on the proper selection and absorption of the right qualities and quantities of raw materials and the proper elimination of wastes. The quality of a product and service depends as much on these things as the quality of a person's life and actions. Let us consider some of the uses and abuses of the corporate body.

The Corporate Home

You can learn a lot about people by visiting their homes and seeing the way they live. The same is true of companies. The layout of offices, the cleanliness and maintenance of buildings and machines, the orderliness of files and inventory, and the atmosphere speak louder than corporate pronouncements.

Winston Churchill once said: "We shape our buildings and afterwards our buildings shape us."[1] Two companies that firmly believe in that principle are Levi Strauss & Company, the world's largest clothing manufacturer, and Deere & Company, the largest producer of farm machinery in the world.

Levi Strauss was a family-owned company for 121 years, until it went public in 1971; and in spite of becoming a $2.5 billion business, it still retains much of its traditional family character. One of Levi Strauss' central beliefs is that "the well-being of the company and the well-being of its people are one and the same."[2]

For almost 70 years Levi Strauss lived in a warm, cozy, four-story building on Battery Street in downtown San Francisco, where it moved after the 1906 earthquake destroyed its previous residence. But rapid growth in the 1960s strained the facility to the bursting point, so in 1973 the company moved to a modern high rise at the Embarcadero Center. Levi Strauss employees were stationed on the lower floors and executives on the twenty-eighth floor, which was accessed by different elevators. Suddenly, executives and subordinates were no longer meeting each other in the halls. People started complaining of a cold, isolated feeling in their glass-enclosed cubicles. A survey of employees revealed that the family feeling and close interpersonal relations were suffering.

Even though the lease had another 13 years to run, the company decided to build its own headquarters complex on an eight-acre site at the foot of Telegraph Hill overlooking San Francisco Bay. Levi Strauss' new home consists of five red brick buildings, which blend into the slope of the hill behind. When you enter Levi Strauss' offices, you have the feeling you are really in a home. On every floor there are three or four very large open-area lounges with cushioned chairs, couches, and kitchenettes, which cover a total area of about 5,000 square feet. Fifty percent of the office space is open, and half of the window exposure is in open areas. In addition, there are dozens of open-air balconies, a 7,000-square-foot health club, and a park. One woman, who was sitting on the lawn eating her lunch, summed up the attitude of employees toward the new offices: "This is mine!"

What was the price the company paid for this luxury? First, Levi Strauss got a building that was 10 percent more efficient in terms of usable office space than the one at Embarcadero. Second, it got higher productivity. Howard Friedman, consulting architect for the company, said: "There's no question. It's very easy arithmetic. There is less employee turnover. The waiting list is tremendous. That's a key. If you reduce your turnover, you increase your productivity." Friedman says that Levi Strauss has made the same effort to humanize its 50 factories around the country, through selection of attractive rural settings; comfortable lighting; good acoustics; air conditioning; pleasant eating and lounge areas; and personal, domestic-type toilets.

In contrast to Levi Strauss' relaxed, casual, people-oriented atmosphere, the headquarters of Deere in Moline, Illinois, radiates an aura of quality and precision engineering, two of the company's dominant corporate values. Levi Strauss shunned the steel-and-glass look; Deere consciously adopted it to express values of simplicity, functional efficiency, cleanliness, endurance, and strength. The building has been called the "Versailles of the cornfields" and is generally considered the best piece of corporate architecture in the country.

Friedman says that Deere's building reflects the belief that "people should work in surroundings that have the same care and attention to design that they give to the products they make and that the character of the place you work [in] is an absolute reflection of the caliber and quality of the product." Deere applies the same principle to its manufacturing plants, even the traditionally smoke- and soot-filled foundries. According to an article in *The Boston Globe Magazine*, "Deere may run the only foundries in North America with not even a cigarette butt on the floor. . . . At Deere, the emphasis on a quality environment for the workers is almost fanatic."[3] Levi Strauss and

Deere mean what they say. They carry their highest values down to the most material level.

Good Housekeeping

Anyone familiar with the history of the leather industry knows that tanneries are as infamous for their dirt and gloom as foundries are for their smoke and dust, especially the tanneries of central Europe 50 years ago. But not all the tanneries. Tomas Bata was so obsessed with cleanliness that he had all his workers wearing clean shirts every day, installed showers, and insisted that every machine and window be washed once a week. One day he walked through one of his tanneries wearing white gloves and rubbing the black machinery as he passed by. After seeing the soot on his gloves, he ordered that all the machinery should thereafter be painted white. He instituted a system for keeping all his factories so clean that it was difficult to find a single piece of wastepaper on the miles of pavement. Even the power plant that he installed before 1911 was kept spotlessly clean. A half-century later his son Thomas explained why: "Cleanliness is something that we have always valued. It maintains a certain discipline in assuring a quality attitude. If you create a clean environment, people react differently. It's something we strive for."

What is so special about cleanliness? Nothing except that the most successful companies seem to take it very seriously and many others just take it for granted. Contrast Bata's factories 50 years ago with this American factory:

> [There is] garbage throughout the plant, since very few employees ever get in the habit of using the garbage barrels provided for their use. . . . Water and oil on the floor will always be a problem in plants. These items were not considered when equipment installations were made; of course there is no excuse for stock on the floor, disorderly stock arrangement, or miscellaneous items lying all over the place. . . . Every time we expected a visit from one of the top officers we spent a minimum of $20,000 to dress up the plant.[4]

This description by a Chrysler plant supervisor in the early 1970s contrasts dramatically with *Fortune*'s description of IBM's "wholly immaculate factories"[5]—in 1940! It is a funny thing how cleanliness and prosperity seem to go together. Cleanliness has a power.

As a corporate value, cleanliness is closely linked with other values. At Anheuser-Busch, Inc. cleanliness is absolutely essential for maintaining the highest-quality beer. "I couldn't impress upon you enough the importance of cleanliness," says Jerry Ritter, corporate vice-president of Anheuser-Busch Companies, Inc. "Cleanliness is probably the most important expression of what you think of yourself, what you think about your product, and what you say to other people. This company has had that attitude from the very beginning. It runs throughout the company. It starts at the top and goes right through the rest of the organization."

At Du Pont cleanliness is closely linked to safety. "You can't have one without the other," says John Page. It is also a key value at General Mills. Gene Sailer, director of manufacturing in the Package Food Operations Division, says, "If you walk through an environment where you feel good—because the parking lot is clean, the yards are clean, the maintenance shops are orderly (we like to say there should be no dust in the air!)—it really sets the tone for the work. It's a signal."

We all associate cleanliness with the value of customer service, so it is not surprising to learn that cleanliness is a high priority in Marriott's hotel lobbies, guest rooms, and restaurants. But Joe Uhl, assistant office manager at a Marriott hotel, says: "The whole hotel, even behind the scenes in the back offices, in the storerooms—everything has to be clean." Why is cleanliness important in places where the customer never goes? Bill Marriott, Jr., says: "It's an indicator of commitment, an indicator of being on top of your job—you know, the Marine Corps policy of polishing your shoes. It's spit and polish. It's indicative of trying to do a good job. We look under the beds. We look in the corners. We look at the back lot. . . ."

The power of cleanliness is best illustrated by instances in which it is not expected at all. Cleanliness was never traditionally associated with low-priced–fast-food restaurants until McDonald's made it one of the firm's primary corporate values. McDonald's clean restaurants convey what no amount of advertising can; namely, that "McDonald's food is really clean and sanitary and healthy—even for the middle class!" Walt Disney Productions did the same thing for amusement parks, making Disneyland into even an upper-class attraction. The clean environment of the park tells customers that they are visiting a respectable, acceptable, wholesome place just like home.

Better Maintenance

Everything in this world responds to attention. Recognition of abilities and development of talents are forms of attention to people; cleanliness and proper maintenance are expressions of attention to machines. In *Zen and the Art of Motorcycle Maintenance*, Robert Pirsig writes about the personality of machines and relates how they, like people, respond to attention: "Each machine has its own, unique personality. . . . The new ones start out as good-looking strangers and, depending on how they are treated, degenerate rapidly into bad-acting grouches or even cripples, or else turn into healthy, good-natured, long-lasting friends."[6]

Of course, all American companies know the importance of proper attention to machinery. Well, judging from this description of a Chrysler plant 15 years ago, perhaps not quite all:

> Much of the equipment was in need of replacement and another large percentage of it in need of repair. . . . It was a constant battle to try to stop the scrap. . . . Failure to keep equipment in good operating condition also caused another big expensive waste of manpower and performance—repairs were excessive. When the repair bank is high, the scrap rate is high. We worked night and day to get defective material repaired. We were well aware that to stop defective material at the source was the real solution to reduce the repair bank. It is very serious in many ways: one, it created excessive inventory that ran into millions of dollars; two, extra manpower required to repair the defective material cost millions of dollars. The equipment did not get bad overnight; we had built 12 million engines on this equipment. *We had no preventive maintenance program.*[7] [Emphasis added.]

The realization of high corporate values and goals requires the support of a firm physical foundation. Proper maintenance of equipment is one essential component. Like cleanliness, the value of maintenance is intimately related to other corporate values. At Anheuser-Busch, Inc. and General Mills, machinery maintenance is an integral part of quality control. As one executive at the beer manufacturer said: "The more shutdowns you have, the more quality-maintenance problems you have. We'd like to have a minimum number of unscheduled, unplanned shutdowns." General Mills is installing a computerized preventive-maintenance program so it can keep more accurate track of all the moving parts in its plants—with a standard part-numbering system! Good preventive maintenance is essential not only for quality but for maintaining punctuality on production schedules. Gene Sailer, of General Mills, says: "A key to reliability of the system is preventive maintenance. A good preventive-maintenance program is worth 5 to 10 percent in terms of the reliability of the systems."

At Du Pont good maintenance is essential for realizing the corporate value (we're sure you know by now). Safety is also a core value at Delta, and Delta's preventive-maintenance program is unsurpassed in the industry. Delta's senior vice-president for technical operations, Don Hettermann, tells his maintenance crew that "safety is everybody's business, not just the inspector or the foreman, but everyone's." Speaking of reliability, Delta's mechanical-dispatch reliability is 99.49 percent—that is the percentage of flights that are not subject to any delay because of maintenance problems. Delta defines a delay as anything more than one minute, whereas some airlines consider a flight delayed only after 15 minutes.

Good maintenance is also closely connected with good customer service at Delta. It is an important reason why Delta has had the best consumer-complaint record among the major U.S. airlines in all but one of the last 14 years—it finished a close second in 1973—and usually has one-third to one-tenth as many complaints per 100,000 passengers as other carriers.

Good Dining

It is well known that the quality of food a person eats is highly correlated with life expectancy and resistance to disease. A similar relationship exists between the raw materials that a company consumes and its long-term financial health. Find a company in financial difficulties and you are likely to find one that is ordering materials it does not require, paying too much for what it orders, accepting defective materials or materials of the wrong specifications or materials it has not even ordered, or perhaps all of these together. When there is a shortage of raw materials or a shortage of funds to purchase them, it is usually a signal that raw materials are being wasted or not utilized as efficiently as they should be.

The problem of high inventory costs has plagued manufacturers ever since the early days of mass production. Henry Ford was the first to devise an efficient solution by creating a moving inventory system. The idea was to project the precise timing of the assembly-line operation and then schedule procurement of raw materials to conform to that schedule, so that there was no need to store them. GM improved on Ford's system by forcing suppliers to conform to production schedules at their own risk.

Coordination of purchasing and production has been lifted to the status of a fine art by the Japanese, with the "just in time" inventory system. Materials and components are ordered to arrive at precisely the time they are required for production, thereby reducing inventory costs to an absolute minimum.

Controlling inventory to minimize production costs sounds easy enough. But to raise the value of cost efficiency through the "just in time" system requires raising performance throughout the corporation, from top to bottom. Planning, marketing, purchasing, and production systems all must be refined and precisely coordinated. Intel introduced the system in 1982. Before that, the firm used to reschedule production runs and orders to vendors every time it got a new order from a customer. Now it projects future orders and sticks to the production schedule. Vendors have become far more reliable and offer Intel lower prices because its orders are reliable. In the process, Intel has reduced its inventory levels by 40 percent, and its own production reliability has increased from 80 percent to 99 percent. Good digestion requires some thought.

The Thing Itself

You can learn a lot about a company from its products, too. People sometimes talk about quality as if it were something that is actually determined on the factory floor, but that is no more true of quality than of profitability. Quality is not something produced by quality circles. Quality is a value. Achieving it depends on the company's total commitment to that value, the strength of its will, the establishment of clear standards, the creation of effective systems, the acquisition of precision skills, the design of appropriate production facilities, the proper maintenance of machinery, the purchase of the right materials, the coordination and integration of these factors, and above all, a corporate attitude at all levels of the company like that expressed by Jerry Ritter of Anheuser-Busch: "The quality of our product is absolutely the ultimate and the No. 1 thought in our minds at all times."

Making quality the No. 1 priority is not quite so simple as it may sound. To really put the importance of the product or service above the importance of profits requires an enormous commitment by management that will be tested every day and can never withstand the pressure to compromise unless quality really is more important to the company than money. As Peters and Waterman discovered in their study of excellent companies, "Profit is a natural by-product of doing something well, not an end in itself. . . ."[8]

In each company we visited, there were values that were placed far above the value of money—in practice as well as in principle. At Merck quality and integrity come first. Quality begins with research. As former Chairman John Horan described Merck's guiding belief: "If you produce something worthwhile, money will follow."[9] Merck's strategy has been to attract top-notch research scientists from the universities and give them a wide latitude of freedom to pursue every lead, regardless of its potential for profit. In the 1940s Merck invested $20 million on an eight-year research project to find a cure for Addison's disease, knowing full well that the drug could never repay the investment. But what researchers actually discovered was cortisone, a revolutionary breakthrough for the treatment of arthritis. This discovery, together with the synthesis of vitamin B_{12} and streptomycin, launched Merck on its way to the top. Merck invests nearly twice as much on research as the average company in the industry—11 percent of sales versus 6.7 percent for the industry in 1983 and a total of $400 million in 1984. For Merck, quality research comes first; the rest follows naturally.

The quality of a product consists of several components: the quality of the materials used to make it, the quality of the workmanship, and the quality of the technology. Whenever a new product comes out on the market, the Japanese practice is to buy one, call all the experts to gather around, and try to make as many tiny improvements on the original as possible. By the time they are finished, the improved version far surpasses the original. That is the infinite potential of technology.

The quality of almost every product can be improved 100 percent by this procedure, especially when those who try to refine it were not involved in the original development and can take a completely fresh approach. Although commercial custom condones such practices and law does not always prohibit them, the act of imitating another's invention, in which enormous investment has been made in research and development, is fundamentally dishonest. It may be a successful strategy for short-term growth, but not for enduring success. American business is founded on the values of creativity and individual initiative, not imitation. Even if we could, we should not imitate the Japanese in this regard—it would kill our creative impulse. What we can do to protect ourselves is to introduce a similar practice within our own companies to improve our own technologies—a department of R, D, & I (research, development, and innovation)—bringing in outside experts to provide fresh perspectives and new ideas before the Japanese do.

Weighing In

As a physical asset, money constitutes part of the corporate body, and, like the other parts, it responds to proper attention. Attention to money is given in the form of proper accounting. Accounting is a system to help the manager understand his or her operations better. When properly used, it is the most effective tool for monitoring corporate performance.

In the 1860s the Pennsylvania Railroad was the largest business operation in the world, and it pioneered many of the management techniques that have since become commonplace. As the first of the big publicly owned enterprises in the United States, the railroads were answerable to a large number of investors, who had the right to know exactly how the firm spent their money. The Penn was the first to introduce modern principles of cost accounting and did it so effectively that a stockholders' committee marveled to find that "a charge or entry of a day's labor, of the purchase of a keg of nails, of the largest order goes through such a system of checks and audits as to make fraud almost an impossibility."[10] Cost accounting enabled the Penn to accurately measure its cost on each and every operation and pinpoint precisely which ones made money and which ones did not. It also made possible cost-based pricing, to assure a profit on every rate it fixed. This apparently mundane achievement was quite a feat for a huge business, at a time when many companies had no idea of whether they were earning or losing until they closed the accounts at the end of the year.

Andrew Carnegie learned cost accounting and other managerial techniques as a superintendent for the Penn and went on to apply them even more effectively at the Carnegie Steel Company, forerunner of the United States Steel Corporation. When he founded his company, he was surprised to learn that none of the steel companies was in the habit of calculating the costs of each production process. Carnegie introduced a comprehensive accounting system to accurately measure the cost of each and every process. This system enabled him to eliminate inefficient processes, rationally evaluate alternatives, replace less efficient equipment, even if it were newly purchased, and thereby bring down his production costs to the lowest level in the world—from $56 per ton in 1872 to $11.50 per ton by 1900.

Long after Carnegie had retired, cost accounting remained a rare phenomenon. Henry Ford despised accounting as "a seedy offshoot of the banking conspiracy"[11] and refused to let accountants touch the company's books. Once he sent a nocturnal raiding party to clear out the offices of a new accounting department, which his son Edsel had installed in his absence. Until Ford's retirement in 1945, no one in the company knew the cost of anything it made or did or even whether the company made a profit or loss the previous year.

Of course, American business has come a long way since Henry Ford, hasn't it? Well, shortly after taking up his new job, Iacocca discovered that "Chrysler had no overall system of financial controls. To make matters worse, nobody in the whole place seemed to fully understand what was going on when it came to financial planning and projecting. Even the most rudimentary questions were impossible for them to answer."[12] Each company can judge for itself whether Chrysler is an exceptional case or not.

The real issue is not whether a company maintains cost accounts but the extent to which these accounts accurately reflect and precisely reveal actual activities at the lowest level of operations. Even today many corporations are not able to break down their numbers to declare precisely how much money each activity, operation, product, or service is earning or losing. Aggregate lump-sum figures provide only a general impression of overall performance. Accounting becomes a powerful and sensitive instrument only when it reflects the actual cost of each separate activity. To do so, accounting systems must be integrated with the production process and based on detailed records of what actually takes place in the factory, store, or office.

Sears is probably one of the best-controlled companies in the United States. It employs a very sophisticated cost-accounting system that is sensitive to minute changes in the performance of each individual department of every store. Standards have been fixed for virtually every item of expenditure, such as stationery supplies per thousand sales transactions, the number of minutes required by the accounting department to balance a cash-register account, cleaning supplies per 1,000 square feet, and so on. The company is constantly working to bring down every cost, even the most routine. In 1984 the cost of janitorial supplies was projected to decrease by 5 percent due to standardization of the products used.

The numbers on a balance sheet are most frequently employed to understand a company's profitability; but they lend themselves to many other uses. More precisely than any other factor, money reflects the amount of energy expended on a product or activity, the direction the company is moving in, and the level of employee enthusiasm. When carefully studied, these figures can reveal at a very early stage of production, or even during the planning phase, whether a product will generate a profit or a loss. If one knows all that numbers can reveal, the soundness of a decision can be tested in no time by casting it into monetary figures. There is no process, no activity, no direction, no result of a company that cannot be revealed by the numbers, provided that the policy, principles, and practices of accounting are properly adapted and organized.

Geneen describes the power of numbers quite dramatically:

> Anyone in business, if he sets up the proper kinds of controls—controls that tell him when any segment of his company is not doing what he expected, and tell him this promptly enough and in enough detail so that he can go back behind the numbers and analyze precisely where it is that he has to take action—then he (or anyone else not mentally incompetent) could run a progressive, profitable, and growth-oriented company. That's what a good set of numbers will do for you.[13]

Vital Signs

The true health of the human body is not measured by its size, strength, and outer appearance, but by certain vital signs that are indicators of the harmonious and efficient functioning of the organs and systems inside and even of the psychological condition of the individual. The sound of the heartbeat, color of the cheeks, and clarity of the eyes tell a physician much more about a person than height and weight. The vital signs of health are the same for all, independent of age and size. A healthy six-month-old infant and a healthy grandmother both have a body temperature of 98.6° F.—it does not vary even a little this way or that.

The same is true of companies as well. There are vital signs of corporate health, which are independent of a company's size and financial strength and more accurately reflect its vitality. A company that regards an open file drawer as a safety hazard, a flight that leaves a minute behind schedule as late, a room with a single piece of paper on the floor as filthy, the number of square feet a janitor cleans as a crucial aspect of productivity, an excessive consumption of paper clips as a cause for concern, a phone call answered on the first ring and a letter replied to on the same day as minimum standards of courtesy, and a machine that starts to murmur a little as an urgent case for repair—that company, regardless of its size, shows the vital signs of excellent health, because its values are actually real. And any company that does not exhibit these signs—regardless of its size—certainly has scope to improve its health.

Corporate Bodybuilding

No one can afford to ignore health. The survival and good health of the body is the essential condition for achievement or enjoyment. But mere physical health is not the be-all and end-all of life. Those who focus an inordinate attention on muscle building and controlled nutrition forget that these are only the means for living and not the aim of life.

The same is true for a company. Corporate bodybuilding is a means to an end, not an end in itself. In the 1920s Ford amassed a huge corporate body, with $700 million in surplus cash, only to come to the brink of bankruptcy a decade later—because the firm forgot that the corporate body is only the most external form of something living, which is inside.

The ultimate value of an organization cannot be measured by its size, the number of buildings it owns, the number of products it makes, or even the wealth it accumulates. The achievements of great individuals, great institutions, and great nations are not measured in these terms. The first duty of a company is to survive, as Drucker said; and for that, profits are essential. But that is only its first duty, not its ultimate goal. We must look beyond the outer physical form for that higher purpose.

CHAPTER 9

Harmony Within

Remember those old, imported European films with the dubbed-in English words that were a fraction of a second out of synchronization with the picture? That infinitesimal error in timing prevented you from losing yourself in the story and gave even the finest acting an air of awkwardness or unreality. Imagine what the effect would be if the delay were a minute or two instead of a second. You would hear people still talking to each other after one of them had already walked out the door. You would hear the bad guy challenging the hero to draw after watching the villain fall dead on the dusty main street. The awkward and unreal would become hilarious and absurd. That is the importance of harmony between words and acts.

Suppose a company performs like an unsynchronized film, saying one thing and doing another—shipping orders after their cancellation dates, purchasing parts for discontinued production models, introducing a technology or fashion after it has already become outdated in the market, paying workers overtime one week and laying them off the next and paying them overtime again the third, borrowing money from the bank at high interest for one division while another division of the same company is depositing its excess funds at low interest, setting priorities that are misinterpreted and executed in reverse at lower levels, adopting high corporate values that are negated in practice by unhelpful attitudes among staff, and so on. An impartial observer of these things is not likely to be very amused. Yet all of these expressions of disharmony in an organization are much more common these days than an unsynchronized film.

Operational Harmony—Coordination

Harmony is essential to all life, whether it be the life of an organism or the life of an organization. The most basic form of physical harmony, what we call coordination, is dramatically exemplified by the routine functioning of the human body. At every moment the body maintains a very delicate balance and precise equilibrium between the intake of oxygen, beating of the heart, flow of blood, digestion of food, excitation of nerves, exertion of muscles, functioning of organs, secretion of hormones, and maintenance of constant body temperature. If this harmony of the body is even slightly disturbed, it means big trouble.

At the operational level, companies function very much like the human body. They expend an enormous amount of energy in a steady stream just to maintain routine activities like purchasing, production, storage, distribution, marketing, maintenance, recruitment, and training. At every moment an organization has to preserve the delicate balance between all of these simultaneous activities. The maximum efficiency of an organization is achieved when all its parts function in smooth harmony with one another.

An organization is a complex matrix of interdependent activities. If purchasing slackens, production slows. If sales flag, inventories rise. If collections fall behind, cash flow suffers. If recruitment or training is inadequate, expansion is retarded. A disequilibrium between any of these functions can cause serious, sometimes irreparable, harm to the health of the organization.

Coordination is physical harmony in the horizontal dimension between activities, systems, and departments at the same level of the organization. Integration is physical harmony in the vertical dimension between activities, systems, and departments at higher and lower levels of the organization. Coordination and integration are basic organizational values, without which other values like quality, efficiency, profitability, and service cannot be achieved. Even the simple act of serving hamburgers at McDonald's requires precise coordination among systems for taking orders, cooking, serving, receiving payments, and cleaning equipment. These systems must also be integrated with other systems for purchasing supplies, recruiting staff, training, and facilities maintenance.

Companies usually establish coordination and integration at key points that are essential for their functioning. But there are many other areas of interaction where these values are frequently lacking. A retired Chrysler plant supervisor related an incident that occurred when he was supervising assembly operations at a Chrysler engine plant. The metal-stamping department always liked to run the highest-priced jobs, regardless of conditions in other departments. On one occasion the stamp plant kept running front fenders even though the metal-finishing department had run out of room to store them and had requested the stamp plant to stop. To cope with the onslaught, metal-finishing personnel were pitching the fenders onto a ten-foot-high pile and damaging them in the process.

This incident, which occurred in the early 1950s, might be dismissed as an isolated occurrence; but another description of Chrysler 25 years later suggests that it was not. When Iacocca arrived at Chrysler, he found that

> the company consisted of a bunch of little duchies . . . a bunch of mini-empires, with nobody giving a damn about what anyone else was doing . . . thirty-five vice-presidents, each with his own turf. There was no real committee setup, no cement in the organization chart, no system of meetings to get people talking to each other. I couldn't believe, for example, that the guy running the engineering department wasn't in constant touch with his counterpart in manufacturing. But that's how it was. Everybody worked independently. . . .[1]

Tuning Up the Company

Many companies are like a box containing all the parts of an unassembled watch. They have all the resources required for successful operations—talented people, a fine product, sufficient capital, a good market—yet somehow they are not able to put it all together and make it run properly. Other companies are like a watch that has been clumsily assembled by an amateur. All its parts are grinding and grating on each other. There is some rough working order, but things are constantly stopping, going wrong, breaking down. Then there are companies that function like a precision-made, well-lubricated watch. All the components are in precisely the right relationship to one another, and movements between them are perfectly synchronized, frictionless, and smooth. These companies have achieved harmony at the operational level.

At about the same time Chrysler's stamp and metal-working departments were fighting over fenders, IBM introduced coordination between its engineering and production departments to facilitate the development of one of its first electronic computers. This coordination resulted in faster and cheaper development of a better-quality product and thereafter became a basic operating principle at IBM.

When John Huck joined Merck as director of marketing in 1958, the company was dominated by a powerful research division. Research developed new products and gave them to the marketing division to sell, in much the same way Chrysler's engineering department used to design new-model cars. At that time, the research and development staff used to call meetings to present new products to the marketing division. These meetings marked the first time that marketing people were exposed to these products or had an opportunity to comment on them. The relationship was all one way. There was no coordination between divisions at an early stage of product development.

Soon after Huck's arrival, a serious effort was made to rectify the imbalance. A joint research-marketing committee system was established to coordinate work even during the research phase. Product managers began to mingle with researchers on the once-forbidden terrain of the laboratories. One good example of a product that benefited by the improved working relationship between research and marketing was a new antidepressant drug with significantly better characteristics than the competition. This drug soon became number one in its field.

Increased harmony at the physical level through coordination not only raised productivity within the company; it evoked a response from the market as well. When Merck launched its effort to coordinate, it ranked among the second half-dozen drug companies in the United States. By the time the move for internal coordination was complete, Merck was a rising star in the industry. As Huck said: "Coordination makes the difference between being really successful and just being pretty good."

The introduction of a new interdepartmental system for coordination was not sufficient to create a harmonious relationship between research and marketing. Attitudes of people at all levels of the company also had to change. It took ten years before people really came to feel that they should fully communicate and cooperate with each other. According to Huck the attitude is more important than the system. "You probably need the system to get going, but that isn't enough. If you have the right attitudes, you could probably do it without the systems." Systems facilitate coordination and harmony at the physical level. But the right corporate attitude generates cooperation, which is a higher and more powerful form of harmony.

Merck has recognized the importance of corporate attitudes for fostering harmony within and without. As it stresses credibility in its relations with physicians, so it stresses trust in its relations with employees. John Lyons likened an organization to an internal-combustion engine. Friction is a major obstacle to the smooth running of them both. Friction dissipates a lot of energy as unproductive heat. It causes wear and tear on the parts, lowers efficiency, and slows speed. To counteract friction in a car engine, a cooling system and a lubricating system are utilized, both of which add extra weight and bulk to the vehicle. Companies introduce many cumbersome systems to reduce friction between individuals, departments, and divisions. Now suppose friction in the engine could be dramatically reduced by some means. All the extra systems could be scrapped. Equipment, operating, and maintenance costs would drop. Speed and efficiency would improve. Engineers have not yet discovered a way to eliminate friction in a car engine. But some companies have found a way to reduce organizational friction by encouraging positive corporate attitudes that generate cooperation and teamwork.

Organizational Harmony—Cooperation and Teamwork

General Mills gets its high-flying, youthful exuberance from the entrepreneurial spirit it fosters within the company. But if that were its only strength, you might find the company shattered by an infinite number of brilliant inspirations and great ideas, each headed in a different direction! The cement that bonds all these individuals together and makes all their energies and ideas productive is the spirit of teamwork and cooperation that has evolved over the years.

General Mills has overcome the functional isolation between departments by establishing interdepartmental task forces, creating systems for coordination, and fostering an attitude of cooperation at all levels. The company has made significant gains in "people productivity" by developing teamwork among research and production, production and marketing, and marketing and sales. The Consumer Foods divisions organize groups for each new product. Representatives from each function (R&D, marketing, and so on) work together as a team. The key to success is an attitude of shared responsibility. "The controllers and the research guy and the market-research woman and the production person all feel that they've got a much greater vested interest in it," one executive explained. Each division has come to recognize that it depends on the others in order to do its job properly.

As we saw in Chapter 5, the gaps between systems possess a great potential power. General Mills focuses on these interfaces and tries to bridge the gaps through team management. Marketing and production people spend a lot of time talking to each other and trying to find ways to do things better. Working on the interfaces can result in substantial gains. The director of manufacturing in the Package Foods Operations Division thinks, "There is a potential for reducing costs by 30 percent."

But the key is the attitude of the team members. "If the total system prospers, then you'll all prosper. If you come with a selfish motive that says, 'I can only be successful if I climb the mountain higher than somebody else,' then you're not going to get there. It requires cooperation. You're trying to build a team while still maintaining individual pride."

Cooperation not only saves money; it saves time, too. Raj Puri, a program manager in Consumer Foods, is involved in the launching of new products. He estimates that the company's team approach can reduce the time from conception of a new product to sales by as much as 40 percent to 50 percent, a savings of two years or more. Interfacing between research and manufacturing starts while the product is still in the laboratory. Once again, the key is attitude—"trying to get people to look at the overall business. It broadens our horizons. Everyone has their boundaries and they have to expand across them," Puri says.

The same close rapport exists at General Mills between sales and marketing, which are traditional adversaries in many corporations. A recent incident dramatically illustrates the power of harmony to evoke a response from the market. During the first eight months of 1984, sales in Consumer Foods were lagging behind the previous year. In September it was proposed that 12 separate food product groups combine their advertising budgets and marketing strategies into a single giant, promotion program, which required each product group to relinquish control over its own budget to a coordinating body.

The $20 million spent on the single promotion was the same amount budgeted for separate expenditure by the different product groups, but the results were far better—the biggest sales month in the history of the foods division. Walt LeSueur, director of sales administration, described the joint effort this way: "It is not a marketing and a sales organization that are fighting each other. It's an integrated sales-marketing operation that works together and understands each other."

The power of teamwork is not something new at General Mills. The founder, James Bell, believed that it was the critical factor in the company's growth during the Great Depression. In 1939 he said: "Because the organization of General Mills is necessarily diffuse and complex, it is all the more important that unity in action, recognition of individual responsibility and the spirit of cooperation prevail. This spirit . . . has been responsible for the company's success, progress and growth throughout a decade marked by depression and uncertainty."[2] And, we can add, through 4½ decades of prosperity since then, too.

Communication

The basis of all harmony is communication between people. At the level of physical coordination, communication is needed to convey information between related people and points in the organization. Coca-Cola is able to control and coordinate activities around the world because it has developed a daily flow of two-way communication between the head office and its overseas subsidiaries. Coca-Cola has the ability to process the information it receives and to respond within 24 hours. It gets profit-and-loss reports from foreign subsidiaries twice a month and has a very accurate reading on monthly performance by the seventh calendar day of the following month, which is lightning fast for a company of this size operating in 155 different countries. As the company's chief financial officer said: "The information flow creates a tremendous strength. The speed and accuracy of it are phenomenal."

Communication is also essential for establishing organizational harmony. The basis of all cooperation between people depends on two things—an understanding and an attitude. Communication can create both. First, people must understand the importance of cooperation and the place of each active participant in the overall scheme of things. Second, they must acquire a willing attitude based on a recognition that cooperation serves the greater good of the organization. General Mills' 12-product promotion was made possible by this understanding and this attitude.

At Northwestern Mutual communication is a vital function, which supports a very high level of organizational harmony. There is a free flow of communication horizontally between related departments and also vertically between higher and lower levels of the company. The horizontal flow is promoted through a system of liaison committees, which serve to bridge the gap between related departments. Whatever may be said of the cumbersome nature of management by committees, they can play an invaluable role in fostering cooperation and teamwork. Northwestern Mutual has made committees an effective channel for coordinating activities, fostering greater understanding, and overcoming negative attitudes within the company. Committees are also used to raise the level of cooperation between the office staff and the company's independent field agents. "We have a pretty good understanding of our mutual interests," says Vice-President Dick Wright.

Northwestern Mutual supplements communication through the committees with educational programs to foster teamwork. A new videotape entitled "In Search for Harmony" is now being used to help the home office staff better understand and appreciate the needs and activities of the field agents.

A harmonious family feeling is not just something management professes at Northwestern Mutual. "You are treated like an individual. You're not just a cog in the wheel," says one middle manager. "They really try to reach down into the clerical level, and I think they do succeed." Top management not only talks; it eagerly listens, too. "There is an upward vertical movement of communication. They really do rely on the input of the people who are on the line. In fact, if they don't hear anything, they'll make [it] a point to solicit a comment. They always ask the service reps for input. That's why it gives you a sense of importance." The effectiveness of communication in fostering positive relationships at Northwestern Mutual can be judged from the results of a 1980 survey, which showed that 85 percent of the staff felt the company kept them well informed, and 97 percent had complete faith in the information they received.

At Marriott teamwork is developed by regular communication through a system of management meetings and employee meetings, so that, as one executive put it: "Everybody knows what we are trying to accomplish and . . . [is] reminded of it and encouraged toward it."

Meetings are a much-maligned thing these days. A 1983 survey of U.S. executives found that 71 percent believe that meetings are a waste of time. But the real problem is not with meetings per se. Successful companies utilize meetings as a highly effective instrument for improving coordination and cooperation. Like any tool, meetings themselves are neutral. Their effectiveness depends on the skill of those who utilize them.

Coordination, cooperation, and communication enable the organization to harness the available energies more efficiently and utilize them more productively. Efforts to increase organizational harmony afford infinite scope for improving corporate effectiveness. As one bank official writes, with reference to meetings:

> The room for advances in productivity through technological means may be growing scarce. It could therefore be that the next leap forward in productivity will come through the more effective management and organization of purely human activities.[3]

Corporate Harmony

Physical harmony is achieved by proper coordination of related activities through a network of interlinking systems. Organizational harmony is achieved when employees acquire a greater understanding of the work done by others and recognize the importance of cooperation and teamwork. But there is still a higher form of harmony, in which the bonding element is a feeling of identification with the company and a sense of belonging rather than a system, an understanding, or an attitude.

There are a few companies in which cooperation, teamwork, and team spirit are raised to the level of a high ideal and core value of the psychic center. The company seeks them in preference to monetary goals, not just as a means to make greater profits. Cooperation and friendliness among peers are then augmented by a deeper sense of the company's commitment to its people and the individual employee's personal commitment to the firm. Cooperation in these companies transcends the necessities of work and the interests of efficiency. Neighborliness goes beyond the limits of mere courtesy and good relations. Harmony among employees and between employees and management is maintained even in the absence of special systems to promote it or peer pressure to enforce it. People are bound together by a set of values that they feel committed to live and work by. Harmony has become a custom or perhaps even a culture in the company.

When outsiders visit a company like this, they can perceive a warm, friendly atmosphere or family feeling in the air. This is how we felt when we visited Delta. So many companies speak about family feeling these days that the phrase is losing its real significance. But at Delta the thing is real and palpable, regardless of what you call it.

Many reasons can be given to explain it. C. E. Woolman was a kind, affectionate man. The company was started in a small southern town. It has a policy of preserving jobs in times of slack business, promotes from within, and pays high salaries. But in our view the single most important element is not these things. It is an abiding sense of security. How do you feel when you are in your own home with your own family? You feel safe and secure. Delta makes its people feel secure.

Security starts at the physical level—with safe airplanes. Delta employees believe that the company has the best-maintained fleet in the industry and will spare no effort or expense to keep it that way. This conviction generates a feeling of confidence and relaxation in a business where the fear of accidents is uppermost in the minds of many. "There is never any thought of compromising safety," says Senior Vice-President Joe Cooper. "There is never any question in the employees' minds that a piece of equipment is not the most reliable thing around."

Economic security is the basis of the company's employment policy. Employees know that once they are accepted into the family, their jobs are secure so long as they put in an honest day's work. Delta has never laid off workers for economic reasons—except a few pilots for a few months back in 1957. "When times are tough, when the industry is going through a bad time, we don't have to think, 'Where are we?' We don't even think about it, because we know our jobs are going to be there," said one flight attendant. Delta has never had a strike. The company offers better compensation than most unions demand, so more than 90 percent of the employees do not bother to join one. As mechanic Lenny Meuse put it, "If we needed a union here at Delta, we'd have a union. But the way they treat you, we don't need one."[4] The company also has a generous retirement program to protect the whole family.

Delta tries to provide psychological security to its employees, too. We asked one senior executive what is the most important thing he tries to communicate to his staff. He replied, "to give them peace of mind." Then he added. "All of us that work at Delta are members of a family-type organization. A lot of people feel that is just a cliché, the Delta family; but our people and all of us really believe it."

But the true measure of family feeling is in a company's acts, not in its words; and at Delta the action comes from an unexpected source— the employees. In 1982 77 percent of Delta's 37,000 employees contributed toward the purchase of a $30 million Boeing 767 for the company. That act expresses their feelings pretty loudly. "You can interview as many people as you want," Meuse told us, "but basically they'll all tell you the same thing: It's a great company to work for. They take care of us, and we try to take care of them."

Harmony Attracts

Harmony is a formidable power. It improves efficiency, reduces waste, minimizes friction, increases productivity, eliminates conflicts, relieves tension, releases enthusiasm, and generates joy. But that is not all. It also possesses the capacity to attract customers and make the market come to the company instead of the company's going to the market.

What makes a person attractive to other people? It is liveliness and charm, energy and harmony of personality. We are naturally attracted to people of high energy because we feel more intense and alive in their presence. If they have cheerful and harmonious personalities, we also feel calm, relaxed, and happy when we are with them.

The same is true of companies. Think for a moment of the companies that you keep going back to in preference to so many others. Sometimes it is because one firm's price is better than the others'. Sometimes it is because of better quality. And sometimes—it is just because we feel better there. We enjoy it.

When a company has a rich, harmonious personality, it becomes more attractive to customers. Sales personnel are more friendly. Service people are more cooperative. Operators are more cheerful. An associate of ours became a dedicated Delta fan long before he knew anything about the company or had ever flown on one of its flights, just because a Delta reservations agent was so helpful and friendly on the phone.

A Merck professional representative explained a similar phenomenon. When the representatives are happy in their work, proud of the company, and have a positive attitude, "it causes a ripple effect like in a lake. They are more effective, more positive, more persistent, more empathetic; and therefore, when the doctor is looking at you, he sees somebody he likes to be with."

Harmony is expansive. When Tom Watson increased the level of harmony at IBM during the 1930s with his policy of job security and job enrichment, not only did productivity and job satisfaction improve; the market responded, too, enabling IBM to grow right through the Great Depression. Harmony is attractive like a fashion. It spreads by itself and creates its own market where there was none before, because it meets a deeper need in people—the need for harmony in their own lives.

Uniting Opposites

We have so far spoken of harmony between activities, people, systems, and departments. But one of the highest forms of harmony is the capacity to reconcile conflicting values. A striking attribute of the companies we studied was their simultaneous adherence to two or more different, and apparently opposite, sets of values.

At General Mills we found a tremendous emphasis on individual entrepreneurship coupled with an equal insistence on cooperation and teamwork. At Merck there is hard-driving, aggressive selling linked with a meticulous insistence on objective, factual presentations—no easy combination. At Northwestern Mutual the highest priority is teamwork and committee-based, consensus decision making—two things that are known to slow momentum and dampen individual in-

itiative—yet the company has achieved the highest level of productivity and speed of response in its industry. Marriott utilizes the most
sophisticated network of impersonal systems to deliver highly personalized and friendly service to its customers and to achieve the highest
levels of profitability in the hotel food business—all at the same time.

Companies that achieve a high level of corporate harmony are
constantly reconciling and harmonizing conflicting sets of values in
their everyday operations. The greater the apparent conflict between
the values they adopt, the greater is the power that issues from harmonizing them.

Corporate Alignment

Anyone who has ever driven across midtown Manhattan at 5 P.M. on
a weekday knows what disharmony is all about. Traffic inches forward,
jams together, and gets clogged at every intersection. Police look on
helplessly. Traffic lights are useless. Pedestrians cross when and where
they can. Trucks double-park to make their deliveries, backing up
traffic for blocks. Everyone is going every which way, focused on individual destinations, in a total confusion and chaos that is certainly
dangerous to people's psychological health, not to mention their physical safety.

Contrast this with the feeling of joy and ease cruising down Seventh Avenue at midnight after a Broadway show, with a long stream
of synchronized traffic lights green for as far as you can see and hardly
a dozen cars on the road. You float through the usually congested
intersections as if on a magic carpet, without even looking to the left
or right, because the lights are with you and it's all clear. You save a
fortune on gasoline by avoiding all those stops and cut down wear on
the brakes and gears. You travel in a few minutes a distance it took
you an hour to cover in the afternoon. You feel safe and relaxed, with
no fear of an accident and no tension on the nerves. Everything is going
your way. That is what we mean by corporate harmony.

The key to the whole thing is the lights—synchronized green
lights running all in a row. Nothing to slow you down. No barriers in
the road. The lights set the direction of the traffic. This is the role that
values play in a company when they are set high enough and seriously
pursued. They act like lights clearly fixing the direction of all the traffic
and helping it flow unhindered in the shortest time, at the least cost,
and with the minimum of friction. The higher the value, the smoother
the flow.

There are an infinite number of elements and points within an organization that can be properly aligned and harmonized with other elements of the same type and of different types, with other points at the same level and at different levels. The innumerable systems for production must be in harmony with each other as well as with the systems for purchasing, storage, accounting, distribution, and marketing. Systems at each level must be properly integrated with related systems at all the other levels above and below. They must also be in harmony with technical skills for production, marketing skills for selling what is produced, accounting skills for proper costing and pricing, and so on. So, too, they must be in harmony with the organizational structure and authority exercised. For instance, the system of unlocked laboratory storerooms at Hewlett-Packard depends very much on the milieu of positive authority in the company's corporate character. Systems must also be in harmony with the beliefs, values, and objectives of the psychic center. What is true of systems is true of the other elements as well. Skills must be in harmony with other skills at all levels, with the product, machinery, materials, marketing strategy, organizational structure, type of authority, values, and so on.

This complex matrix of interacting elements can be depicted dramatically by a series of arrows, each arrow representing a different element in the organization and the direction of the arrow symbolizing the degree of its alignment with other elements.

For instance, in Figure 6 we have a simple case of disharmony between values and skills. Perhaps the company wants to establish a high level of coordination and teamwork, but its managers lack the level of interpersonal skills required to do so.

Figure 7 represents a company whose values are not in harmony with its equipment. Perhaps the value is safety, and the equipment is subject to hazardous breakdowns. Or the value may be quality, and the equipment is not given the attention necessary to achieve it.

Figure 8 depicts a situation in which the company has set good customer service as a high priority. It has created the necessary systems and acquired the necessary skills. But it tries to positively motivate employees to give cheerful service using negative forms of authority such as rigid discipline.

Henry Ford had the mission of making a low-priced car for the masses. He acquired the necessary systems and technical skills. But as the market expanded, times changed, and his own organization expanded thousands of times; he clung to old-fashioned attitudes about banks and accountants and continued to run the company in the autocratic fashion of an aging proprietor. The resulting disharmony nearly destroyed the firm (Figure 9).

Figure 6.

Figure 7.

Figure 8.

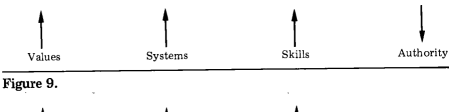

Figure 9.

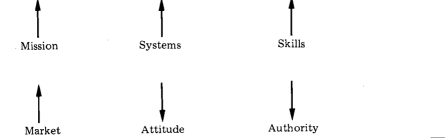

Figure 10.

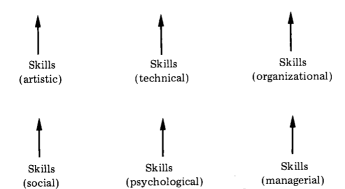

The mission of Walt Disney Productions is to make people happy. It requires a lot of skills to do that: artistic skills to design amusement parks and write film scripts, technical skills to build the park attractions and produce films, organizational skills to handle crowds of 10,000 people at peak periods and provide sufficient food for their consumption and merchandise for sale, social skills to please the customer, psychological skills to motivate staff and make their work enjoyable, managerial skills to keep the entire operation functioning as a profitable commercial organization. When all these skills are present, there is harmony at one level (Figure 10).

Suppose a company really believes that serving the customer is its most important value, and its staff members have acquired the attitude that pleasing the customer is a high priority. There is harmony between the value and the attitude. If top management makes plans to improve the speed and quality of service, objectives are also in harmony. If the structure is loosened to encourage individual initiative, if the incentive system is refined to reinforce positive behavior by the staff, if training is given to better equip customer-contact personnel with the physical and social skills for high-quality service, and if the physical premises are made cleaner and more comfortable, then we could say the company has a string of green lights for improving customer service—as in Figure 11.

Of course, in reality, things are more complex than this. There are many more elements that contribute to corporate behavior, and there are a very large number of behaviors all taking place simultaneously. A more complete but still very partial representation of corporate harmony containing 21 elements is shown in Figure 12.

Making Harmony Last

There are moments in the life of every company when harmony rises to a higher level. Often such a moment comes in response to a threatening crisis, as it did at Chrysler a few years ago. When things take a sudden and dramatic turn for the worse, people become more alert, flexible, dynamic, and cooperative. They stop insisting on their opinions, stop standing on prestige, brush aside their grievances, and forget their feuds. Everyone pitches in to save the situation. Activities are better coordinated, departments cooperate with each other, people work with a team spirit, and work flows smoothly. A company that

Figure 11.

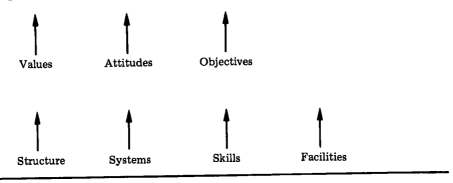

Figure 12.

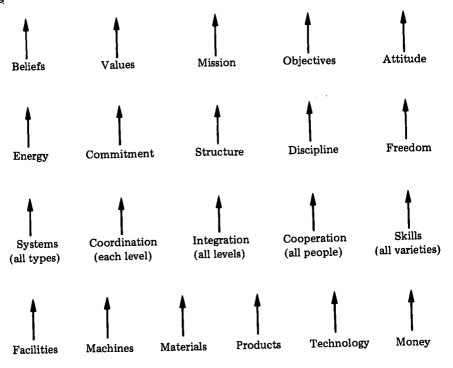

appeared to be in the throes of death suddenly revives with an unexpected freshness and vivacity.

The sudden opening up of a new opportunity can also push harmony to new heights within an organization, as it did at Apple during
the first phase of the company's life. In such an expansive period, no
one has a moment to think about job security, because the company
is hiring as fast as it can and does not even have free personnel to
handle recruitment. Every secretary and sales rep is given maximum
freedom and responsibility because there is more work than anyone
can handle. Every day brings fresh surprises and fresh triumphs that
send thrills through the organization. Cumbersome bureaucratic procedures are streamlined in the rush to meet deadlines. Inefficient systems are upgraded and refined to handle greater activity faster. Negative opinions and nonwork attitudes are drowned in a sea of optimism
and success. The whole staff feels a sense of pride and joy at being part
of a successful, rapidly expanding venture. A harmonious team spirit
pervades the organization. The company responds to the market by
increasing its internal harmony, and the market responds to that harmony by becoming more expansive.

The types of harmony generated by a crisis or an opportunity are
both inherently limited by the fact that they arise in response to the
pressure of external circumstances, which is usually temporary. In a
crisis the harmonious atmosphere is likely to last only so long as the
crisis itself. In an expansive period it is likely to last only so long as
the opportunity is expanding faster than the organization can adapt
to it. Once growth slows down or levels off, divisive tendencies that
have been held in check come to the surface.

For harmony to become a permanent attribute of the corporate
personality, it must be generated from within the organization itself
as an aspiration to realize some inspiring ideal—a higher value or
lofty goal. The internal pressure of that constant quest generates harmony. The higher the ideal, the greater the harmony that results. A
corporate ideal like rapid growth or high quality generates a force for
harmony within departments. A social ideal like the well-being of employees (Delta) or service to society (AT&T) generates a power of harmony at the corporate level that can integrate and unify the entire
organization.

When harmony becomes a permanent attribute of a corporation,
the response of the market becomes permanent, too. The market reveals to the company a scope for endless expansion and enduring success.

CHAPTER 10

Harmony Without

All things are interwoven with one another; a sacred bond unites them; there is scarcely one thing that is isolated from another. Everything is coordinated, everything works together in giving form to the one universe.

—Marcus Aurelius[1]

At the beginning of this century, an English scientist working in India conducted a bold and dramatic experiment that confounded the medical profession. He selected a herd of healthy Indian cattle, designed hygienic accommodations for them, and fed them a properly blended diet along with clean, fresh water. When veterinary officials came to inoculate the animals, he refused to permit it. To the surprise of the veterinarians and the neighboring farmers, his animals did not catch any of the diseases prevalent even among inoculated cattle in the area. And to the utter amazement of everyone, his animals remained free of disease even when they were put in physical contact with diseased animals. His animals were so healthy that the disease that scourged the countryside could not affect them. That is the power of harmony within.

Survival and Growth in Hard Times

There are equally astonishing stories about companies that maintained their position or even continued to grow in an unsupportive or hostile business environment because of the harmony they had established within their organizations and their capacity for rapid adjustment to changes in the world around them. When Alfred Sloan took over as president of an ailing GM in 1920, the company was in chaos and struggling for survival. Within five years he built it up into the world's largest automaker, surpassing Ford, which was entering a period of decline. Sloan transformed GM into America's first decentralized big business organization based on centralized policy making, strategic planning, sophisticated systems of financial and operating controls, and market forecasting. He created a high level of internal harmony by coordinating all activities within each subsidiary and integrating many diverse businesses within a single, unified organizational structure.

Sloan regarded periodic business slumps as inevitable and believed that the true test of an organization was its ability to prosper during these difficult periods. When the Great Depression set in, GM sales tumbled by two-thirds in three years. But by this time the company had built up its systems for coordination to such an extent that it was able to respond quickly to the disastrous slump in the market and adjust its purchasing, production, inventory, and employment levels accordingly. As a result, GM made profits and paid dividends every year during the 1930s, a period that almost proved fatal to Ford Motor Company.

GM's remarkable performance was possible because of its high level of internal coordination coupled with its very close contact with the market, utilizing sophisticated market-forecasting techniques first developed at Du Pont. In other words, the company had developed internal harmony and harmony with its market—harmony within and harmony without.

While Otto Doering was tying the golden knots that bound Sears' mail-order system together, something equally or more important for the company was taking place down in Panama, where Robert Wood was working on the construction of the Panama Canal under General Goethals. Due to the scarcity of good books in Panama, Wood developed the habit of perusing successive annual editions of the U.S. statistical abstracts; and between the monotonous columns of figures, he observed three significant trends: the automobile was making America mobile, farmers were migrating to the cities, and the urban working class was acquiring middle-class tastes, purchasing power, and buying habits.

The net result of Wood's unusual taste in books was that when he joined Sears in 1924, he reformulated the company's mission. "We're going to offer values to the great middle class buying public of American citizens."[2] Then he opened the first of Sears' large suburban retail stores, conveniently accessible to the increasingly mobile middle class.

By 1929 Sears had 268 stores with combined sales of $175 million, which represented 40 percent of the company's total revenues.

During the early years of the depression, retail trade in the United States dropped by nearly 50 percent. Even department stores, which were usually located in downtown urban areas, suffered a 40 percent fall in sales, and it took them a decade to recover to their predepression level. Yet throughout this period, Sears' sales and income continued to grow. By 1931 its retail business had larger revenues than its mail-order division. Sears succeeded because it sensed the changing temper of the times. It attuned itself to meet an unfulfilled need of the society that was increasing, even at a time when the economy as a whole was shrinking. Harmony without has an extraordinary power.

A Gigantic Golden Gap

Another good thing happened to Wood while he was in Panama. He discovered the importance of reliable supply lines and learned how to establish them. General Goethals put Wood in full charge of supplies for building the canal, with one simple admonition: "The day we run out of cement, you're fired."[3]

This fortuitous circumstance placed on Wood the burden of re-cruiting, housing, and feeding nearly 50,000 people while simultane-ously maintaining an uninterrupted supply of cement, which could not be stored for any length of time owing to the tropical climate. His experiences under Goethals formed the inspiration for the unique buy-ing system that Wood introduced at Sears—a system based on harmony with suppliers.

By this time, mass production and mass distribution were both established systems of activity in the United States; yet the link be-tween these two powerful but independent systems was tenuous. Wood discovered a golden gap in the interface between them that contained far more gold than Otto Doering's integrated mail-order systems.

The basis of Wood's buying system was the principle that both the mass manufacturer and the mass distributor could make more money if they worked together harmoniously for their common benefit. By purchasing raw materials in bulk on behalf of all its suppliers, Sears was able to obtain substantial discounts on the huge volume of ma-terials it required, which none of its suppliers could get by purchasing the materials themselves. By working closely with the manufacturers to improve the quality of their products and the efficiency of production techniques, Sears was able to buy better merchandise at a lower price, and the manufacturers were able to earn more on what they produced. By guaranteeing manufacturers orders far in advance, suppliers were able to maintain more stable production schedules and avoid the costly waste from frequent start-ups and shutdowns. By eliminating the need for advertising and large sales divisions, the manufacturers cut their total costs by 15 percent to 20 percent on sales to Sears and could pass on part of that savings to their customer.

The cumulative result of these mutual advantages was that both Sears and the manufacturers prospered beyond anyone's expectations. In one dramatic instance, Wood offered financial assistance and a guaranteed market to an ailing manufacturer of locomotive parts if it would switch over to the production of refrigerators instead. The descendant of that company is Whirlpool Corporation, which ranks among the top 150 industrial firms in the United States, with $2.6 billion in revenues. The benefit that Sears derived was even more dramatic. Competitors simply could not match the merchandise values and prices Sears could offer because of its harmonious system.

Wood guided the destiny of Sears from 1924 to 1954. Even at the time that he assumed command, the company was the nation's largest retailer. During the next three decades, its sales grew 15-fold, from $206 million to $3 billion, and its profits grew 10-fold, from $14 million to $141 million. This phenomenal expansion, which took place despite the intervention of the Great Depression and World War II, was largely the result of one thing, harmony without—harmony with a rapidly changing society and harmony with suppliers.

A New Frontier

Over the decades Sears has displayed a remarkable ability to perceive, before most other companies, the significance of changes in society and to adopt new strategies suited to tap the commercial opportunities that these changes opened up. This capacity to remain in harmony with the needs of society has unquestionably been the company's greatest strength.

When Wood opened Allstate Insurance Company units in retail stores, the financial experts of the day were highly skeptical of the move. Today, under the direction of Edward Telling, Sears is in the process of an even more dramatic shift in strategy to take advantage of what it perceives to be an enormous untapped commerical opportunity created by changes in society. The recent acquisition of Dean Witter Reynolds Inc., one of the largest U.S. securities brokerage firms, and Coldwell Banker, the nation's largest full-service real estate company, and the establishment of integrated financial-service centers in its retail stores are the core of that strategy.

What prompted Sears' most recent new departure? Edward R. Telling, chairman and CEO of Sears, explains: "We are facing up to the *new realities of the American marketplace.* The American economic, political, and social condition has undergone a radical change; a change that calls out for new products . . . new services . . . new ways of doing business."[4] A major Sears strategy to respond to these changes is a new approach to the marketing of financial services.

As in the past, many people have scoffed at or been bewildered by what seems to be a sudden shift in Sears' strategy. Even the companies that Sears acquired did not fully comprehend the underlying rationale for the move and the incredible potentials it has uncovered until some months after the acquisitions had taken place. There were many so-called sophisticated New Yorkers who even laughed at the idea that a commoner from Chicago could possibly understand something about financial markets that Wall Street failed to perceive. But laughter is rapidly giving way to a mixture of awe and fear.

Sears is quick to present its credentials for such a venture. After all, the company started offering installment credit on farm equipment and major appliances without collateral way back in 1911, at a time when most banks refused to make such loans. Wood started Allstate Insurance Company in 1931 to sell car insurance through Sears' retail stores and mail-order catalog with an initial investment of $700,000. Fifty years later Allstate is the second largest property-casualty insurer in the country, with more than $12.7 billion in assets, $8 billion in revenues, and earnings of $555 million in 1983. Sears has also operated a commercial real estate company since the 1950s, and it owns saving banks in California and Delaware. In addition, the company presently lends $12 billion to American consumers through its credit-card system.

But all these qualifications are really secondary. Sears' best credential for the move is its historic capacity to stay in tune with the needs of middle America. It is not any extraordinary acumen that enables it to do so. Sears possesses the objectivity, humility, and common sense to maintain harmony with the world in which it lives, grows, and prospers. Carl Hulick, vice-president of Dean Witter, calls it "a self-effacing intelligence."

Sears simply looked at the numbers and read the writing on the wall. About 85 percent of all American households with incomes of

$30,000 or more, 70 percent of those with incomes of $36,000 or more, and nearly 75 percent of all households doing business with New York Stock Exchange firms are current Sears customers.

The typical customer of the investment houses is in the upper-income, higher-net-worth group. But there are millions of prosperous American households with billions of dollars in savings that find the off-the-street, uptown New York or downtown Beverly Hills investment firm inaccessible and too imposing to approach freely. But when you put that account executive in a Sears' store, the psychology changes, and a powerful chemical reaction occurs.

Since the first Sears financial center was opened, Dean Witter has found that 35 percent to 40 percent of all its new business is coming from the stores, and the average account executive in the stores is opening twice as many new accounts as those in Dean Witter's own offices. About 62 percent of these new accounts are first-time customers of a brokerage firm, and another 18 percent are reactivated accounts—that is, 80 percent are additional customers for the investment industry. More than half of them are women. As a test case, Sears opened one financial center in a middle-income, blue collar neighborhood in Chicago. This store turned out to be the most successful of the initial eight centers. As Hulick said, in that store "we had discovered a pocket of mattress money." And the same results repeated in other cities around the country.

Sears has been able to capitalize not only on its retail store infrastructure and its ongoing relationship with half of all American households but also on the familiarity and confidence customers feel in dealing with the company renowned for its money-back guarantee. One lady walked into one of the financial centers and said she had never invested money before because she did not trust brokers. When the broker explained that he was a Dean Witter stockbroker, she replied: "No, you aren't. You're with Sears!" What Allstate's Chairman Donald Craib said of his company is proving true for Sears' new partners, too: "Our greatest strength is our affiliation with Sears, Roebuck and Company. It was, is, and will be, because we draw from that same core of customers, and it's a huge one and a loyal one."

The move into financial services signifies a further modification in Sears' corporate mission. The company is broadening its scope to serve more of the needs of the American household—merchandising, insurance, real estate, brokerage, and consumer credit. Sears hopes that it can sell Americans their homes, furniture, and automobile spares, as well as insurance, stocks, and bonds, and ultimately become a consumer bank. Hulick recalls when the magnitude of Sears' idea suddenly dawned on him. "I can remember sitting in the meeting when the light bulb went on. There is an absolutely huge potential. My gut feeling is that it could be bigger than anyone can conceive of right now."

The potential Sears has uncovered was not created by the invention of a new technology or the production of a new product. It is the result of an effort that every company can make—an effort to establish greater and wider harmony with the ever changing needs of society.

Infinite Opportunities

Tomas Bata was fond of telling the story of two shoe salesmen who went to explore the market potential in an African country. One cabled back to the home office: "No one here wears shoes. No market." The other cabled: "Everyone here is barefoot. Infinite potential." Bata saw that potential long before much bigger firms in the West and went on to create the largest shoe company in the world.

One need not go to Africa in search of such potentials. They are there all around us in every industry for every company. For some it may be creating a new product or developing a new technology. But there are equally vast opportunities to be tapped simply by changing one's perspective, one's strategy, or one's attitude. Sears has done it very consciously three times in its 100 years of business, Coca-Cola did it almost accidentally in the last century, when its product came to be identified with the social aspirations of the common people.

The phenomenal development of the personal computer market was not simply the result of a new technology for reducing the size and price of computers. It was the product of a revolutionary new way of thinking about the computer and its role in society. Even long after new technologies were available for bringing down the price and simplifying use of the computer, the traditional computer makers were slow to see the potential.

Computers were originally thought to have applications only for big businesses and governments. In the late forties the most reliable market research indicated that the world market could absorb 1,000 computers by the year 2000. By the midseventies 50,000 computers had been installed around the world. In 1984 alone computer sales were about 2 million units. This incredible expansion was due to the capacity of companies like Apple to identify themselves with the needs of social groups that fell far outside the traditional market for computers—the individual, the family, the small business, and the school.

While companies and educational institutions were gearing up to the onerous task of teaching people how to communicate with the computer in a multitude of strange languages, Apple was doing an admirable job of simplifying the interface between people and computers. Apple bridged the intellectual and psychological gap that separated people from the machine. According to *Fortune*, "No company has done more than Apple to dispel the notion that computers are inscrutable beasts."[5] Apple's Macintosh personal computer, writes *Business Week*, "is so easy to handle that many people do not even bother to read the instruction manual. . . ."[6]

Companies that exploit existing markets reap rewards in proportion to their efficiency, the size of the market, and the strength of the competition. But companies that convert unseen market potential into actualities expand at a phenomenal rate, as Apple has.

What Apple has done in a product business, Federal Express has done in a service industry. It identified a need that stalwarts in the field had failed to meet. It created a new $1.4 billion business for itself and a new $5 billion overnight-delivery industry out of the existing parcel-delivery industry that UPS entered in 1907.

Marriott is now making a parallel move with its life-care communities, which are designed to cater to the needs of America's growing population of healthy senior citizens. This service combines the independence of the private residence with the convenience and security of centralized recreational, food, and medical facilities. It is a natural extension of Marriott's existing business and a natural outgrowth of changing social requirements.

Exploding the Myth of Limits

The concept of a fixed, limited market is an illusion. When a new product is introduced that caters to a real need of the society—such as the automobile, telephone, radio, TV, or computer—the market grows until it saturates the society at one level. Introduce one new variable—like lower price, new applications, better quality, smaller size, more pleasant service, greater convenience—then the need for the product increases, and a new market opens. To be in harmony means to discover these latent needs of the marketplace and adapt the product to meet them.

The same thing is true of service businesses as well. There are two parts to the delivery of any service: a physical part, like food or a seat on an airplane, and a social part, which relates to satisfying the customers through courtesy, convenience, and personal attention. There is a balance between these two. The fast-food restaurant delivers a low-cost product. Speed and price are primary. The high-class restaurant serves better-quality food, but it also places greater emphasis on comfort, elegance, and pleasant behavior. There is only so much you can do to the physical quality or the desirability of a hamburger or a seat on an airline. But there is infinite scope for varying and improving the social and psychological qualities surrounding the service. The most successful service companies are those that put themselves in harmony with the nonphysical needs of their customers. Delta does it through warmth and friendliness, Disneyland through cheerfulness, Dow Jones & Company, Inc. through authenticity, and McDonald's through cleanliness and courtesy.

Society not only has physical needs; it has social and psychological needs as well. At a time when the family has been fragmented, personal isolation is constantly increasing, and nervous tension has become endemic, the nonmaterial needs of modern society are as great and pressing as the physical requirements of many developing countries. Companies can address these needs by providing job security for their employees; creating a family feeling in the office; offering friendly, personalized service to customers; acting as genuine agents of goodwill in the society; or providing products and services that entertain, educate, and relax consumers and protect their health.

How well is American business tuning in to its environment? According to a survey by Opinion Research Corporation released in 1984, there is ample scope for improvement. Only 14 percent of those polled expressed a high level of trust and confidence in large American companies. Large companies rated very poorly on ethics and morality, job creation, protecting the environment, and meeting the needs of society. The survey revealed that 69 percent of the public believe that business is a social as well as an economic entity, that it has an obligation to help society, and that it is presently neglecting society's problems.[7]

The answer to this negative image is not more or better public relations activity or greater philanthropic activity, however worthwhile that activity may be in its own right. The greatest service that business can perform for the nation is to meet its seen and unseen, felt and unfelt real needs more and more efficiently, effectively, honestly, pleasantly, and harmoniously. As Drucker has written, business has to learn "how to convert the major social challenges facing developed societies today into novel and profitable business opportunities. . . ."[8] The opportunities for that conversion are as rich and vast as American society itself.

When a company is in harmony with society, the growth potential is unlimited; the scope for expansion is infinite. Take the greatest commercial successes in American history and plug them into the formula. A good number have done nothing more spectacular than to serve.

Social Unity

The lesson of harmony is a very simple one. But too often it is forgotten. Chrysler blatantly ignored it during the 1960s and 1970s by alienating its customer base with drastic changes in styling and by overloading most of its intermediate-size cars with 500-horsepower gas-guzzling engines, even after the fad for the racer image had ended and the oil crunch had begun. The crisis that the company passed through a few years ago was a direct result of this error and, one would think, enough to teach anyone the lesson. Chrysler's president, Harold Sperlich, constantly repeats a new refrain: "You really have to cooperate with your environment . . . . You have to cooperate with the market."[9] Cooperation means harmony.

Chrysler really saw the power of harmony in 1980 when it approached the very brink of bankruptcy. Literally the entire society came to its rescue. The U.S. government granted $1.5 billion in federal loan guarantees, and Canada gave $200 million more. Banks provided the company with $642 million in new loans, deferred interest, or interest give-ups. State and local governments came up with $357 million in support. Suppliers and dealers granted $63 million in concessions. And the United Auto Worker's agreed to a three-year labor contract that would save Chrysler $462 million in wages and benefits.

None of these benefactors was acting solely out of philanthropic compassion for an ailing company. All of them recognized that they constitute a single, unified, productive entity called society and that their interests are inseparably intertwined. The positive attitude of cooperation and support has been generally ignored by experts trying to explain Chrysler's successful recovery. Harmony between many interdependent units was the essential key to it all.

Life Without Limit

Throughout this book we have drawn an analogy between the life of an individual and the life of an organization. However, in one critical respect the person and the company differ. The life of the individual is limited; the life of a company can continue as long as the society in which it lives. It can continue even longer perhaps by transplanting itself to another society, as Bata Shoe Company did when the Communists took over in Czechoslovakia.

At the time of their birth, both the individual and the organization are children of the society in which they are born. They acquire its ideas, values, attitudes, norms, customs, habits, behaviors, and lifestyle. These things form the basis for the development of their personalities. But meanwhile, the society continues to change. It accepts new ideas, modifies its values, adopts new customs, accepts new forms of behavior, and so forth. The individual finds after four or five decades that the beliefs and values so easily accepted in youth are no longer prevalent. Many people discover the truth in the adage that a person can move from being a flaming liberal to a deep conservative to a complete reactionary in one lifetime, frequently without any fundamental change in viewpoint. The individual may remain the same, but society moves on. As the gap widens between the two, the individual is relegated to a back seat, so that another generation can carry on the forward march.

Old age and obsolescence are not inevitable for an organization if it continues to remain in harmony with its parent society. Companies can and do extend their lives, revitalize their energies, and transform themselves to meet new challenges and opportunities, as Sears and AT&T are doing today. This process of renewal is the process of corporate evolution, a constant inner growth and continuous outer adaptation to ongoing changes in society. It opens up the possibility for the organization to continuously expand and develop as the society expands and develops without end or limit.

CHAPTER 11

The Significant Individual

One essential question remains unasked and unanswered. We have spoken about the importance of beliefs and values, mission and objectives, attitudes, hierarchy, discipline, freedom, systems, skills, material things, coordination, integration, and harmony. But what about the most important of all organizational resources—the individual? What is the significance of the individual in the life of a corporation?

Historically, the most significant individual in the life of a company has been the founder or an outstanding CEO who came later. Such people have imparted the values and formulated the mission that set the company's direction. They have molded the corporate character and invested all their energies to make the organization come alive. Leaders like Rosenthal and Wood, Vail and Sloan, Woolman and Woodruff, Bata and Marriott and their descendants have created organizations as extensions of their own personalities and given them an independent existence. These people identified themselves so closely with the life of the organizations that, as it was observed of Tom Watson, it is difficult to say where the personality of one ends and the personality of the other begins.

It was not money or position that made these leaders significant. It was attitude and effort—a willingness to give themselves to the organization and to work hard. Work was their religion. With characteristic humor and understatement, Woodruff once remarked: "It was not so difficult. It was mostly a matter of working all the time."[1] Watson almost made it sound easy: "It isn't a hard thing to build up a business if you are willing to do a reasonable amount of work."[2] Make no mistake about it, Watson's idea of "reasonable" was not 9 A.M. to 5

P.M. Nor was Bill Marriott, Sr.'s. He said, "No one can get very far in this life on a forty-hour week."[3]

It is easy to attribute the accomplishments of these leaders to some rare talents or genius, but nearly all of them have frankly denied anything of the kind. Woodruff was quite notably ordinary. "Bob has no particular talents," as one of his dearest admirers and successors at Coca-Cola said. Woolman was a lovable workaholic, but hardly extraordinary except in that regard. James Buchanan Duke, the founder of the American Tobacco Company, was quite explicit about it:

> I have succeeded in business not because I have more natural ability than those who have not succeeded, but because I have applied myself harder and stuck to it longer. I know plenty of people who have failed to succeed in anything who have more brains than I had, but they lacked application and determination.[4]

Edison's well-known remark sums it up best: "Genius is 1 percent inspiration and 99 percent perspiration."[5]

Despite the understandable tendency of those around them to admire these leaders and even deify them, it was more an extraordinary effort than an exceptional talent, more a right attitude than a brilliant intellect, that led to their success. The attitude, like the effort, was total and unwavering, a decision to act, a determination to achieve, and an enthusiasm for the challenge. As Duke explained shortly before his death:

> I resolved from the time I was a mere boy to do a big business. I loved business better than anything else. I worked from early morning until late at night. I was sorry to have to leave off at night and glad when morning came so I could set at it again.[6]

Admittedly, these individuals did share one characteristic in greater than normal measure, and that was energy. But where did their energy come from? It was itself a product of a decision, a determination, and an enthusiasm. Effort and commitment are the twin keys that release the energy stored up within the human personality. The effort and commitment are the result of a decision. The decision is the expression of an idea. The idea is an idealistic value or a high, distant goal. The idea fixes the direction, the decision sets it in motion, the effort and commitment carry it forward, and the enthusiasm lifts it to success. A high idea, a clear decision, a firm commitment, and an overflowing enthusiasm released the energy of these individuals and transformed it into intensity.

Becoming Significant

The process these leaders passed through in achieving success is familiar to us, for it is exactly the same in the individual as it is in the company. Individual personality and corporate personality follow the same path in their development. It has been the thesis of this book that any company that has the knowledge of the process and is willing to make the effort can achieve enduring success. Therefore, it is only logical to ask: Can any individual with a similar knowledge and making a similar effort achieve lasting significance? He or she can indeed. Enduring success for a company and lasting significance for the individual both have the same source. It lies in the undiscovered potentials of personality, individual and corporate.

In truth, the greatest discovery that significant individuals have made was not the unlimited power of organization, though all of them released at least a tiny portion of it, but rather the unlimited potentials of human personality within themselves. They were not so much great leaders possessing great power as they were individuals in whom great power was released, making them appear great.

Any company that really wants to achieve enduring success can achieve it. Any individual who really wants to become significant can become so. The emphasis is on the word *wants*, because it is "mostly a matter of working all the time," as Woodruff said.

Individual Growth and Corporate Success

How do people become significant? They become significant when they decide to fully develop their capacities and improve their personalities as much as they possibly can. They become significant to the company when they grow. Peter Drucker has written in *The Practice of Management*:

> Man is distinguished from all other resources in that his "development" is not something that is done to him; it is not another or better way of using existing properties. It is growth; and *growth is always from within*. The work therefore must encourage the growth of the individual and must direct it—otherwise it fails to take full advantage of the specific properties of the human resource.[7] [Emphasis added.]

Contrary to what many believe, life in an organization presents excellent opportunities for individual growth, because people grow primarily through work and social interaction, which are the basis of corporate existence. The greatest benefit an individual can derive from work is the growth of his or her personality to make the person better, stronger, more productive, and happier. The greatest benefit a company can derive from its people is to foster their personal growth, so that their energies and talents can be made fully available to enliven and enhance the life of the organization.

General Wood once reminded his staff at Sears: "We must always consider our 150,000 employees as 150,000 individual human beings, with personalities of their own . . . who have faith in their leaders, who believe not only in their ability, but in their fairness and justice, and who in return give of their best, freely and willingly. If all of Sears is animated by this spirit, *nothing can stop us.*"[8] [Emphasis added.]

Who Is Significant?

What makes an individual significant? We are all significant individuals in our own personal lives; but although most of us like to think so, very few are really significant in the life of a company. Sure, many of us do excellent work, receive recognition, move closely with our boss. Some of us have made a very important sale for the company on occasion or helped develop a new product or a new process. When a special talent or skill is required, many are sought out for their capacity—a crack sales rep to handle a big customer, a bright lawyer for a tough negotiation, a brilliant engineer to solve a difficult technical problem, a knowledgeable accountant to bring order out of chaotic numbers, a manager with a way with words to handle an irate employee or customer, a secretary with a flair for creating advertising copy or drafting letters, a supervisor who inspires subordinates to work hard.

These are notable accomplishments for any employee, but they are not what we mean by being a significant individual in the company. A significant individual is one whom the company needs for its work, not one who needs the company for his or her living. Bill Marriott, Jr., is a significant individual who everyone agrees works harder than anyone else in the company. Why, we asked? To set an example, "so everyone else will work hard," he replied. Telling and Brennan are significant individuals at Sears, who have a vision of the future and are guiding the company to realize it. Goizueta is a significant individual who has directed Coca-Cola into new fields. So is Steve Jobs at Apple.

All these leaders happen to be presidents and chairpersons of the companies they work for, but that is not the real criterion by which to judge their significance. Many chairpersons and CEOs, even of large companies, really do not play a very significant role in the lives of their companies—especially when their contribution is viewed from a historical perspective. Anyone can be significant at any level or in any position. Whoever the significant individuals are, they have these essential attributes:

1. They feel the work is more important than they are, and they sacrifice their personal convenience in favor of the work. That is why significant people are never nine-to-fivers for five days a week. They are like C. E. Woolman, of whom it was said, "Delta Air Lines was his life."[9]

2. They always think about the work that is yet to be done and do not dwell on past achievements.

3. They are not really looking for external recognition and rewards, although both always come in abundant measure. Their real motive for work is the challenge of accomplishment and the sheer joy of growing. They love work because it is its own fulfillment. "I had always enjoyed going to work," said Geneen. "In fact, I never thought of it as work. It was a part of my life, a part of the environment in which I lived and breathed. . . . Business could be a great adventure, a lot of fun, something to look forward to every day, and the rewards went much further than one's annual salary and bonuses."[10]

4. They do not just work long hours or spend all their energy. They constantly strive to acquire new skills and to shed present weaknesses, so that they can perform at the *highest possible level*. They are never satisfied with themselves and always want to be better than they presently are. They try to continuously raise the peak level of their performance.

5. They are constantly being sought after by the company to take on new and higher responsibilities and constantly being catapulted to higher levels of the organization or to larger organizations and greater rewards.

Many individuals possess one or two of these attributes. There are a number of people who come to work an hour early and leave three hours after closing and work on weekends, too. But that alone is not enough to be significant. They must also work at their highest possible level all the time by developing new capacities, not just work hard and long at what they know or do best. There are many who like their work and the people they work with, the travel, the conventions, the challenge of making a sale or designing a better product, but that, too, is not enough unless they feel the joy that comes from constantly growing.

There are people who may even meet the first four criteria—they may be hardworking, always striving to improve, thinking only of the work still to be done, and feel refreshed and enthused by what they do—yet still not find new opportunities and greater rewards thrust upon them because they do not understand the process by which people grow. They have the goal, the willingness, the urge, and the right attitude, but not the knowledge of how to convert their hidden talents into developed capacities and to effectively express them in action for the good of the company and their own personal growth. This book is especially intended for companies that really want to achieve enduring success but do not know the process. This chapter is especially meant for individuals who really want to become significant but do not know how.

The Way

No individual by virtue of birth, family, wealth, or social position has a monopoly on achievement, any more than any company by virtue of size, resources, or influence has a monopoly on success. Any company at any level can prosper and grow to one, ten, a hundred, or a thousand times its present size. Sears started with nothing and accomplished it over half a century. Apple started with nothing and did it in less than a decade. Whatever the size, whatever the field, there are no limits to growth.

We have all known many people—childhood friends, college roommates, office colleagues, or neighbors—who seemed to be just like us; yet inexplicably, by some stroke of good fortune or particular talent, they shot up in life to a far higher level. To the astonishment of long-time Sears employees, Edward Brennan was promoted to head the merchandise group at the young age of 46 and became president at 50. Brennan started as a salesman in a Wisconsin Sears store in 1956. Ron Allen, an engineer, joined Delta in 1963 doing part-time drafting work and came up through the personnel division to become president in 1984. Don Craib joined Allstate as a claims adjuster in 1950, then became a field manager, and gradually worked his way up till he reached the chairman's post in 1980. Roberto Goizueta, Coca-Cola's Cuban-born chairman, joined the company as a chemist 30 years ago and moved up through the ranks of middle management. At General

Mills we met a young marketing director who joined the company just eight years ago as an intern while still in graduate school. She has already been promoted four times and seems headed for a vice-president's job in the near future.

If your own career has not been quite so meteoric, still there may have been a period when you made rapid progress. If you recall now what happened at the time, the urge that drove you forward, the effort you made, the self-discipline you exercised over yourself, the steps and stages you passed through in developing a talent or acquiring a skill, then you get a glimpse of the process by which individuals become significant.

There is a process by which people rise, though many may not be consciously aware of how they have done it. It is not a process meant only for one in a million. It is available to all who really want to achieve and are willing to make the effort. According to psychologists, people utilize only 10 percent of their mental capacities in living a normal life. They also use only a tiny fraction of the energy and abilities their personality is capable of expressing. When individuals release this potential energy and develop these latent talents, they grow. When they channel all that energy into work and express all those talents in their jobs, they become significant.

According to Richard Wytmar, president of an executive recruiting firm, any manager can become an "indispensable executive,"[11] provided that the manager is willing to make the effort to develop his or her capacities and that he or she takes a positive attitude toward the work. There is a way.

The Prerequisites

There are certain conditions and prerequisites required to become eligible for any great opportunity in life. The opportunity to become significant is no exception. First of all, you have to know where you are and where you want to go. You have to ask yourself, as Wytmar suggests, What are my strengths? What are my weaknesses? How do my skills compare with those of others who have risen to higher levels in the organization? Do I possess all the skills that my boss possesses or that his or her boss possesses? "If you want to move ahead, you've got to look around your organization and ask yourself what kind of skills you need in order to make the move to other positions," says Wytmar. "Then you must acquire those skills and demonstrate the ability to handle broader responsibilities."[12]

What are the attributes required to become significant in any job? There are many, and they are well known: punctuality, orderliness, systematic functioning, a capacity to make decisions, a willingness to delegate authority and responsibility, an ability to communicate clearly and pleasantly and to motivate people, self-discipline and self-restraint, cooperation with others, loyalty, integrity, and so forth.

1. *Recognizing strengths.* All managers possess certain of these attributes in some measure, and by virtue of these qualities, they have reached their present positions. Exercising one's existing capacities is living, but it is no way to grow. Expressing a known ability is acting out of habit. It is easy and gratifying, but not challenging and energizing. It is energy that makes for growth and advancement, and energy comes from the effort to release latent capacities and to acquire new skills, not to repeat what one already does well. People who always seek out opportunities to express their present skills may be very successful at the present level, but they are likely to remain there. Their bosses may even openly say, "You are the only one who does this work well. I cannot afford to let you go to any other job." Such people have the satisfaction of knowing they are appreciated and wanted, not the challenge of growth and the opportunity for advancement. In other words, progress comes from developing new capacities rather than exercising old ones.

2. *Identifying weaknesses.* Developing new skills and capacities is not enough for continuous progress. One must also continuously seek to overcome one's present weaknesses. Knowledge of your strengths must be balanced by a knowledge of your weaknesses as well. As most people like to exercise their existing talents, they also like to avoid doing anything they are not good at. Often they do so under the excuse, "That work does not suit me."

Weaknesses are of many types. Each one corresponds to an absence of a positive attribute listed above. Some people are perennially late; others, notoriously sloppy. Some have disorderly desk drawers; others, disorderly minds. Some are lax with their subordinates; others are lax with themselves. Some are poor communicators; others never stop talking. Some are too harsh in dealing with people; others are too soft. Some do whatever is asked of them even when they know it is wrong; others do not like to follow an instruction even when they know it is right. Some insist on doing by themselves work they should delegate; others delegate responsibilities that they should look after themselves. Some managers ignore the genuine personal problems of their subordinates; others get too personally involved to be effective managers.

There are many other weaknesses that directly undermine efficient functioning and prevent a person from advancing. Any and all of them can be removed by a determined effort. When even a single new skill is acquired and one weakness is removed, individual energy and performance increase enormously and the person moves up in the organization, usually several levels at a time and far beyond all expectations.

3. *Psychological effort.* Becoming significant is not just a question of working hard or being busy all the time. Almost everyone is busy all the time doing something or other. The effort required here is to work always at the highest level possible rather than simply putting in long hours doing routine work. It is more a psychological effort than a physical one. It requires a constant exertion of the will, not just the muscles. It involves exercising control over one's own temperamental traits, restraining unwanted behaviors, and making the effort to act in the most appropriate manner. It demands discipline of old habits and active initiative to acquire fresh ones. It involves becoming better informed, thinking things through before you act, and making decisions expeditiously. When people work hard physically, their present functioning improves. When they make a psychological effort, they rise to a higher level of functioning.

The Elements of Enduring Success

The task of managing a multinational corporation involves managing the components of which the company consists—ideas, organization, systems, skills, technology, finance, products, and markets. The task of managing a division of that corporation involves managing exactly the same components; only the quantities and degree of responsibility may differ. The same is true of managing a department of the division. At all levels, from the very top to the very bottom of an organization, the components of management are the same.

Each of these components consists of several subunits. Ideas include beliefs, values, missions, objectives, standards, policies, plans, and attitudes. Organization consists of departments and the people within them, hierarchy and authority, rules and regulations, and so forth. When all of these subunits are analyzed further, they can finally be reduced to certain basic, essential elements of management—time, people, information, money, machines, materials, and energy.

Regardless of the level of the organization, these are the essential elements, and effective management of them requires certain capacities. These capacities are defined by the corporate values referred to in Chapter 3. For convenience they are repeated here:

Physical	*Organizational*	*Psychological*
Cleanliness	Discipline	Respect for the individual
Orderliness	Freedom	Pleasing the customer
Punctuality, regularity	Motivation	Harmony (family feeling)
Efficient use of money and materials	Standardization	Decisiveness
Maintenance of equipment	Systemization	Integrity
Quality of product, service, or work	Coordination	Loyalty, trust
Maximum utilization of time	Integration	Commitment
Optimum utilization of space	Communication	Personal growth
Safety	Cooperation (teamwork)	Service to society

The values of a department and the values of a corporation are the same. In the last analysis, what do individual managers do? They strive to be clean and orderly, to be punctual and use the time available in the most efficient manner, to conserve materials, to utilize space properly, to maintain equipment, to improve quality in every aspect of work, to function systematically, to coordinate with colleagues, to integrate with those at higher and lower levels of the organization, to minimize expenditures, to discourage negative behavior and encourage positive behavior among subordinates, to serve customers, and so forth.

The same values that govern the company, the division, and the department govern the conduct of all managers in carrying out their jobs. Corporate values, departmental values, and individual values are the same. For the manager of a department, that department is the company, and the manager is the CEO of that department. The manager's task is to manage corporate values within the department. The manager's position is exactly analogous to that of the CEO outlined in Chapter 3. The manager has to accept those values, decide to implement them, create a suitable structure for implementation, define performance standards for each value, design or operate systems to achieve the standard, recruit the appropriate people and impart the necessary skills for implementing the values, coordinate and integrate activities, communicate with subordinates, and relate realization of the values to the personal growth and fulfillment of each person in the department. All that has been said in this book about the company applies to the individual as well. Value implementation begins with the CEO and ends with every individual in the company. Every person who identifies with the values of the corporation and strives to implement them can become a significant individual in the life of the company.

There is no capacity that is required for management beyond what is embodied in these corporate values. There is no work that cannot be accomplished through them. The task of all managers is to manage the organizational resources put at their disposal—including their own time, ideas, systems, people, decisions, skills, and so on—as well as they possibly can. Those that strive to personalize the corporate values as values in their own life and for their own personal growth find themselves identified with the psychic center of the corporation, one with it in value. Their actions are closely attuned to the corporate objectives. Their personal attitudes are in harmony with the attitudes of the corporation. Their personal growth is linked to the growth of the company. As it rises, they rise. As it becomes successful, they become significant. The more they give of themselves for the benefit of the company, the more valuable and significant they become in it. The more sincerely they serve it, the more rapidly they rise within it. They do what was done by IBM's CEO, John Opel, who "achieved the top post by molding himself to be just what the company wanted, because that is exactly what he wanted too."[13] And if by circumstance these individuals find themselves within a company that is not willing to grow or appreciate their service, they find greater opportunities calling them elsewhere. They continue to rise, even if the company does not.

Unforgettable Moments

Take an ordinary day at work. The boss calls you in to find out how things went wrong or why the target has not been reached. Your subordinates question your instructions, and your colleagues criticize your decisions. Your assistant tells you that your most original idea is merely "all right." An important customer complains about slow delivery or poor service.

What if all these ordinary moments could be converted into great ones? Suppose your assistant, who never appreciates any of your ideas, comes forward to say they are "wonderful." Suppose your boss calls you in to praise you for a job well done. Suppose your colleagues commend all your decisions, and your subordinates execute them with enthusiasm. Then ordinary moments become unforgettable; work becomes fresh and fulfilling. Life becomes rich and rewarding. You become a center of intensity. For that, there is a process—the process of translating values into actions in one's own life.

Putting Values to Work

Values are the criteria by which we measure the quality of our actions. In the individual as in the company, there are a series of stages through which we pass in the process of fully establishing any value in our lives. The process of value implementation in a company is analogous to the process of personal growth in an individual. In both cases the personality develops, becomes more organized, better utilizes its capacities, and expresses them more effectively in action.

Consider, for example, a simple corporate value like punctuality. "Punctuality," says the proverb, "is the soul of business." Without it, service cannot be prompt, efficiency cannot be high, prices cannot be low, and profitability cannot be maximized. As obvious as this may sound, punctuality—in starting work, attending meetings, completing schedules, answering letters, returning phone calls, producing products, attending sales calls, shipping goods, invoicing customers, maintaining accounts, and paying bills—is not so very common as one might think. A recent issue of General Mills' *Family* magazine dramatized this point with an article entitled "What Time Does a 10 O'clock Meeting Start?" It requires a comprehensive and perpetual effort of the entire organization to maintain this one simple corporate value.

Punctuality is a value as important for a manager as it is for a company and as difficult to establish and maintain. For instance, take Bill, a fictional but typical manager representative of many we know. Bill commutes by train 40 miles into New York every morning and consistently arrives 10 to 15 minutes late. One day he finally gets tired of displeasing his boss and being laughed at behind his back. He decides to make it a point to arrive on time. To do so, he has to catch the next earlier train, which leaves his hometown 30 minutes before his present train. For that, he has to wake up and shower a half-hour earlier, too, which just happens to coincide with the time his wife takes her bath. She agrees to readjust. Under the new schedule, Bill's wife is bathing while he is dressing, and there is no one to cook his breakfast, so he has to get up even earlier to scramble the eggs. By the second or third day, he is feeling quite fatigued from losing 45 minutes of sleep every night, and he sleeps right through the alarm. Bill then realizes that he must adjust his bedtime and retire earlier in order to get enough sleep, which requires a number of adjustments with his wife and children regarding dinnertime, keeping the TV volume down, and other family matters. After a week he really wonders whether it is worth such an effort and inevitably decides that it is not.

What Bill failed to observe was that his effort made him more alert and brisk during the day, a better listener in meetings, a little faster with the paperwork. He had activated his will to achieve a goal and been energized by the endeavor. Had he persisted and extended the discipline of punctuality to other areas of his work like attending meetings and replying to letters, he would have found his overall efficiency raised by 5 percent to 10 percent. All his colleagues and subordinates would have been commenting that he was a "changed person," without being able to pinpoint what was actually different.

Twelve Steps to Significance

Fortunately, our manager decides to try again with greater determination in order to establish punctuality in his life. His effort takes him through the following stages.

1. Until his boss started to complain and his colleagues began to joke with him about always being late, Bill was not even aware of his own deficiency. Previously he had thought that he was about as punctual as anyone else, but he now begins to notice that most other people are actually far more punctual than he is. Thanks to pressure from his boss and his peers, he gradually becomes conscious of the fact that lack of punctuality is one of his *weaknesses*. He has acquired a new *knowledge*.

2. After observing himself and others for some more time, he recognizes that punctuality is a far more important value than he had thought. He realizes that he must acquire it if he is to move up in the company. He feels a strong urge to overcome his deficiency, and he resolves to do so. He has made the *decision* to acquire a new value.

3. He speaks of this decision to his family and a few friends and is surprised when almost all of them laugh at his resolution. They are all sure he will soon forget it and remain the same old person. Their ridicule strengthens his resolve. He makes a promise to himself that he will become punctual. He has converted his decision into a firm *commitment of his will*, and he begins to practice his resolution seriously.

4. The more he thinks about his past behavior, the more he realizes how many problems and how much tension are generated by this one bad habit. The very thought of overcoming it makes him feel happier. Each time he succeeds in being on time, he feels a sense of accomplishment and greater confidence. He is exhilarated by the challenge of becoming a punctual person, and his *enthusiasm* is released for the effort.

5. One day, after complimenting himself for arriving at work ten minutes early, he sees a note on his calendar reminding him to file his quarterly department report the following day. He has not even begun to draft it. It suddenly dawns on him that punctuality is a value that applies to every aspect of his work, not just arriving at the office and attending meetings on time. He decides to draw up a list of each recurring task he has—like replying to letters, filing travel expense reports, and returning phone calls—and he establishes a *standard* for completing each one of them within a stipulated time.

6. During the first week of his effort, our manager stays at the office every night until 8:00 or 9:00 working on the day's correspondence and other tasks that he could not complete during normal working hours. He realizes this cannot go on forever. He begins to examine his working day to find out how all his time is being spent and discovers that much of it is taken up by small talk with colleagues in the corridors, unscheduled intrusions by subordinates, and meetings that spill over the allotted time. He decides to eliminate all unnecessary distractions. Setting aside a fixed hour every day to answer correspondence, he issues orders that he not be disturbed during that period, except for urgent matters. When colleagues fail to end meetings at the appointed time, he promptly excuses himself—even in the middle of an interesting story about the CEO's troubles with his wife. When subordinates come in to complain endlessly about others, he disciplines himself to end the discussion quickly. He has learned to set *rules and regulations* governing his own conduct in order to be punctual.

7. By this time our manager has already become the talk of the whole division. He looks five years younger, walks briskly, needs less sleep, and thinks more clearly. But still he runs into problems maintaining punctuality on many occasions, such as when customers call

on the phone, a colleague comes in to chat, or he has to write a report—reports were never his strong point. But gradually he discovers ways to handle phone calls politely in less time. He learns how to lead a casual conversation with colleagues onto a serious topic that is useful or bring the discussion to a quick end. He asks a friend to help him improve in report writing. He acquires new *skills* needed to implement his value.

8. Though vastly improved, he still finds he is late to 25 percent of meetings and behind schedule on work 30 percent of the time. He realizes that he needs to organize his entire day more carefully and develop means to complete his work more quickly. He works out *systems* for processing mail, issuing instructions, delegating tasks, and receiving reports. His productivity improves dramatically.

9. His own routine work is now under fairly good control. But when it comes to work with his boss, subordinates, and colleagues, things do not fit into his systems. His assistants keep interrupting him to deal with their problems. His colleagues keep calling him at unscheduled times to discuss interdepartmental affairs. He asks his boss to allot him a specific appointment several times a week to discuss the affairs of his department. He decides to allot 15 minutes at a fixed hour every day for each of his assistants to meet him to discuss their work. He arranges a regular 30-minute meeting with colleagues once a week to discuss subjects of mutual concern. He has *coordinated* his systems with the activities of colleagues and *integrated* them with the activities of people working over and under him.

10. By now he is able to achieve his standard for punctuality 80 percent to 90 percent of the time. He finds that he no longer has to rely so much on rules and systems to be prompt. He always makes a conscious effort to be punctual in everything he does. The value has become *institutionalized* as part of his behavior, something he always expects and demands of himself.

11. After some time, he finds that he no longer has to strain himself and struggle to be on time. He notices that punctuality has become a customary way of behaving, something he accepts as an essential part of doing his job properly. Even when his boss is away on a trip, he continues to maintain punctual behavior and succeeds 90 percent of the time. By now he has become known as a serious worker, an upcoming star, a man who is going places in the organization. His whole department functions briskly. Work flows smoothly. Productivity reaches a new high.

12. One day he suddenly realizes that he never thinks of being punctual any more. It has become natural to his way of functioning. But he also has become less rigid and obsessive in his concern for being

on time. He has noticed that often the most wonderful opportunities come as an interruption precisely at the moment when he is striving to keep to a schedule. He realizes that punctuality is only one among many corporate values and that sometimes it has to be sacrificed to others that are more important. When his assistant comes in with a very serious personal problem, he puts away his watch and forgets his schedule. When a customer gives him a very good idea for a new product, he cancels three meetings in order to follow it up at once. Our manager has made the value of punctuality one of his own *personal values* and integrated it with the other important values of his personality.

Our manager, who less than half a year before was being laughed at by his peers and scolded by his boss, is now a different person. His efficiency has vastly increased. He feels younger, more energetic and alive. His work is no longer a pressure or a strain. It has become a constant source of enjoyment. Like Duke and Geneen, he goes to sleep every night eager for morning and for another day to begin. By the way, do not look for him in his old office anymore. He was called long ago to a higher job, where he is now struggling to acquire another one of the company's most important corporate values.

These are the stages the manager passed through in acquiring the new value:

1. He became conscious of his weakness and acquired knowledge of the importance of the value.
2. He made a decision to adopt the value.
3. He made a commitment of his will to express the value in his life.
4. His enthusiasm was released for the effort of acquiring the value.
5. He established standards by which to evaluate his own performance with respect to the value.
6. He devised rules and regulations for his own conduct to help him reach the standard.
7. He developed systems to organize his activities in order to achieve the value.
8. He acquired the skills needed to implement the value.
9. He coordinated and integrated his systematic activities with those around, above, and below him.
10. He maintained the value by a constant, conscious effort in everything he did, no longer needing a particular system for support. He acquired an institutionalized behavior of the company.

11. He no longer had to struggle or strain to implement the value. It became a customary habit in all his work.
12. He identified with the value as a personal one in his own life and naturally sought to express it in everything he did. It had become an integral part of his personality.

The Odyssey Continues

This apparently herculean achievement of becoming punctual is actually only the starting point of our manager's quest for significance. He has discovered the process and acquired some experience. He begins to understand himself, his companions, and the company better. The way opens before him.

By this time our manager is being talked about around the company as a truly exemplary person for his punctuality. He feels gratified and better for the effort. But in the process he has become aware of so many other areas in his work personality that need improvement. After all, punctuality is only a physical value, while he is working in a social environment where social skills and values are important. He also sees that to really perfect punctuality, he has to develop other capacities as well.

One important area he has identified is communication. He has discovered, in the course of trying to manage time better, that he manages communication very poorly. For one thing, it always seems to take twice or three times as long for him to give instructions to subordinates or explain a point to colleagues as it takes others he has observed. Gradually he becomes aware that he is a perpetual repeater. He never feels he has fully communicated his point until he has repeated it three, four, or five times and notices his subordinates on the edges of their chairs or his colleagues rising to leave the room. He not only repeats a lot but often raises his voice very loud in order to emphasize a point. He begins to realize that the less sure he is of what he is saying, the louder he tends to speak; and the less clear he is about an idea, the more he tends to repeat it, as if to clarify it in his own mind by repetition to others. He also has observed that the president of his company is very soft-spoken, a man of few words, but those words carry a clarity, determination, and power for implementation. The manager vows to acquire this value, too.

Anyone who meets our manager a few months later is amazed at the change. By a serious effort he has almost stopped repeating himself.

He has read a few books on communication, attended a brief course on discussion skills, and practiced diligently. He has instructed his colleagues and subordinates to remind him whenever he starts to repeat and whenever he raises his voice above the normal level. He finds that people listen to him more closely than before and follow his instructions better. He has been able to reduce the time of an average meeting by 30 percent to 40 percent, making it much easier for him to stick to his time schedule. He works more efficiently and thinks with greater clarity. His boss has even commended the brevity and precision of his explanations.

The manager has made significant gains in this area by a strenuous, constant effort. He has become conscious of more and more areas where he should improve in order to communicate effectively. He discovers that his communication skills are better when his desk is orderly and his thoughts are well organized. He notices at times that when he is too casual, lax, and informal with his subordinates, they do not listen carefully. When he maintains a certain distance, communication is more effective. At other times he sees that when he is in an irritable or angry mood, it disturbs the communication process. People respond more to his mood than to his words, so he struggles to control himself and be more pleasant. A proper blend of friendliness and seriousness seems to work best. He has found that a simple act of communication depends on many other values, like orderliness, authority, self-control, pleasant behavior, and so forth.

Our manager also discovers to his surprise that often he does not listen to what other people are saying, and the discussion gets prolonged and confused by his lack of attention and receptivity. He finds that many mistakes are avoided, time is saved, and problems are caught before they become serious when he disciplines himself to be a good listener. For all the improvement, he still admires the great ability of his CEO to accomplish work effectively with far fewer words, in less time, and with greater ease than he himself is capable of.

Sometime later when you seek out the manager, you learn he has again been promoted. He receives you very pleasantly in his new office, asks about your affairs, replies briefly and clearly to your questions in a relatively low voice, appears cheerful and relaxed during the discussion yet serious and businesslike even so. He not only listens closely to what you say but has acquired the capacity to look at things from your point of view rather than his own. He anticipates your concerns and evokes a strong sense of trust and confidence in his relationship with you. He has a new poise about him, a confidence and an energy that mark him as an unusual individual. You learn from one of his subordinates that he is looked up to by his staff and has vastly improved the performance of the department since he took over.

Although we have abridged the narration of how the manager so dramatically raised the quality of communication in his work, he had to pass through all the 12 stages he completed earlier to become punctual. The only difference in this case was that he had more confidence in his ability to change and accepted the challenge with greater enthusiasm. He also saw much more dramatic results in his work because he was now striving to acquire a social value rather than a physical one.

Further Adventures

In the course of this effort, our manager has stumbled upon an earthshaking discovery about himself. He realizes that he does not know how to make decisions. His capacity for decision making is even less developed than his capacity for punctuality was when he began his effort at self-improvement. By now he also realizes that upgrading performance on a psychological value like decision making is far more difficult than improving performance on a physical or social one. But he also knows that the results of succeeding will be far more dramatic, both for his career and for his personal growth.

With the experience gained so far, he proceeds to observe himself very closely in this realm and uncovers an area where he is completely disorganized and chaotic—his thoughts. He notices that each time a situation is presented to him for a decision, his first tendency is always the same—to postpone. Over the years he has acquired a whole array of very rational-sounding reasons for not making decisions. One of his favorites is, "I don't have enough information." He is surprised one day to come across a remark by Lee Iacocca that "most managers have too much information."[14] Suddenly he realizes that lack of information is usually just an excuse for not making a decision. He also finds that he has a tendency to delegate to his subordinates decisions that he should really make himself, not out of a desire to help them develop but out of an inability to decide for himself. He hears one day that his boss had permitted a programmer in the computer department to select a $500,000 computer for the division, which turned out to be a very poor choice. When the mistake was finally recognized a year later, it cost the company several million dollars in terms of lost productivity and consulting fees to rectify it. The manager resolves not to make the same mistake himself.

The manager's desire to be more punctual has prompted him to become a better communicator and a better decision maker. In the process he has learned to save an enormous amount of time. Each value depends on and supports the others.

Our manager passes through several of the stages described earlier and by a very intensive effort achieves a moderate level of success. He has discovered that decision making is a skill that can be acquired by training. He also discovers that there is a system for it, a mental system, which can be developed by writing down the issues and the facts required to decide and taking action to gather the necessary facts. This clarity of thoughts enables him to abridge many long meetings with subordinates to a few minutes.

Our manager has become far more decisive, yet in the process has uncovered another problem. Decision making not only requires information and clarity of thought; it demands a strong will, too. He finds that often he hesitates to make a decision that affects a subordinate because he lacks the strength to carry it out. He learns that confusion and indecisiveness often mask weakness.

Fortunately, his efforts to date have already made him a far stronger, more confident, and more energetic person. He has learned that each time he exercises his will to make a greater effort, more energy is released, and he grows a little stronger. So, applying the same principle, he makes a tremendous effort to decide issues according to what he knows is right, even when it presents difficulties for him in execution. He sees that often he has told a small lie or permitted someone to suffer unfairly or has done something he knew was not really honest because he lacked the strength to be completely true to his convictions. Though the effort is enormously difficult, he feels a wonderful sense of relief, fulfillment, and joy, because he is doing the right thing and he is becoming a better person.

When we last saw our manager, by prior appointment in his executive office, the experience was quite overwhelming. He was very open, friendly, relaxed, and personable. Though he assumed no airs or formality, he exuded confidence and strength. When he looked at you, his eyes were direct and penetrating, with a sparkle of life in them. He laughed easily and spoke softly, but warmly. Though he said only a few words, his every gesture and expression conveyed his meaning and intentions. When confronted by a subordinate with an important decision, he paused for a moment to review the facts, gave an instruction, and returned to the conversation as if nothing had intervened. He was alert, cheerful, fully alive. His being radiated a calm joy and quiet intensity. We knew we were in the presence of a very significant individual.

The Driving Force

The process we have described here with respect to three important corporate values can be repeated for them all. Although it may take a long time for some people to express a single new value in their behavior, those who apply themselves very seriously can accomplish it in a month. Managers who attempt it may observe that in the process they are acquiring many other values in greater measure, too. If they make a similar effort to express other corporate values as well, they will find that in the process those capacities they already possess will become more perfect.

The growth of a company like Apple from $1 million in sales in 1977 to $1.5 billion in 1984 required an enormous effort by countless individuals. The effort required is proportionate to the result desired. If a person wants to rise ten levels higher within a company, the effort he or she must make is tenfold greater than before. Normally, people and companies make such efforts only in times of crisis to preserve their jobs or avert bankruptcy. This is what Lee Iacocca and Chrysler Corporation did in the early 1980s. Had Chrysler made the same effort earlier, the crisis would never have arisen in the first place.

According to Rick Wytmar, an executive search consultant, there has been a 30 percent reduction of middle management positions in the United States over the past ten years. Therefore, he urges managers to make the effort to improve their productivity and become indispensable in the face of increasing competition for their jobs. An effort based on insecurity and fear can certainly generate results. But the moment the sense of insecurity is removed, the effort will cease, because it is only a reaction to pressure from outside. A negative motive like fear cannot sustain a long-term effort for personal growth.

The effort to become a significant individual can also be motivated by a drive for personal achievement, by ambition. If managers are truly convinced of the results that can be obtained, they may make the enormous effort required. The material results will be substantial, but the effort itself will be tedious and exhausting.

The most favorable motive for making this effort is a desire to become a better person. When the driving force in the individual is an urge for personal growth and self-improvement, the experience becomes self-rewarding and self-motivating, independent of what other people say or do about it. It has been said, "If you want to raise a child, be prepared to be exhausted for five years." The process will be like that, exhausting but fully enjoyable and fulfilling in itself.

The Choice

Every person has a capacity to improve, sometimes vastly. The one essential thing is to really want it. It is up to each individual to choose. Many managers live a casual, carefree, relaxed existence that others may joke about behind their backs—one in which they continuously accommodate to the wishes of their subordinates, friends, and family, always adjusting to others, never deciding or willing for themselves, playful in their behavior, but often unhappy and insecure within. The alternative is a life of challenge and effort and continuous accomplishment, a briskness of energy, alertness of mind, clarity of thought—to be one who is respected by subordinates as an example to be followed, one who is supported by family members with ready cooperation, one whose natural disposition is happiness and whose normal reward in life is success.

Those who do make the effort find that their professional life and private life are no longer separated by an artificial barrier of time or conflicting commitments. They reinforce and support each other and become integrated. The energy, freshness, and strength these individuals acquire in work spills over and removes much of the tension, flatness, and conflict in their personal lives as well. They become better people at home as well as at the office, better parents and spouses as well as better managers. It is not their work alone that is improved and uplifted, but their whole lives that are raised to a higher level of intensity and satisfaction. They become more significant individuals in the companies they work for and in their homes, too.

Becoming a significant individual means identifying yourself fully with whatever work you do and giving yourself totally to it. The process of accomplishing the work and the process of improving yourself are the same. As Chris Steiner, of General Mills, said: "I think the biggest obstacle we can run into a lot of times is ourselves. It really demands a lot of energy. To do your job well, you really have to put a lot of yourself into it." It involves a commitment, an act of self-giving. As Sue Espinosa said: "You really get involved at Apple. You don't mean to, but you really do." And the result? John Machuzick, of General Mills, summed it up best: "I love it!"

Earlier in this chapter we stated that in most companies the significant individual is the CEO. We can add here that anyone who makes the effort to become significant can become a CEO. If the company is stagnant, he or she rises to the top levels. If the company is growing, the individual grows with it until he or she acquires the level of authority and responsibility that the CEO once possessed at an earlier stage of the company's development.

The Role of the Individual in Corporate Success

When managers make this effort, it is not their personal progress alone that is the result. The entire work for which they are responsible is energized and becomes more productive. They have attuned themselves to the central values of the corporation; therefore, the decisions they make and the actions they initiate are more likely to be in harmony with the overall direction of the company. They have discovered and developed their own inner capacities; therefore, they will be better able to identify and develop the hidden talents of their subordinates. "A superior who works on his own development sets an almost irresistible example," as Drucker said.[15] They release inner springs of energy from their own personalities and express it in their work; therefore, they will be better able to release the energy of their subordinates, to excite and enthuse them, to help them grow, and to channel their energy into work.

The relationship between individual growth and enduring corporate success has been noted before. Tom Watson, Jr., wrote in *A Business and Its Beliefs:*

> I believe the real difference between success and failure in
> a corporation can very often be traced to the question of how
> well the organization brings out the great energies and talents of its people.[16]

The key to enduring corporate success is not to imitate Japan but to release the unlimited potentials of an organization's greatest resource—its people. The effort of individuals within a company to grow is the most powerful and lasting impetus for the growth of the company itself. As Drucker put it:

> Self-development of the effective executive is central to the
> development of the organization. . . . As executives work towards becoming effective, they raise the performance level
> of the whole organization. They raise the sights of people—
> their own as well as others'.[17]

A company that recognizes the unlimited reservoir of energy and talents it posesses in its people and takes the personal growth of every individual within the company as a central value of the corporation will be constantly enlivened, invigorated, and carried upward by the perpetual flow of fresh energies emanating from its people.

CHAPTER 12

Energizing the Corporation

People have the capacity to stand by nonchalantly witnessing a miracle, then walk away as if nothing unusual had ever happened, taking the incredible for granted. That has been the typical response of managers to Chrysler's dramatic recovery. Everyone knows about it, appreciates it, and admires it, but how many really understand how it happened? Much attention has been given to Lee Iacocca's sudden rise to fame, the government loan guarantees and their early repayment, the success of the K-car and the minivan. But these are only the external trappings and results of a process that should be of intimate concern to all managers—the process by which corporations are energized and launched on the road to enduring corporate success. The facts surrounding Chrysler's remarkable achievement are known, but the process itself remains shrouded in a veil of obscurity and confusion.

Of course, Chrysler's miracle is not the first or only one to occur in the American automotive industry. Sloan performed an equal or greater miracle at GM in 1920, when it was on the verge of succumbing to a crisis precipitated by the postwar recession. Sloan created a new, decentralized organizational structure at GM and performed magic in the marketplace. During the eight years from 1921 to 1928, the company's unit sales volume grew more than eightfold, and its market share increased from under 15 percent to over 45 percent. From then on GM has never looked back.

Ford Motor Company performed an equally dramatic miracle after the Second World War, when Henry Ford II took over control of the ailing company, which had lost two-thirds of its market share over the previous 20 years and found its very survival in question. Within 10

years Ford recovered its No. 2 position in the industry and was transformed into a major growth company.

   These three miracles are all expressions of a single process, a process that governs the growth and development of every company, regardless of its size—the process by which corporations are energized
and evolve. How is it that these companies, which were on the verge
of extinction, were able to recover so rapidly and grow so dramatically
after coming so close to collapse? Where did the energy come from to
fuel their recovery? What was the mechanism they employed to convert
a life-threatening problem into an opportunity for growth? In another
year or two, Chrysler's accomplishment will become a part of history.
While it is still fresh in our minds, it is worthwhile learning all the
lessons it has to teach us.

Déjà Vu

A sudden fall in market demand had a devastating effect on the company, which was already plagued by poor-quality products and poor
management. Manufacturing cars without dealer orders and in spite
of the plummeting sales, the company accumulated enormous inventories of poor-quality cars on its lots. The company tried unsuccessfully
to force the dealers to buy the unwanted stocks. Concerned bankers
pressed for reform.

   A new president was appointed. He cut the price on the unsold
cars to clear the inventory, drafted outside talents to upgrade quality
and improve design, persuaded creditors to wait and bankers to lend
the company more money. Within five years all the outstanding debts
were repaid, nine years before their due date. One journal called this
remarkable recovery "the biggest reclamation project the automobile
industry has witnessed and practically the christening of a new business."[1] The new president was Walter Chrysler. The year was 1925.

   Everyone knows the story of Chrysler under Lee Iacocca, when
the company struggled for its survival between 1979 and 1984. But
few people are aware of how this story mirrors the saga of Chrysler
under its founder, Walter P. Chrysler, when the company struggled to
be born between 1920 and 1925. These were the "auspicious" circumstances under which the corporation assumed its present name but
inherited a past that it is still unable to shake off, even after 60 years.

   The crisis in 1920 and the crisis in 1980 are remarkably similar.
In some essential way, Chrysler remains the same after 60 years of

alternating growth and decay. The same corporate character and personality still preside over its destiny.

Crisis is a natural, though not an inevitable, part of growth. In Chrysler's case it was a birth sign and a ruling planet. The United States Motor Company, of which Chrysler is the ultimate descendant, was constituted in 1910, bringing together a number of independent car manufacturers, wistfully described as "a collection of pronounced failures."[2] The new conglomerate did not fare any better than its several parents. Two years later it declared bankruptcy. Soon afterward it re-emerged under the name Maxwell Motors, prospered briefly during the boom that followed World War I, and then collapsed along with the market in 1920.

When Walter Chrysler was called in by the bankers to save the company, there were 26,000 unsold cars crowding company lots and freight yards. When Iacocca joined the company, there were around 80,000 unsold cars in what the company euphemistically called its "sales bank," and the figure soon passed 100,000. Walter Chrysler instituted a policy of building cars only against firm orders from dealers, a system Iacocca had to reintroduce 60 years later. In 1920 the company had $33 million in debt obligations. Chrysler persuaded the bankers to lend it another $15 million. The company recovered so rapidly that all the debts were liquidated by January 1925, nine years ahead of schedule. A few months later Maxwell Motors was taken over by the newly christened Chrysler Motors Corporation, and the company was launched on a period of rapid growth that saw it reach the position of the nation's second largest automaker, a position it held until 1953.

In the 1980s the debt was much bigger and the government was directly involved in saving the company, but here, too, the recovery was incredibly swift and the loan guarantees were retired seven years before they were due. Once again there was talk of a new Chrysler Corporation; although the name did not change this time, there was a widespread conviction that the nature of the company had somehow changed. However, the remarkable Chrysler Corporation was and still remains somewhat of a mystery.

The Leaning Tower

The origin of all Chrysler's problems through the decades was an imbalance in the constitution of the company resulting from the conditions of its birth and the personality of its founder. Unlike most leaders of large business in his day, Walter Chrysler rose from the ranks of manual labor. After graduating from high school, he declined an opportunity for a college education and went to work in a grocery store. How apropos was Iacocca's remark that Chrysler was still being run in 1978 "like a small grocery store"![3]

Walter Chrysler became an apprentice machinist on the railways, then a mechanic, and eventually a superintendent. When he joined Buick as works manager in 1912, he brought to his new job his experience with large-scale metalworking for utilitarian purposes and introduced improved processes and greater efficiencies into the nascent auto industry. By 1916 he had become president of Buick, where he remained for four years.

Chrysler's humble origins and lack of education made it extremely difficult for him to appreciate the revolution in management and organization that was taking place. In keeping with his experience as a mechanic, Chrysler, like Ford, approached automaking as essentially an engineering job, to produce the best technical design most economically. He recruited talented engineers to create a company with "an extraordinary engineering intelligence,"[4] placed heavy emphasis on research, and built up a strong tradition of technological innovation and engineering excellence.

Technology is an inexhaustible resource. There are innumerable ways that technology can be improved, modified, or adapted to make it more competitive, to widen the existing market, or to create entirely new markets. Ford reduced the price of the automobile through technological innovations in production and thereby created a new market among those who could never before afford a car.

At Chrysler technological innovations like the high-compression engine, hydraulic brakes, and automatic transmission provided a constant source of fresh energy to nourish the company's life and spur its growth. Over time, engineering excellence became the primary value, the mission of the company, which it pursued in preference to all other values.

But technology is only one of the key components of corporate existence and not, as Walter Chrysler believed, the only key. His strong bias for engineering was accompanied by a failure to develop the other essential components in equal measure—a failure that sometimes amounted to gross negligence. The potentials of technology were often tapped at the expense of the other components and to the detriment of harmony between them. As a result, the company developed in a partial and unbalanced manner. It grew into a leaning tower.

Technology for Technology's Sake

The most visible effect of this imbalance was on Chrysler's approach to the market. The market contains unlimited potentials. It consists of all the needs, desires, interests, fashions, and fads of society. They are innumerable. There are basic physical needs like transporation, which can be met in an infinite variety of more convenient, comfortable, and attractive ways. There are also social needs, such as for recognition and status, which generate greater demand for material objects. There are psychological needs, as well, such as security or dominance, which create demand for products and services.

In the early days of the automotive industry, the car was primarily a means of transportation that met a physical need for a faster, more convenient, more comfortable way to travel. The challenge faced by the car manufacturers was to produce the most mechanically advanced vehicle in the largest numbers at the lowest price.

But gradually a shift took place in the market. Having accommodated itself to the newfangled invention, the public started to look for more subtle refinements in styling and design. The automobile began to appeal to social needs for status and attention and psychological needs for power, a sense of self-importance, and even masculinity.

William Durant was one of the first to see this new trend. He conceived of a company that would manufacture a wide variety of cars that appealed to the public's social as well as physical needs. Durant created GM and gave it the mission to build cars for every purse and purpose. When he took over at GM, Sloan, too, recognized that styling had become the most important marketing consideration.

As Walter Chrysler was introducing his very first model, based on the new high-compression engine, Ford's Model T was nearing the end of its days. Chrysler understood that people wanted something new, but he thought they wanted new and improved technical design, when in fact what they wanted was new styling. In the mid-1930s the company introduced a new, aerodynamically designed model with the first automatic overdrive transmission. It was an engineering masterpiece but a marketing disaster. Chrysler was in tune with the latest advances of technology but already losing touch with the market.

Chrysler's bias for engineering rather than marketing considerations continued unabated after the Second World War. The company's management insisted on practical, mechanical advances with a "disdain for whimsical fashion" at exactly the time customers were eagerly awaiting new annual style changes.[5]

Over the years, technology came to dominate market considerations. Engineering determined the size, styling, content, and cost of the cars that the company made. When Chrysler's management wanted to build a rear-engined compact in the late fifties to compete with GM's Corvair, the engineers refused, because they could not design one to meet their own standards of styling and comfort. The company's former chairman, Lynn Townsend, remarked, "There was no way this management could have even ordered that engineering department to do a rear-engined car."[6] In the late sixties, a similar fate befell plans for a subcompact. As recently as 1975 Townsend commented, "The engineering department is the most dominant influence in this company."[7] *Fortune* wrote at the time: "Overreliance on engineering as the company's strategy has had calamitous consequences. Chrysler responds to its engineers' inventions, not to the wants of its market."[8] Instead of developing new technology to meet a market need, Chrysler developed technology for the sake of technology.

The market was not the only thing that took a back seat to engineering at Chrysler. Organization did, too. Perhaps Walter Chrysler believed that building factories, making engines, and assembling cars were all there was to creating an organization, but that is far from the truth. Chrysler was essentially an engineer rather than a manager or an organizer. The company he built focused primarily on engineering design and assembly of parts produced by suppliers. Except for the engines, Chrysler did little manufacturing of its own in the early years. Even a managerial task like negotiating with the union was handed over to a law firm. The organization Chrysler created was small in size, simple in structure, similar to that of much smaller and less complex businesses, with himself and a few associates at the center personally managing all key operations. Chrysler was one of the early breed of empire builders, who, like Henry Ford, utilized vast material and human resources but "had relatively little interest in devising schemes to assure a more efficient over-all management of these resources."[9] In other words, Chrysler believed in the power of technology and production but ignored the enormous power of organization.

By contrast, Alfred Sloan was a builder of organizations. While Walter Chrysler was concentrating on technology, Sloan was building up a powerful, decentralized organization at GM with autonomous operating divisions coordinated and controlled by a centralized executive staff, interdivisional committees, and a sophisticated system of controls. Sloan did not have specialized technical talents, but he created an organization that attracted all the design, production, and marketing skills he himself lacked. GM's decentralized organizational structure became a pillar of strength for the company and a model for American business. Organization proved more powerful than technology.

In the early 1950s both Chrysler Corporation and Ford Motor Company attempted to reorganize along the lines Sloan had established at GM. Ford succeeded in great measure, although Henry Ford II perpetuated something of the autocratic tradition established by his grandfather.

By this time, Chrysler's organization had crystallized into a group of independent and isolated divisions, each in contact with the executive offices at the center but with little communication or coordination between them. The division heads possessed little authority and were responsible primarily for sales, purchasing, and cost control. There was no overall system for coordination, as at GM. The original corporate character was so well entrenched that it successfully resisted the attempt at reorganization. The net result was a move toward ever greater centalization of authority and control rather than decentralization— an organization held together by the strength of the chief executive rather than by internal cohesion. After Walter Chrysler's retirement, the organization lost the centripetal force that united its parts. It became what Iacocca termed "these little states—duchies. They would not report to central authority. . . . Everybody had his own little empire. Twenty little companies and nobody to pull them together."[10]

The company did acquire a decentralized character, but it nearly lost the character of being an organization. Organization means first and foremost coordination, but at Chrysler everyone was "working in a vacuum," as Iacocca remarked. "All of Chrysler's problems really boiled down to the same thing: nobody knew who was on first. There was no team, only a collection of independent players. . . ."[11]

With or without a strong coordinating organization, the primary components of a company are indissolubly linked together and interdependent. The failure to fully develop the powers of organization ultimately had repercussions that seriously affected Chrysler's most precious possession, its reputation for engineering excellence. In the late 1950s and then again in the mid-1970s, the company was faced with a serious problem of poor quality. Many of the defects could be directly attributed to "poor coordination between engineers and manufacturing"—that is, lack of organization.[12]

The original bias for engineering had introduced a crack in Chrysler's original organizational structure. As the company grew, the crack became wider, until it represented a nearly unbridgeable gulf between the different parts of the firm. The basic principle of a central organizational will directing and controlling all the parts was undermined from the start by the inordinate importance and freedom given to the engineering division.

Untapped People Power

Chrysler not only failed to tap the potentials of the market and organization; it failed to release the boundless energies and talents of its people as well. People have an infinite capacity for development. They can be disciplined to work harder and more efficiently. They can be motivated to be enthusiastic and cooperative. They can take on greater responsibilities and exercise authority constructively. They can acquire greater knowledge and skill. They can become innovative and creative, loyal and dedicated. Their work can be made an opportunity for personal growth and fulfillment. When any of these potentials of people is enhanced, the productive power of the company increases enormously.

Chrysler failed at the very first step—discipline. Executives using the president's office as a passageway from one office to another and factory workers who do not bother to use the trash barrels for their garbage are clear signs that the most rudimentary form of discipline is lacking. Iacocca called it "a state of anarchy."[13]

Chrysler's ideas on labor relations were as outdated as its concept of organization. Long after the UAW was an established power in Detroit, recognized and accepted by GM and Ford, Chrysler refused to cooperate with the union. The bitter feelings generated in the early days set the tone for the labor unrest that pursued Chrysler in later years. Absenteeism, low morale, racial tensions, disputes between workers and managers, and wildcat strikes were more common than at GM and Ford. These recurring problems seriously affected the efficiency of operations and the quality of the cars. Workers at one plant failed to punch in and out for lunch hour and then broke the time clocks when management insisted. As one UAW official commented, "Inside the Chrysler plants there was just about every kind of problem you could imagine"—theft, gambling, protection rackets, prostitution, and even a murder.[14]

The absence of a strong central authority made it difficult to control people and impossible to harness their full capacities for productive work. Talented individuals were assigned to jobs that they had not been trained for. Potential talents were ignored or suppressed rather than being actively encouraged. A rich pool of human resources was neglected for want of an organization to develop it.

Unmined Wealth

In the absence of a well-developed organization, the productive potentials of capital cannot be mobilized. The efficient use of money by elimination of unnecessary and wasteful expenditure is one way to release its productive power. The use of cost accounting to determine the optimal pattern of investment and the precise gain or loss from each activity is another. But these potentials relate only to the use of money. There are also creative financing techniques that make capital available far more readily than in the past—techniques like lease-purchase, credit cards, venture capital, stock offerings, bonds, and so forth.

Chrysler neglected its financial potentials as much as it did its human and organizational ones. Until 1957, when a comprehensive cost-control program was introduced, one division head complained that he could not find out the cost of the cars built by his division. Twenty years later Iacocca found that there was still no overall system of financial controls.

The productive potential of creative financing techniques was dramatically demonstrated in the sixties. In 1962 Chrysler introduced the first 5-year or 50,000-mile warranty, at a time when Ford and GM offered only 12 months or 12,000 miles. Two years later Chrysler Credit Corporation was established to provide funds to dealers and retail customers. Between 1962 and 1968 the company's market share in the United States grew from 10.3 percent to 18.1 percent, and sales tripled, from $2.5 billion to $7.4 billion.

The impressiveness of this achievement is only mitigated by the fact that GM had established a similar credit organization 43 years earlier, in 1919, and Ford had followed suit in 1950. The gains made by Chrysler in the sixties from creative financing could have come much sooner and been cumulatively much greater if only it had imitated what had proved successful for its competitors long before.

The company's greatest error with regard to finance was to intensively pursue profit as a short-term goal, producing cars it did not need in order to meet budget targets, juggling figures to make it look as if cars in the sales bank had actually been sold, adjusting accounts to conceal the financial weaknesses of the company, and sacrificing long-term investments and essential R&D expenditures to boost present profits.

Of course, the greatest error a company can make is to run out of cash. And Chrysler did this several times—once as the United States Motor Company; once as Maxwell Motors; again in 1958, when it had to rush to the banks for a $120 million emergency credit line; and yet again in 1979. Each time disaster had been averted it has returned in far greater proportions, until finally only the U.S. government could save the company from collapse. If the cycle is allowed to repeat, next time even the government may not be able to help.

The Second Resurrection

This was the constitution of Chrysler when Lee Iacocca became president. Its problems were gargantuan and seemingly insurmountable. The company owed $1.3 billion, had no cash, and, in the collective opinion of Chrysler and its bankers, its assets could not be sold for anywhere near the amount of its debts. As if this were not enough of a problem, there were others: some 100,000 unsold cars valued at $600 million in the sales bank that were poorly made and deteriorating outdoors; enormous overheads and declining sales that were generating millions in losses every day; a dissatisfied and alienated customer base, which was discouraged from further purchases by the growing public conviction that the company would not survive long enough to service its own warranties; and an undisciplined, demoralized workforce frightened by the specter of unemployment. The voice of the financial experts was nearly unanimous. Chrysler will not survive.

Chrysler not only survived the crisis but posted one of the most incredible recoveries in corporate history. The company that had lost $1.7 billion in 1980, the largest loss of any corporation till that time, earned an estimated $2.4 billion in 1984, more than it had earned in all of the previous 59 years of its existence. When Chrysler made a stock offering in early 1983, the entire 26 million shares, with a market value of $432 million, were sold within an hour. The company's stock, which had fallen below $4 a share a year earlier, rose to $36 a few weeks after the offering.

How was such a dramatic recovery possible? Where did the energy and resources come from to accomplish it? What was the process by which a crisis was transformed into an opportunity for growth?

The simplest answer to these questions is to give all the credit to Lee Iacocca or the government's $1.5 billion in loan guarantees. Whenever we do not understand an event, it is easy to explain it away as the work of a genius or superhuman leader or the obvious result of the indomitable power of money.

However great Iacocca's achievement, he frankly admits that he lacks either intellectual genius or superhuman power. The extraordinary thing about him is the commitment and effort he made and the good commonsense knowledge of organization he exhibited. Iacocca is a hardworking, dynamic, experienced automobile executive, a charismatic person with a keen sense of the market, but he is not, as he is the first to admit, a superman.

As for the loan guarantees, certainly Chrysler would not have survived without them. But it would have been no surprise to anyone if the company had failed even after receiving them. In fact, it almost did. Eighteen months after the guarantees were issued, Chrysler ran out of cash—it came down to its last $1 million at a time when daily expenses were $50 million—and in 1980 and 1981 its total losses were $2.2 billion, which was more than the value of the guarantees. Money alone was certainly not the answer. Then what was?

Steps to Success

The steps taken by Iacocca at Chrysler, the changes made within the organization, and the dramatic reversal of the company's fortunes are expressions of the process we have been presenting in this book, the process by which corporations evolve. The advantage of examining a case like Chrysler's is that the enormous pressure of dire external circumstances forced the company to intensify its effort for change, so that the process was accelerated and is therefore easier to perceive.

In the previous chapter we stated that the individual is a microcosm of the organization. The process of individual growth is one of releasing and converting energy into productive power. That process begins with an awareness of a weakness to be overcome or a higher goal to be achieved. It commences with a decision by the individual to grow, a commitment of the will, and enthusiasm for the effort. Then it passes through several more stages, which culminate in the development of the individual's personality to incorporate new personal values.

Corporations are individuals, too. They develop inwardly in their capacity to generate, transmit, and utilize energies for productive work. The process that governs their development is the same as that which governs the development of the individual. It is the process by which personality grows.

Knowledge

The first step in that process is to acquire knowledge of the growth that needs to be achieved and of the weaknesses that have to be overcome. By weakness, we mean an inadequate or below-average capacity in some particular area, which has to be strengthened. Weaknesses occur in areas where the personality is not developed.

But there are some personality defects that are the result of wrong development rather than no development, wrong organization rather than disorganization. The problems faced by Chrysler were not those of an immature corporate personality that had not yet developed a distinctive character. They were expressions of a personality that had developed, but developed in an asymmetrical manner. There was a formed character, but it was based on many bad corporate habits. Because the personality was developed, it was able to successfully resist the attempts to modify it in the 1950s.

Iacocca's immediate task at Chrysler was not to build up the organization, but to forcefully eradicate innumerable negative habits that had become entrenched. The first necessity was not soul-searching and self-scrutiny, but just plain discipline. Energies that were being squandered and resources that were being wasted had to first be brought under control before they could be utilized productively. A lack of discipline pervaded Chrysler, and the only possible remedy was "a dose of order and discipline."[15]

The Crucial Decision

Iacocca's first act at Chrysler, and probably his greatest, was not his plant closings, cost cutting, or appeal to the government. It was a decision—a decision so momentous that it sapped all his energies and left him "seeing double." It was the decision to eliminate this lack of discipline, to remove the entrenched negative habits that had generated the crisis in the first place. Without that, no growth was possible, and even the company's survival was highly doubtful. That decision—made progressively as the true nature of Chrysler's problems became fully evident to Iacocca, reaffirmed and strengthened by each additional revelation of disorder, and solidified into a complete determination and commitment of his entire personality—was the indispensable prerequisite and essential seed of all that followed. Because the obstacles were so large and the resistance so great, nothing less than a total commitment commensurate with the weight of the task could be effective.

Once that decision had been fully made, it had to be communicated to all levels of the organization, accepted by them, and converted into a commitment of the entire management, and it had to generate a willingness and enthusiasm for change. Even Iacocca's total determination could not have been fully effective if he had attempted to fulfill it through authority alone, because the organization lacked the authority required to correct its own misguided course. Iacocca chose to rely on education and persuasion rather than force in order to enlist the sympathies of his people and convince them in turn to make commensurate decisions at their own levels to eliminate substandard behavior and poor performance. He succeeded in winning the support of his people and persuading them to confirm his decision in their own minds and actions.

Iacocca's decision called forth all his energies and threw them into action. It also released the energies of those around him. He had not merely to communicate a decision to his associates; he had to inspire them with confidence, make them commit themselves, and release their energies and enthusiasm. The fact that many highly placed executives sacrificed secure positions at Ford and other companies to join Iacocca shows that he did succeed in releasing their enthusiasm for a challenge and an adventure. "My mother was horrified when I left a good job at IBM to join Chrysler, and so were the mothers of some of the others who joined the Iacocca team at that time," recalled Frederick W. Zuckerman. Zuckerman joined Chrysler in October 1979 as assistant controller/financial controls and today is vice-president and treasurer. Walter Chrysler was known as an energetic and courageous risk taker. The tradition still lives at the company.

Revitalizing the Organization

Energy was released by a decision and reinforced by the commitment of a determined management team. But in order to become effective, it had first to be converted into a force or will of the corporate character. The decision had to change the structure and functioning of the organization.

This change was accomplished in several ways. The organization was restructured along more rational lines, eliminating such anachronisms as having a single executive responsible for both manufacturing and sales operations. Separate operations were isolated from one another so that they could be individually evaluated. There was a massive reshuffling of the organization chart. Nearly the entire executive team was replaced by new faces, mostly recruits from outside. Talented individuals were promoted from below, and an effort was initiated to uncover and encourage latent talents that had been suppressed by the old, encrusted organizational setup. Highly competent and trusted people were brought in to head priority operations like finance, quality control, and marketing.

The reorganization instilled a sense of discipline at the higher levels of management, where it had been sorely lacking. New policies were instituted, new standards of performance were established, and new rules were formulated to eliminate the grosser violations of corporate self-restraint.

The sales bank for unsold car inventory had engendered a lack of discipline in the sales force, since production could continue even when orders flagged, and the cars could be stored in the sales bank until they were disposed of on a clearance sale. The abolition of the sales bank and the introduction of a make-to-order production policy forced the sales department to sell cars in order to keep the plants open instead of just to keep the sales bank from overflowing.

A significant aspect of the reorganization involved closer coordination and greater cooperation with the UAW, necessitated by the requirement for union wage concessions in order for the company to qualify for the government loan guarantees. The appointment of the UAW president, Doug Fraser, to Chrysler's board marked a reversal of the company's historical efforts to distance itself as far as possible from the union. This reversal not only won the necessary wage concessions but also enabled the company, in cooperation with the union, to tighten labor discipline. For instance, they worked out new rules to reduce absenteeism at the plants. "Putting Fraser on the Board was symbolic that we are all in this thing together," Zuckerman said.

The decision of the CEO and commitment of top management energized the company. The reorganization transformed that decision into a force for change. But in order for that force to be effective, new systems were required to convert force into organizational power.

One of the most basic of these systems was for reporting financial data. Discipline requires control, control depends on monitoring of activities, and monitoring is done most effectively through information systems. Those that existed earlier at Chrysler were incomplete and only partially operative. The new management insisted on analyzing the performance of each separate operation in terms of timeliness, quality, and financial viability. A comprehensive reporting system, a centralized system of financial controls, and a quarterly performance-review system were among those introduced.

For conversion of this organizational power into corporate results, the company needed the right skills at the right place. But over the years Chrysler had developed the habit of shuffling managers so frequently that very few were found in positions they were actually qualified to manage. Iacocca found it necessary to fire or retire most of those who had been associated with lax operations and bring in strong, experienced executives to insist on disciplined functioning.

While elimination of undisciplined behavior was an essential prerequisite for any positive achievement, it represented only a part of the momentous decision Iacocca made and implemented. In moves of as great or even greater significance, he defined, communicated, and implemented several key values. Foremost among these values were quality of product, efficiency of production, punctuality of scheduling, coordination among departments, cooperation with dealers, and harmony with the market. The process of implementing each of these values followed the steps outlined earlier in this book.

Implementing Quality

Chrysler had been plagued by quality problems for years. Poor quality was taking a heavy toll on the company's market share and hiking up warranty costs. Everyone was aware that quality was a weakness. The decision to improve was essential to recovery. "From day one, Iacocca drove home the message that you must never scrimp on quality," Zuckerman told us. "Iacocca pounded this message over and over. It gave him a great opportunity to make a 'Let's Win One for the Gipper' speech, which he does very well."

The first step was to evolve a strategy, the Quality Improvement Program, and then to create an organizational structure to implement it. Iacocca brought in a retired quality-control expert as a consultant, established a new department to oversee quality, and hired 250 people to staff it. In order for the program to be effective, many systems had to be introduced or upgraded. Purchasing was an area where quality control was very lax. Paul Bergmoser was hired away from Ford to head the department, and a team of skilled quality-control people was added to the purchasing department.

Many quality problems were introduced by the inordinately large number of parts the company used on its various models. New policies were introduced, which reduced the number of parts from 70,000 to 40,000, and a streamlined inventory system was installed.

Poor quality also resulted from the lack of coordination between design and manufacturing. The designers were specifying parts that could not be produced. Systems for coordination between these two departments eliminated design errors before they became production defects. The company coordinated with the UAW on a quality-circles program that significantly reduced manufacturing errors.

Independent studies undertaken before the quality program was introduced found that Chrysler typically had 30 percent more customer complaints than Ford or GM. As a result of the program, the quality of Chrysler's cars improved dramatically. Between 1978 and 1980, one study showed a 32 percent improvement by Chrysler. A confidential GM marketing report in 1980 indicated that customer satisfaction was higher at Chrysler than at any of its competitors. By 1983 Chrysler's warranty costs had fallen by 40 percent.

Implementing Punctuality

Another problem area had been delays in the introduction of new products. Punctual introduction of new models required precise timing, close coordination, and tight discipline from the point of conception to the completion of production. Punctual development timing was a priority value for the new management.

Specific standards were established and deadlines set for each phase of the development schedule. Standards had existed earlier, but they had often been ignored. Bergmoser called it "a matter of discipline."[16] Now clear lines of authority and decision-making responsibility were established for approval of design concepts, and a master system was introduced to ensure proper coordination between all participating departments, especially design and production.

As a result of the development-timing program, new-product scheduling was radically improved. Three years is the standard development cycle for new models in the automotive industry, even when they do not involve major changes in the engine and transmission. In 1983 Chrysler released three new models on which the time from approval of design to release ranged between 6 and 12 months. Such quick reflexes were a direct result of the improved discipline and streamlined systems.

Implementing Efficiency

The decision to acquire greater production efficiency was not a choice. It was a compulsion. It was compelled by the company's financial crisis. Discipline alone was not enough to achieve it. It required a comprehensive strategy for value implementation that touched every aspect of the company's functioning. It involved a major restructuring of the organization—the closing of 23 plants—a drastic reduction in the workforce and all levels of management, elimination of the sales bank, centralization of accounts payable (which was previously handled from 30 different offices), creation of oversight committees, reorganization of the controller's office, and other structural changes.

The organizational will for greater efficiency was empowered by a multitude of systems that coordinated quality control, purchasing, inventory, design, and manufacturing functions to achieve greater economies. All these operations were integrated with the controller's office by the improved reporting and financial control systems.

Coordination between purchasing and manufacturing alone enabled the company to cut inventory costs by $750 million with a "just in time" inventory system and a reduced number of parts. For decades Chrysler's engineering department had been boosting production costs by the addition of sophisticated design elements the customer was unwilling to pay extra for. Now coordination between engineering and marketing helped produce economies such as the reduced transport costs for the K-cars achieved by limiting their length so that more of them could fit on a standard freight car.

The net result of this value-implementation program was a 23 percent reduction in fixed costs over five years and a reduction in the company's breakeven point from 2.3 million cars to 1.1 million.

Implementing Harmony Without

One of Iacocca's major objectives was to overcome Chrysler's loss of contact with the market, to re-establish harmony between what the engineers designed and what the market wanted, and to restore customer confidence in the quality of Chrysler cars and the stability of the company.

First he had to reverse a corporate habit of cutting new-product development funds whenever money became tight. At the height of Chrysler's financial crisis, he committed $700 million three years in advance to fund development of the highly successful minivan.

At the same time, he had to restore market confidence in the company and its products in order to ensure that they would even be around three years later. To restore public faith, the company engaged the advertising firm of Kenyon & Eckhardt. Breaking all precedents in the industry, Chrysler established extremely close coordination with the ad agency, even allowing agency representatives to sit on the company's marketing and production-planning committees. Together they developed a series of newspaper advertisements that openly acknowledged all of Chrysler's problems and effectively communicated management's commitment to rectifying them. The words by themselves would not have inspired the market, but they were backed by a radically new policy (new for the industry—but which Sears had popularized 80 years before)—a 30-day money-back guarantee on the purchase of new Chrysler cars. The policy instilled faith where words alone could not. Sales soared, and less than 0.2 percent of the cars sold under the guarantee were returned.

Of course, advertisements and guarantees would have been of little value if the company's new K-car had not been what the market wanted. But under the pressure of a crisis, Chrysler's development engineers had uncharacteristically bent their ears to the market and heard correctly what it wanted. After his arrival Iacocca took personal charge to ensure that they continued to do so.

The right car was not enough. Chrysler's dealers had been mistreated by the company for years. Their cooperation was essential for elimination of the sales bank and restoration of customer confidence. The new management made a major effort to improve relations with the dealers, to listen to their grievances, assure them that quality would improve, and inform them of the internal changes taking place. At the same time it had to deal firmly with dealer discontent over abolition of the sales bank, which had been a continuous source of discount-priced cars for the dealers.

The response of the market to these initiatives was remarkable, especially in view of the competition from Japan and the leveling of demand. In 1978 Chrysler sold 1.2 million passenger cars in the United States and the percentage of Chrysler car owners who intended to buy a Chrysler as their next car dropped to 36 percent, just half the 72 percent figure of GM. By 1984 volume had risen to 2 million cars.

In addition to the good design of the K-car and Iacocca's TV advertisements, there was another factor responsible for the improved market response. Energy attracts, and intense energy attracts powerfully. During the last five years, Chrysler has released an enormous amount of potential energy to ride out the crisis and spur recovery. That energy has not only wrought changes within the company; it has evoked a response from the market as well.

Twelve Steps

Chrysler has not just survived a crisis. It has grown substantially and is a stronger company today than anytime in the recent past. Crises followed by growth are common enough in all fields of life. Growth depends on energy, and the effort made to survive a crisis often releases far greater energy than is required for mere survival. Crises generate an intense pressure that compels people and organizations to make greater efforts than they would otherwise be motivated to make left to themselves. As we saw in Chapter 1, regardless of whether it is generated externally by a crisis or an opportunity or internally by a determination to grow, the effort—if sufficient—energizes the organization and spurs its growth. The process of that growth is the same in all three cases.

We can identify all the major steps of that process in Iacocca's work at Chrysler. They are similar to the steps taken by our manager in Chapter 11 to become a significant individual.

1. *Identify weaknesses and eliminate them.* Knowledge of imperfections and a willingness to remove them are a prerequisite to growth. Often it requires a crisis to motivate companies to such an effort. In Chrysler's case the problems were so deeply entrenched that only a crisis could generate sufficient pressure to overcome them.

2. *Decide on your values and goals.* Knowledge of one's weaknesses and problems is essential for remedial action, but knowledge becomes powerful only when it is accepted and endorsed by the will and converted into a decision to act. It is not enough to know what needs to be done. There must also be a resolute decision to do it. That decision releases energy.

After understanding Chrysler's problems, Iacocca identified some of the essential corporate values necessary for its recovery and success: discipline first; then quality, economy, and efficiency; punctual product development; standardization and systemization; internal coordination and communication; cooperation with the union, dealers, and suppliers; integration of the company's operations around a central organizing and controlling executive team; harmony with market needs; and public confidence. His decision, in effect, was to do everything within his power and the company's resources to improve performance in all these areas.

3. *Make a real commitment to change.* For the decision to influence others and enlist their cooperation, it had to be backed by a genuine personal commitment to achieve what had been decided. Since Iacocca was asking everyone else to sacrifice, he began by sacrificing his entire salary for a year. Since he was asking others to work harder, he committed himself to sacrifice personal leisure and comfort to see that the job was done. More than his words, that personal commitment persuaded others to leave secure jobs to join him at Chrysler and evoked the respect and cooperation of company employees.

4. *Generate enthusiasm.* When people obey an order, they contribute their physical energy to the work. When they understand the importance of the work and decide it should be done, they lend their mental energies for its accomplishment. But when their emotions are aroused and they become enthused by the challenge and eager to accomplish it, the entire energies of their personalities are released and pour forth into the work.

A task as onerous and difficult as Iacocca faced at Chrysler could never be accomplished by a grim or half-hearted determination. It demands a total commitment of energy and an enthusiastic effort. The most effective way to release enthusiasm in others is to be genuinely enthusiastic oneself. Because Iacocca really believed in what he was doing and really wanted his program to succeed, his full energies and enthusiasm were released. His enthusiasm spread to others, instilled confidence, released their energies, and enlivened the organization.

5. *Create the right structures.* Every value needs a structure for its implementation. Values without structures are like precious jewels without settings. You can keep them in a drawer, but cannot put them to any use. The structure may be one job position, a team, or a whole department. Iacocca created innumerable new structures and altered many existing ones to give greater form and force to the values he sought to implement. He restructured the engineering, manufacturing, marketing, purchasing, accounts payable, and controller functions. He established a new quality-control department. He also eliminated unproductive operations that were dragging the company down.

6. *Set standards and establish rules.* Values cannot be properly implemented unless they are translated into specific standards of performance with respect to each and every aspect of work to which they apply. Standards must be supported by rules. Standards tell people what you want, but in many cases you have to tell them exactly how to do it, too—and, more important, how not to do it. Clear rules backed up by authority are critical to success.

Iacocca introduced higher standards in areas of operations such as discipline, product quality, efficiency, return on investment, timeliness, and worker productivity. New rules were formulated to define appropriate conduct, like the more stringent rules to reduce worker absenteeism.

7. *Recruit the right people.* People are the real raw material of business. They are loaded with hidden talents, capacities, and unexpressed energy. Tapping that resource is like a free pass into Fort Knox.

Iacocca brought in several dozen talented and experienced people to constitute his new management team—people he felt he could trust. He also retired or fired almost the entire front line of existing executives, who had become entrenched in or habituated to the old ways of functioning and would find it difficult to adjust to radical change. He delved deeper into the organization and discovered a rich reserve of dynamic, young, talented people, "people with fire in their eyes,"[17] raised them to the light of day, and gave them freedom and responsibility to express their capacities in their work.

The true significance of Iacocca's accomplishment can be fully perceived only when it is realized how much of it was fashioned out of the company's existing resources—particularly its people—which the earlier management had not properly utilized.

8. *Create systems for everything.* There is no business activity that cannot be reduced to a system. There is nothing a dynamic CEO or a skilled manager can do that cannot be done much better by a system. The enduring successes of IBM and GM are testimony to this truth. Every company has hundreds of systems, but that still covers only about 60 percent of their activities.

Iacocca was shocked to find some key systems missing at Chrysler and many existing ones fallen into disuse, which amounts to the same thing. For every value he sought to implement, he introduced new systems or modified existing ones. A reporting system, financial controls, and systems for purchasing, inventory, product development, scheduling, sales, and quality control all had to be revamped and upgraded to achieve a higher level of value implementation.

9. *Train for every skill you need.* If you make a list of all the skills needed to do the job of a CEO effectively, the skills that can be acquired by training, it will come to more than 100. Every executive, every manager, indeed all the people in an organization need all these skills to be fully effective at their jobs.

Chrysler Corporation had achieved its original prominence in engineering largely because of the Chrysler Institute, established by Walter Chrysler in 1930 to train automotive engineers. The institute supplied talented staff not only to Chrysler but to the entire industry.

Iacocca found that there were a lot of other people at Chrysler who needed training—training to meet quality standards and time schedules and to operate systems. For instance, a training program had to be instituted to teach the sales force how to use the new ordering system.

10. *Make all the right connections.* A company is like an army. Unless you coordinate every activity and integrate every level, you end up firing on your own troops or starving them to death. The departments at Chrysler were doing both.

Improved coordination between engineering and production cut product-development time, reduced quality problems, and helped eliminate impractical designs before they reached the production phase. Similar gains were made by coordination between engineering and marketing and between production and purchasing, as well as between the company and other organizations, such as its ad agency and suppliers.

11. *Communicate.* Disseminating factual information, sending clear messages, issuing clear instructions, listening to what others have to say, and spreading better understanding are necessary to ensure that the decisions made by top management are understood by those below and that the greatest possible measure of acceptance, commitment, and enthusiasm is evoked for their implementation. Ultimately, value implementation depends on the actions of the lowest level of workers in an organization. Communication is the means for creating awareness, willingness, and enthusiasm at that level.

12. *Institutionalize the values.* The first 11 stages outlined above are steps that can be taken by management to release the energies of an organization, instill higher values, and utilize the energies to implement those values in work.

In Chapter 3 we spoke of three further levels of value implementation that begin after the organized effort is completed. When the values become so deeply ingrained in the people and the organization that external systems of enforcement are made obsolete because appropriate conduct is enforced by peer pressure, then the values have become institutionalized as a part of the corporate milieu. At a later stage the values are accepted by the individuals in the company as an essential part of their jobs and are implemented even in the absence of peer pressure. They have become customs in the organization. Finally a stage can be reached when the individuals identify with the company's central values as personal values in their own lives. A mature corporate culture develops.

Institutionalizing Value Implementation

The transition from the first 11 steps to the three stages of the last step in value implementation usually takes a long time. But time is not the only thing necessary, for in many companies that transition is never made at all. There are other conditions. First, the active effort at value implementation through stages one to 11 must be fully completed, without the omission of any step. If any element is missing, the process does not mature; and it may even lose ground later on, as it has many times at Chrysler after a period of energetic effort and progress. Second, the effort at value implementation must itself become an institutionalized activity of the organization. It must become a conscious goal of the entire company, supported by the appropriate decisions, structure, systems, skills, and continuous, ongoing activities.

At Chrysler value implementation is still a personal activity of top management, compelled by the external pressure of a crisis situation, propelled by the dynamism and commitment of Iacocca and his staff, imposed on the organization by force of circumstances, managerial authority, and persuasion. How far these values have actually been accepted at lower levels of the company, how deeply the effort has penetrated the corporate character, and what will happen after the external pressure recedes and Iacocca retires remain to be seen.

In spite of its size, Chrysler has always functioned more like a personal company than an impersonal organization. Walter Chrysler ran it like an old-time proprietor trained in a corner grocery store. Iacocca found it was still that way 60 years later. Observing the quick, personal decision-making process at Chrysler, *Fortune* very recently commented that it is still run "more like a corner grocery store"—even today.[18]

History shows that the Chrysler corporate personality strongly resists change except in times of crisis, and that corporate personality remains largely intact. Unless that personality is changed at its core, and unless that change is carried down into the smallest acts and attitudes of the company, sooner or later the old personality will reassert itself and the old problems will re-emerge.

The Process of Development

The revival of Chrysler is a remarkable achievement, but it still remains a revival, not a transformation. That achievement follows a process—the same process that enabled Bata to emerge from the crisis of 1922 and grow into a multinational corporation, the same process that enabled Marriott to take advantage of the opportunities presented by an increasingly mobile American public and convert a local group of Hot Shoppes into a worldwide chain of hotels. This is the same process that enabled Apple, Coca-Cola, Delta, General Mills, IBM, Merck, Northwestern Mutual, Sears, and so many others to rise from tiny origins, grow and grow, multiply and expand in a movement of corporate development that need never end.

In Chrysler and most or perhaps all of the others, the process is only partially conscious. It is largely directed by common sense, life experience, and trial and error. It is haphazard, fraught with omissions and false starts, subject to considerable delays—though everyone will gladly acknowledge that Iacocca took a remarkably short time to accomplish his task at Chrysler. This means that the process can generate even greater results, more quickly and with a less taxing effort, if it is fully understood and implemented systematically.

The science of management has developed many powerful tools and techniques for increasing the productive efficiency of an organization. To be efficient is to fully utilize the available resources. But today many corporations are no longer preoccupied with problems of efficiency. They have mastered the skills and techniques for smooth organizational functioning and are searching for ways to accelerate the pace of growth. What they need are not more efficient operational tools but more powerful energizing processes for continuous expansion and rapid development.

In this chapter we have looked at the process by which the activities of a corporation are energized for growth. In the previous chapter we looked at the same process with respect to individuals, how their lives and work can be energized and made an occasion for personal growth. Both are expressions of the same process. Not only individuals and corporations but every single action they undertake can also be energized.

Individuals become significant by identifying themselves with the values and interests of the organization and serving the organization through the work. That work becomes a field for their personal growth. They grow by giving. Corporations achieve enduring success by identifying themselves with the values and needs of the society and serving the society through their work. That work becomes a field for corporate development. They grow by giving, too.

In the same way, every action and activity performed by an individual or a corporation is an opportunity for growth, provided it is approached in the right way. Every act can be done either in a substandard manner or in an efficient manner or in a way that energizes and generates growth. The key is to approach the act from a wider perspective.

When C. E. Woolman decided to leave a Delta flight so that one more passenger could have a seat, he was not just being polite. He was sending a signal to everyone in the entire organization to look at their work from the customer's point of view. The Delta flight attendants who today share their food with hungry passengers are acting as Woolman did—thinking of the customer first. As a result, many airline passengers are constantly thinking of Delta, too.

When Woodruff encouraged a policy of trying to provide the maximum profits to Coca-Cola bottlers, he was viewing his work from their point of view. The bottlers not only earned enormous profits; they were also energized to spread Coke to the distant corners of the world and send home untold wealth to the parent company. Woolman's was a small, insignificant symbolic act. Woodruff's was a lifetime policy. They both had a similar effect.

When the Northwestern Mutual agent tries to find a way to help a policy owner whose policy has lapsed, when a Sears manager exchanges five-year-old Craftsman hand tools with a smile, when a Merck representative spells out the negative qualities of the firm's newest product, when a young General Mills product manager is given exceptional freedom to plan out an advertising campaign for Cheerios, when a Du Pont gate guard reminds departing drivers to buckle their seat belts—these are all tiny, insignificant acts carried out by looking at things from another person's point of view. They may be tiny, but they are incredibly powerful acts, energizing acts.

In every company there are hundreds of functions—replying to a letter, cleaning a machine, answering a phone, addressing a subordinate, meeting a customer, making a product, paying a bill, arranging a purchase. Each and every one of them can be done in a substandard or efficient or energizing way. Sears has energized purchasing by identifying with the interests of its suppliers. Apple has energized its people by giving them maximum freedom for self-expression.

Energizing the Corporation

All the components of a company—people, organization, technology, markets, and money—can be energized in this way. When a manager focuses on getting work done through people, that manager acts efficiently. When a manager concentrates on relating to the people as individuals through their work and trying to foster their personal growth, that manager is energizing them (and, incidentally, raising efficiency to peak levels). Attention to people is an expansive movement that releases their energies and potentials and stimulates corporate growth.

When an organization is structured to carry out each separate task systematically, it is efficient. When it views each task as part of a greater whole and coordinates it with all other related activities, those activities are energized. Creation of smooth, harmonious interrelationships is an expansive movement for the activities and the organization.

When technology is evaluated in terms of its design and productivity, more efficient technology is developed. When it is viewed in terms of the needs of the market and continuously refined to improve customer satisfaction, the vast potentials of technology reveal themselves. Looking at technology from the customers' point of view is an expansive movement that energizes the corporation.

When an intensive and comprehensive effort is made to exploit every conceivable means to increase sales of a product, the market for that product is efficiently utilized. When every effort is made to understand the needs of the society and serve those needs by providing a product or service, the market is energized. Serving the society through the market is an expansive movement that unleashes enormous energy and opens the way for unlimited growth.

When money is properly utilized and carefully accounted for in order to minimize wastage and maximize profits, it is used efficiently. When money is viewed as a measure or index of corporate development rather than as the ultimate goal to be pursued, money has a great power to energize the organization. Working for the development of the company utilizing money as a tool or an index is an expansive movement that generates the maximum growth and the maximum profits in the long term.

Relating to people through work in order to help them grow rather than to take more from them; coordinating and integrating all the activities and systems of an organization; viewing technology from the customers' point of view; working for the benefit of suppliers, distributors, customers, and society at large; using profits as an index of growth rather than a goal—these are all expansive movements that release latent energies and potentials.

Conversion of Energy into Power

The growth of a corporation, like the growth of an individual, depends on the continuous release, transmission, and conversion of fresh energies into work. The energy has to be generated and released, mastered and harnessed, directed and controlled, and transformed into productive power.

The process begins with the generation of fresh energy. The generation of electrical energy in physics depends on the creation of a voltage differential between two points. The greater the differential, the greater the energy generated. The same principle applies to an organization. Here the differential is created between where the company is now and where it wants to go, between the values and goals it is committed to achieve and its present level of performance. The higher the values and goals that are genuinely accepted, the greater is the energy released. Profit is a very limited goal, which can inspire only top-level executives. The psychological values listed in Chapters 3 and 11—harmony, personal growth, service, and so on—are ones that can inspire and release the maximum energy from all the people in the organization.

The energy released has to be transmitted through the structure and systems of the organization. The will of the organizational character acts like a relay or booster station. The systems are the transmission lines. The efficiency and speed of transmission depend on the extent to which organizational values like discipline, coordination, and teamwork are present. Without these values, the energy released is not properly directed, controlled, and utilized. It is dissipated in unproductive friction or wasted in uncoordinated activity.

The energy released and transmitted has to be converted into action by people and machines. The amount of electrical energy that a bulb converts into light is limited by the wattage of the bulb, no matter how high the voltage is in the line. The conversion of energy into work in an organization is limited by the skills and attitudes of the people and the condition of all the elements of the corporate body. The greater the skills in the organization and the higher the level of physical value implementation—cleanliness, punctuality, maintenance, quality, efficiency—the greater the energy that is converted into work.

Each time any value is raised to a higher level, greater energy is released, transmitted, or converted by the organization. That energy can be used to build up all the parts of the corporate personality and establish a new harmony at a higher level. As the corporation grows, the level of energy continues to increase, and more and more of it is institutionalized as the intensity of the corporate personality. That constant conversion of fresh energy into greater intensity infuses life into the organizations and makes it come alive.

Every company adopts certain values that it recognizes as important and seeks to implement. As we have tried to illustrate through the examples from successful American companies, there is really no limit to the scope for implementing each value. Training at IBM, systems at Marriott, safety at Du Pont, teamwork at Northwestern Mutual, family feeling at Delta are all taken to a level far beyond that even conceived of by most companies. But there are many values, not just one or two, that can be raised to these peak levels, so that even the biggest and the best have an infinite scope for further growth.

When an individual succeeds in life, often that individual and other people are unaware of the process by which that success was accomplished. The same is true when people fail. We usually ascribe success to either talent, luck, or efficiency and failure to one of their opposites. But always there is a process behind them that we overlook.

The process that Iacocca followed at Chrysler is the process by which all companies evolve, consciously or unconsciously. When knowledge of the process is fully conscious and complete, the process can be vastly accelerated and infinitely extended. It can be reduced to a program and converted into a specific action plan for implementation by any company.

CHAPTER 13

The Vital Difference

The greatest strength of this country has always been the freedom and opportunity it provides to all its citizens to rise in life as high as their aspirations and effort can carry them. During the early decades of American history, this strength remained largely in potential, conceded in principle for all but recognized as a real possibility only for a minority and actually realized in their own lives by just a few individuals who possessed some exceptional talent or made an extraordinary effort. There were very few Thomas Edisons, Andrew Carnegies, and Henry Fords even a hundred years ago.

But this is no longer true. Today the possibility of unlimited achievement has become real in the minds of most Americans, a fervent aspiration in the hearts of many, and an actual realization in the lives of a significant number. The highest levels of education, social status, political power, and commercial achievement have been attained by thousands and tens of thousands of people whose ancestors immigrated to the shores of America a century or less ago, outcast, impoverished, and illiterate. Today there are more highly educated people in every small town than most states contained a hundred years ago. In 1870 only one doctoral degree was conferred in the entire United States. In 1970 more than 29,000 were conferred. Today there are more important and influential people in every major city than the entire nation once contained. The number of M.D.'s has increased nearly 6-fold in the last century and the number of dentists 15-fold. From 1900 to 1970 the number of engineers increased 40-fold. Many companies have made almost as many millionaires in the last few decades as the whole nation produced during the entire nineteenth century. Apple has traversed the ground between a garage-scale operation and a multi-billion-dollar corporation in 8 years, arriving in the exclusive *Fortune* 500 club faster than any company before it and making more than a hundred of its employees millionaires in the process. Tandem Computers, Inc. produced at least 25 millionaires while climbing to the *Fortune* list in just a decade. Nor are the achievements confined to electronics. Federal Express grew from nothing to a $1.4 billion business in just 13 years.

All this goes to show one thing: Opportunities in every field are greater today than ever before. And if we still persist in being more conscious of the obstacles than we are of the potentials, it only reflects the limitations imposed by our vision and our attitude, not the actual limitations to our growth. At the turn of the century, there were about 50 major corporations in the United States. Today *Fortune* lists 500. In another 50 years, there may be 5,000 or even 50,000. There is no inherent bar to growth, because growth is creative. It creates new opportunities, new technologies, new markets, and new wealth, which support further growth.

Apart from statistics, there are other facts right before our eyes that we usually ignore. When a market is expanding, many companies prosper, but not all. Those that fail in a buoyant market are labeled incompetent or unfortunate. When a market is shrinking, many companies fail, but not all. Those that survive in a period of declining market are labeled efficient or lucky. But what about companies like IBM, Sears, Delta, Marriott, Northwestern Mutual, and General Mills, which have not only survived during harsh times but continued to expand? All our labels prove inadequate. We can dismiss as luck a company's growth through one or two troublesome periods for its industry or the economy as a whole. But we cannot explain away the fact that of the top ten companies on *Fortune*'s most admired list in 1984, only one of them ever reported an unprofitable year, and that was way back in 1921. Where we cannot attribute someone else's success to luck, our next recourse is to concede that it was accomplished by people of extraordinary genius or talent. We have been at pains to show, as Edison said, that genius is mainly a question of hard work.

Still it is very difficult to conceive that those individuals and companies that have achieved phenomenal success and multiplied it thousands of times over decades do not possess something extraordinary. And, in fact, they do. It is not an extraordinary ability, it is an extraordinary knowledge. In some, that knowledge is partially or completely unconscious. It is expressed as a feeling or a hunch or strikes them as just plain common sense. But if you closely observe the lives of America's most successful corporations and do not get caught up in their words and strategies and explanations, you will find that their success falls into a pattern and follows the process that we have described in this book.

Development of Corporate Personality

Energy is converted by an organization into products and services for customers, welfare and well-being for employees, profit for sharehold-ers, and service to the national economy or the society at large. Profit is the easiest of these results to measure, and therefore, it is the clearest index of corporate success. But actually, successful companies tend to produce all of these results in far greater measure than average com-panies do. In Chapter 3 we quoted statistics to show that this is true even of their contribution to society.

But these are not the only expressions of energy in a company. Energy can be converted into short-term material results. It can also be invested and absorbed by the organization for its own development, for the growth of its personality and capacities, just as an enormous amount of energy is absorbed and invested in the development of a child's body and mind.

We recognize that the primary purpose of childhood is for the child to grow and to develop its personality, not to achieve any immediate success in life. All its achievements later in life depend on and are limited by that early development. Even after the body is full-grown, we recognize the importance of a continuing investment of energy to increase one's knowledge and skills. When you stop growing, you start dying. Yet in the lives of companies, we focus on material results from day one and usually neglect the most critical task of all—the devel-opment of the powers and capacities of the corporate personality. Ul-timately it is the strength and capacities of that personality that set the limits on corporate achievement. For sustained corporate success, there must be an ongoing and continuous effort at corporate self-de-velopment.

And the force and consistency of that effort, through the years and through the generations, is what makes the vital difference between companies.

A corporation grows as its personality develops. The development of corporate personality involves two movements—the release of latent energies from the components of the company and the conversion of that energy into productive power.

In companies with a well-developed corporate personality, ener-gies are released by the psychic center when it takes an expansive attitude or adopts higher values for implementation. Once the energy is released, the psychic center sets the direction for the conversion of those energies into productive power by the rest of the corporate per-sonality.

But not every company has a mature personality, and no company begins its life with one. Personality has to develop over time. In the early stages, the release of energy and its conversion into power through value implementation are done by the founder or a dynamic CEO, who lends his or her own personality to the corporation for its development. The founder or CEO taps the potentials of people, organization, technology, the market, and capital and utilizes the energy they contain to raise the level of value implementation in the company and launch it on a period of rapid growth.

The decision to adopt a higher value and implement it requires enormous energy. Therefore, energy is an essential prerequisite for value implementation. On the other hand, the adoption of higher values also releases energy, and the implementation of these values harnesses the enormous latent potentials of the company for its growth.

The Process

The release of energy from the components, the implementation of higher values, and the development of the corporate personality are actually three inseparable aspects of a single process, which occur simultaneously and complement one another.

When raw energy is generated and released, controlled and disciplined, organized and refined, harnessed and utilized for the development of the corporate personality, it is converted into organizational power. When sufficient power collects and is gathered, focused, and directed for the translation of high corporate values into physical practices, that power is expressed as a solid mass of radiating intensity like that observed in mature, highly successful companies. The constant conversion of energy into intensity for the continuous development of the corporate personality and the perfection of all its activities is the process that generates sustained corporate success. That process has been described previously in this book. It consists of movement in two directions: from action to ideal and from ideal to action.

In every action, we release and express energy. By giving greater attention and concentration to each action, we execute it more perfectly. The energy is upgraded into skill. Each single skilled movement is only one link in a series of actions. By systematically linking skilled actions with the proper timing and sequence, the activity can be accomplished far more efficiently. The skilled acts are combined to form systems. Isolated systems of skilled activity can be coordinated and integrated with other activities to form an organized and unified whole. Systems are united to create an organization. This mass of interrelated and interconnected systematic activities needs to be controlled, coordinated, and directed from a common center. As an organization becomes more integrated and unified, it develops a psychic center, which determines its direction and guides all its activities. The upward movement from raw energy to skilled action to systematic activities to coordinated and integrated organization to creation of a psychic center is the process by which personality develops through action.

The process also moves in the other direction. The ideal values or goals of the psychic center are transmitted down through the organization to be expressed as more perfect actions. The psychic center accepts a new value or goal, or it increases its commitment to the values and goals it has previously accepted. It translates that commitment into an enthusiastic determination to upgrade its own performance. It then creates new organizational structures, standards, rules, and systems to achieve higher performance on the value; or it upgrades existing structures, standards, rules, and systems to the level required. It acquires new or improved skills that are necessary. Finally it expresses its higher level of commitment, organizational capacity, and skill as improved physical performance—better-quality products or technology, faster service, cleaner facilities, better-maintained equipment, and so on. The results of this process are higher sales and profits, more satisfied customers and employees, and a contribution to the economic or social development of the nation.

The entire process can be reduced to five key ingredients:

1. A committed management and skilled, enthusiastic staff.
2. A systematic and coordinated organization.
3. Superior technology and quality products.
4. A harmonious relationship with the market.
5. Optimal and creative utilization of financial resources

When any of these components is raised to a higher level, it is as a result of the process described above, even though a company may not conceive of it in these terms when it acts. The growth of any one component increases the overall capacity of the corporate personality; but unidimensional development of one part can have only limited benefit for the whole. Growth must be balanced and harmonious in order to be continuous and yield maximum results.

By raising the other components up to restore harmony with the fastest-growing part, the organization expands in capacity and grows even further. By continuously adopting higher levels of value implementation as the goal and following the steps outlined in Chapter 12, each part can be continuously raised higher. More and more energy is generated, transmitted, and converted by the corporation, producing greater material results and greater growth of the corporate personality. When the process is continuously followed, endless expansion and enduring success are the inevitable result.

Converting the Process into a Method

The process we have described here with reference to the development of corporations is the same process by which individuals and societies grow and evolve. It is the process of human development. This process occurs spontaneously, inevitably, and irresistibly whenever the essential conditions for it are met, just like a chemical reaction. But normally the development of personality is slow, sporadic, and partial, because all the essential conditions for growth are not always present or not present in the proper proportions and combinations or not blended together in the proper manner by force of circumstances.

In other words, the process occurs unconsciously and incompletely. Some energy is released by external conditions—crises and opportunities. Some values are implemented partially and haphazardly by force of necessity or to improve performance. As a result, the organization moves forward, bounds upward to a higher level, and again levels off.

This is the process by which the corporate personality evolves naturally and unconsciously. It is a process initiated from outside, which results in an inner growth. But the same process can also be consciously initiated. It can be initiated from within by the psychic center to the degree that the psychic center is developed and is conscious of the process. This is what happens to some extent in mature companies like Northwestern Mutual when they set for themselves a greater challenge in the absence of compelling outer circumstances. The process leads to growth of the company and further development of the corporate personality.

When the process becomes fully conscious and is consciously implemented, it is converted into a method for continuous development of the corporate personality and expansion of the company. Since the conscious method is more complete than the unconscious process, the growth is greater and more rapid.

In the early stages of corporate evolution, the psychic center is not developed enough to consciously initiate this process on its own. It can only respond to external events. But a founder or CEO with a developed personality can lend a personality to the company and initiate the process of growth to the extent that the CEO knows it.

For growth to become a permanent and enduring feature in the life of an organization, this process must be institutionalized. What has been done at times by the founder or a CEO must become a permanent activity of the psychic center, continuously releasing and converting energy for endless expansion and enduring success.

Where to Begin

This process can be utilized by every company. How the process is utilized depends on where you want to go and how serious you are about getting there. It depends on your goal and your willingness to make the effort required to achieve it. Though the process is relatively simple, the effort is arduous—it is in direct proportion to the height of the goal. A tenfold expansion requires a tenfold greater effort.

No hardworking person is suddenly capable of a tenfold greater effort than before. But all are capable of improving the quality and quantity of their effort to 100 percent of their capacity and sustaining it at that peak level *if they really want to*. The effort to achieve and maintain performance at peak capacity releases, not tenfold, but a hundredfold greater energy over time. The key is to fully exhaust the present capacity.

Long-Term Goal

For those who are willing to make that total effort, there is no limit to the goals they can achieve, no end to their expansion. But there are several preconditions for that effort.

Choose your goal. The decision must be complete, the commitment total, the willingness enthusiastic.

Know what it involves. You must conceive of the amount of effort required to achieve the goal and be willing to make it. You must recognize all the skills needed to realize the goal and be ready to acquire them. You must understand the type of organization demanded for that higher level of functioning and be ready to create it. You must be aware of the higher level of motivated staff the achievement demands and be willing to raise people's enthusiasm to that level. You must know the values that can help you realize the goal and enthusiastically accept them.

Learn the process. Growth is usually achieved without understanding. Understanding comes later. But when knowledge of the process precedes experience, the process is far easier, and the progress is much more rapid. The process has to be conceived in practical terms, as it has been described in Chapter 12.

Work happily to achieve it. Growth is fastest, easiest, and greatest when the effort is made happily and wholeheartedly. High results are hard to achieve with a grudging or complaining attitude. The effort itself should become self-fulfilling and self-rewarding.

Implement comprehensive strategies. To achieve your highest goal, implement as many of the following strategies as you can. The more you implement, the faster and farther the growth.

1. The CEO should endeavor to become a significant individual.
2. Encourage every manager to become a significant individual.
3. Implement all the corporate values completely in every department and activity of the company.
4. Create and implement a plan for maximum development of all the potentials of people, organization, technology, market, and capital.
5. Upgrade all substandard operations to the level of maximum efficiency and energize all efficient operations, so that performance on every one of the company's 500 to 1,000 functions is improved in some measure.
6. List all the functions of the company and arrange them in a hierarchy of levels. Place each function in its proper order of sequence and identify all the other functions with which it should be coordinated or integrated in order for operations to be perfectly harmonious. Using this list as a goal and the present operations as a starting point, work out a step-by-step action plan for increasing the level of coordination and harmony at all points.
7. Identify the highest multiple of growth that you believe the company is capable of achieving and you are willing to work for. Draw up a detailed plan of how the company would be constituted and function if that goal were achieved. Compare that plan with the company's existing level of functioning. Work out an action plan to bridge the gap between the two.

Short-Term Goal

Not every company is in a position to make a comprehensive effort for growth at a particular point in time. If conditions do not permit implementation of comprehensive strategies, the same method can still be utilized to double a company's present level of profits. Partial strategies such as the following should be considered:

1. Take any one value and implement it to the highest level of perfection conceivable in every single aspect of the company's functioning, as Du Pont has implemented safety and Marriott has implemented systems.
2. Or take every corporate value listed in Chapter 3 and increase the company's level of performance on each one by 5 percent to 10 percent.

Small Steps Leading to Great Results

For immediate gains that are disproportionate to the effort required, implement as many of these isolated strategies as possible:

1. Increase slightly the level of attention given to people at all levels.
2. Improve slightly the quality of products and/or raw materials.
3. Raise the average level of education in recruitment.
4. Impart one new skill to each manager and worker.
5. Improve coordination of two major systems or coordinate all systems that relate to a single activity.
6. Offer incentives for continuing education or training, innovation in technology, innovation in office or production procedures, and/or greater knowledge of the market.

For All

Some things are good in themselves, regardless of whether or not they are expressed; knowledge is one of them. We believe that even an understanding of the process described in this book can make an individual a better manager and a corporation a better company.

Infinite Potential

There is an inexhaustible potential within the organization. It is inexhaustible because the more it is drawn from, the greater it grows. The more enthusiastically it is tapped, the more it increases at its source. The more it is enjoyed, the more it expands.

People and companies have grown to where they are—and they continue to develop—by drawing from this boundless potential. Those who have used this potential to unleash the powers of sustained corporate success have learned how to make a vital difference, in their lives and in the lives of their organizations. The first qualification is to want it. The more you want it, the more you grow. The more conscious you become of it, the more it beckons you to further growth. That is the essential message of this book.

Notes

The quotations in the text that appear without note numbers were obtained in the course of personal interviews. The sources for all other quotations are indicated in these notes.

CHAPTER 1

1. Edmund Morris, *The Rise of Theodore Roosevelt* (New York: Coward, McCann & Geoghegan, 1979), p. 20.
2. Ibid.
3. Stefan Zweig, *Balzac* (New York: Viking Press, 1946), pp. 112–13.
4. Robert Conot, *A Streak of Luck: The Life and Legend of Thomas Alva Edison* (New York: Seaview Books, 1979), p. 463.
5. Robert O'Brien, *Marriott: The J. Willard Marriott Story* (Salt Lake City, Utah: Deseret Book Company, 1977), p. 166.
6. Anthony Cekota, *Entrepreneur Extraordinary: Biography of Tomas Bata* (Rome: International University of Social Studies, 1968), p. 157.
7. Michael Moritz, *The Little Kingdom: The Private Story of Apple Computer* (New York: William Morrow and Company, 1984), p. 240.
8. Ibid., p. 223.
9. Bill Marriott, Sr., quoted from a videotape prepared by Marriott Corporation.
10. Damon Darlin, "Executive Style," *The Wall Street Journal* (September 17, 1984). Reprinted by permission of *The Wall Street Journal*, © Dow Jones & Company, Inc., 1984. All rights reserved.
11. Thomas Peters, "Strategy Follows Structure: Developing Distinctive Skills," *California Management Review*, Vol. 26, No. 3 (Spring 1984), p. 114.

CHAPTER 2

1. William Shakespeare, *King Lear*, Act I, Scene iv.
2. From Winston Churchill, *Great Contemporaries* (New York: Put-

nam's). Cited in Richard Nixon, *Leaders* (New York: Warner Books, 1982), p. 330.

3. Will and Ariel Durant, *The Story of Civilization: The Age of Napoleon* (New York: Simon and Schuster, 1975), Vol. II, p. 579.
4. Morris, *Rise of Roosevelt*, pp. 26–27.
5. "Intel Course Culture Manual," p. 5.
6. "Apple Bites Back," *Fortune* (February 20, 1984), pp. 98 and 100.
7. "Apple's New Crusade," *Business Week* (November 26, 1984), p. 148.
8. Brooke Tunstall, *Disconnecting Parties: Managing the Bell System Break Up* (New York: McGraw-Hill Book Company, 1985), p. 144.
9. Chris Argyris, *Personality and Organization* (New York: Harper & Row, 1957), p. 21.
10. Ibid., p. 24.
11. Durant and Durant, *Story of Civilization*, Vol. II, p. 776.
12. Ibid., p. 259.
13. Ibid., p. 247.
14. Harold Geneen, *Managing* (New York: Doubleday & Company, 1984), pp. 20 and 133.
15. "International Business Machines," *Fortune* (January 1940), p. 37.
16. W. D. Lewis and W. P. Newton, *Delta: The History of an Airline* (Athens: University of Georgia Press, 1979), p. 33.
17. "To Pause and Be Refreshed," *Fortune* (July 1931), p. 65.
18. E. J. Kahn, Jr., *The Big Drink: The Story of Coca-Cola* (New York: Random House, 1960), p. 63.
19. "The Coca-Cola Industry," *Fortune* (December 1938), p. 155.
20. "To Pause and Be Refreshed," p. 65.
21. From *Beverage Digest*. Cited in "Putting the Sparkle Back into Coke," *International Management*, Europe (October 1984), pp. 4 and 7.
22. Robert Sobel, *The Entrepreneurs* (New York: Weybright and Talley, 1974), p. 240.
23. For fuller discussion see Tunstall's *Disconnecting Parties*.
24. Brooke Tunstall, "Rites of Passage," *Bell Telephone Magazine*, Vol. 62, Nos. 3–4 (1983), p. 76.
25. Frederick R. Kappel, *Vitality in a Business Enterprise* (New York: McGraw-Hill Book Company, 1960), pp. 3 and 5.

CHAPTER 3

1. Lewis Carroll, *Alice in Wonderland and Through the Looking Glass* (New York: Grosset & Dunlap, 1977), p. 64.

2. Thomas Moore, "The Fight to Save Tylenol," *Fortune* (November 29, 1982), p. 45.
3. Lawrence G. Foster, "The Johnson & Johnson Credo and the Tylenol Crisis," *New Jersey Bell Journal*, (Spring 1983), p. 2. © 1983 New Jersey Bell. Reprinted with permission from the *New Jersey Bell Journal*.
4. James E. Burke, "Ad Council Speech" (delivered on November 16, 1983), p. 6.
5. Foster, "Johnson & Johnson Credo," p. 4.
6. Burke, "Ad Council Speech," p. 8.
7. From "The Tylenol Trouble," *The Wall Street Journal* (October 18, 1982), editorial page. Cited in a special report published by Johnson & Johnson. Reprinted by permission of *The Wall Street Journal*, © Dow Jones & Company, Inc., 1984. All rights reserved.
8. Statement by Benjamin C. Bradlee, *Washington Post* executive editor, quoted in *The New York Times* (April 7, 1984), p. 37. © 1984 by The New York Times Company. Reprinted by permission.
9. Quoted from a column by Alex S. Jones in *The New York Times* (April 6, 1984), p. 37. © 1984 by The New York Times Company. Reprinted by permission.
10. Warren Phillips, "How It's Done at *The Wall Street Journal*," *M* (November 1984), p. 71.
11. "Sears' Sizzling New Vitality," *Time* (August 20, 1984), p. 90.
12. Quoted from a talk by George W. Merck at the Medical College of Virginia at Richmond (December 5, 1950).
13. *Safety and Occupational Health: A Commitment in Action*, published by Du Pont, 1984, p. 4.
14. Leon C. Schaller, "Effective Management of Safety and Occupational Health," delivered at Cost Containment Seminar in Las Vegas (November 8–9, 1984).
15. John Gurda, *The Quiet Company: A Modern History of Northwestern Mutual Life* (Milwaukee: Northwestern Mutual Life Insurance Company, 1983), Introduction, p. 1.
16. Ibid., p. 293.
17. Ibid., p. 20
18. Ibid., p. 17
19. Ibid., p. 251
20. Ibid., p. 253.
21. Kappel, *Vitality in a Business Enterprise*, pp. 37 and 71.
22. Foster, "Johnson & Johnson Credo," pp. 5–6.
23. Figures taken from data provided by Johnson & Johnson's office of corporate public relations ("Public Service Companies—30

Years of Growth," *Johnson & Johnson's Corporate Financial Analysis* [November 14, 1983]).
24. Peter F. Drucker, *The Practice of Management* (New York: Harper & Row, 1954), p. 261.

CHAPTER 4

1. Harold C. Livesay, *American Made: Men Who Shaped the American Economy* (Boston: Little, Brown and Company, 1979), p. 217.
2. O'Brien, *Marriott*, pp. 154–55.
3. Livesay, *American Made*, p. 228.
4. Cekota, *Entrepreneur Extraordinary*, p. 175.
5. Ibid., p. 164.
6. Ibid., p. 189.
7. Ibid., p. 179.
8. Ibid., pp. 263 and 264.
9. Lee Iacocca with William Novak, *Iacocca: An Autobiography* (New York: Bantam Books, 1984), p. 53.
10. Ibid., p. 152.
11. Robert Levering, Milton Morkowitz, and Michael Katz, *The 100 Best Companies to Work for in America* (Reading, Mass.: Addison-Wesley, 1983), p. 158.
12. Ibid., p. 153.
13. Thomas Peters and Robert Waterman, *In Search of Excellence: Lessons from America's Best-Run Companies* (New York: Harper & Row, 1982), p. 318.
14. Alfred D. Chandler, Jr., *Strategy and Structure: Chapters from the History of the American Industrial Enterprise* (Cambridge, Mass.: The M.I.T. Press, 1962), p. 269.
15. Pierce Hollingsworth, "General Mills: Winning Market Share with New Products," *Prepared Foods* (September 1984), p. 56
16. Arthur Pound, "Up from the Grass Roots," *Atlantic Industrial Advertising* (August 1935), p. 255.
17. James Gray, *Business Without Boundary: The Story of General Mills* (Minneapolis: University of Minnesota, 1954), p. 250.
18. "General Mills: The General and Betty Crocker," *Forbes* (October 1, 1963), p. 24.
19. "How to Manage Entrepreneurs," *Business Week* (September 7, 1981), p. 67.
20. Ann M. Marrison, "The General Mills Brand of Managers," *Fortune* (January 12, 1981), p. 105.

21. James C. Worthy, *Shaping an American Institution* (Chicago: University of Illinois Press, 1984), p. 134.

CHAPTER 5

1. Worthy, *Shaping an American Institution*, p. 28.
2. Ibid., p. 31.
3. Allan Nevins with Frank E. Hill, *Ford: The Times, the Man, and the Company*, Vol. 1 of *Ford* (New York: Scribner, 1954), p. 461.
4. "To Pause and Be Refreshed," p. 108.
5. Henry Schimberg, quoted from Tim Davis, "The Coke Enterprise: Out Front and Pulling Away," *Beverage World* (July 1984), p. 35.
6. "AT&T: Hot Products, High Costs," *The New York Times* (August 5, 1984), p. F4. © 1984 by The New York Times Company. Reprinted by permission.
7. Gurda, *The Quiet Company*, p. 163.
8. Ann Przybola, "General Mills' R&D: Forerunner in New Technology," *Prepared Foods* (September 1984), p. 60.
9. Chandler, *Strategy and Structure*, p. 373.

CHAPTER 6

1. *Yoga means conscious evolution.* Quote is from *The Bhagavad Gita,* Chapter 2, Verse 50.
2. *Review of Reviews* (May 1933).
3. Iacocca with Novak, *An Autobiography*, p. 246.
4. Ibid., p. 245.
5. Lawrence A. Appley, *A Management Concept: Lectures by Lawrence A. Appley* (New York: American Management Association, 1969), p. 122.
6. "The Colossus that Works," *Time* (July 11, 1983), p. 40.
7. Geneen, *Managing*, p. 82.
8. Ibid., p. 7.
9. Iacocca with Novak, *An Autobiography*, p. 50.
10. Cekota, *Entrepreneur Extraordinary*, p. 221.
11. Geneen, *Managing*, p. 97.
12. Iacocca with Novak, *An Autobiography*, p. 23.
13. Confucius, *The Sayings of Confucius*, trans. James R. Ware (Confucius Publishing Company), p. 148.
14. Cited in Nixon, *Leaders*, p. 56.

15. G. B. Tennyson, *A Carlyle Reader* (Cambridge, England: Cambridge University Press, 1984), p. 275.
16. Geneen, *Managing*, p. 78.

CHAPTER 7

1. "International Business Machines," p. 130.
2. Ezra Vogel, *Japan as Number One: Lessons for America* (Cambridge, Mass., and London: Harvard University Press, 1979), p. 27.
3. Peter F. Drucker, *Management: Tasks, Responsibilities, Practices* (New York: Harper & Row, 1974), p. 766.
4. Ibid., p. 767.
5. "International Business Machines," p. 131.
6. "America's Most Admired Corporations," *Fortune* (January 9, 1984), p. 54.
7. Robert Sobel, *IBM: Colossus in Transition* (New York: Bantam Books, 1983), p. 279.
8. "The Colossus that Works," p. 42.
9. Iacocca with Novak, *An Autobiography*, p. 155.

CHAPTER 8

1. "The Odyssey of Levi Strauss," *Fortune* (March 22, 1982).
2. Walter A. Haas, Jr., *Managing Corporate Social Policy at Levi Strauss & Co.* (December 1980), p. 15, published by Levi Strauss.
3. M. R. Montgomery, "Making It RIGHT," *The Boston Globe Magazine* (October 3, 1982).
4. Edward A. Gallaway, *Accountability* (Philadelphia: Dorrance & Company, 1975), pp. 54–55.
5. "International Business Machines," p. 36.
6. Robert Pirsig, *Zen and the Art of Motorcycle Maintenance* (New York: Bantam Books, 1982), p. 39.
7. Gallaway, *Accountability*, pp. 66–67.
8. Peters and Waterman, *In Search of Excellence*, p. 284.
9. Daniel D. Nossiter, "Blue Chip Bet on Research," *Barron's* (November 8, 1982).
10. Livesay, *American Made*, p. 102.
11. Ibid., p. 248.
12. Iacocca with Novak, *An Autobiography*, p. 154.
13. Geneen, *Managing*, pp. 195–96.

CHAPTER 9

1. Iacocca with Novak, *An Autobiography*, p. 152.
2. Gray, *Business Without Boundary*, p. 228.
3. "The Effective Meeting," *The Royal Bank Letter*, Vol. 65, No. 5 (1984), published by the Royal Bank of Canada. Reprinted with permission of the Royal Bank of Canada.
4. "Delta: The World's Most Profitable Airline," *Business Week* (August 31, 1981), p. 71.

CHAPTER 10

1. Marcus Aurelius, *Meditations*, trans. Maxwell Staniforth (New York: Penguin Books, 1966), Book 7, p. 109.
2. Worthy, *Shaping an American Institution*, p. 92.
3. Ibid., p. 7.
4. From an address by Edward R. Telling before the Economic Club of Chicago (February 25, 1982), p. 18.
5. Peter Nulty, "Apple's Bid to Stay in the Big Time," *Fortune* (February 7, 1983), p. 36.
6. "Apple's New Crusade," p. 146.
7. "The Opinion Climate for Business," *ORC Public Opinion Index* (March 1984), p. 13.
8. Peter F. Drucker, "Good Works and Good Business," *Across the Board* (October 1984), p. 13.
9. "Conversation with Harold K. Sperlich," *Organizational Dynamics* (Spring 1984), p. 27.

CHAPTER 11

1. "To Pause and Be Refreshed," p. 111.
2. Sobel, *IBM*, p. 102.
3. O'Brien, *Marriott*, p. 210.
4. Sobel, *Entrepreneurs*, p. 169.
5. Livesay, *American Made*, p. 153.
6. Sobel, *Entrepreneurs*, p. 194.
7. Drucker, *Practice of Management*, p. 266.
8. Quoted from Wood's address before the On-to-Chicago Meeting, Chicago (May 4, 1950).
9. Lewis and Newton, *Delta*, p. 241.
10. Geneen, *Managing*, p. 129.

11. "Executive Obsolescence: What Can You Do to Prevent It?" *AIPE Facilities Management, Operations and Engineering* (September/October 1984), p. 6.
12. Ibid., p. 8.
13. "The Colossus that Works," *Time* (January 11, 1983), p. 42.
14. Iacocca with Novak, *An Autobiography*, p. 59.
15. Drucker, *Management*, p. 427.
16. Thomas J. Watson, Jr., *A Business and Its Beliefs: The Ideas that Helped Build IBM* (New York: McGraw-Hill Book Company, 1963), p. 4.
17. Peter F. Drucker, *The Effective Executive* (New York: Harper & Row, 1967), p. 170.

CHAPTER 12

1. *Automobile Topics* (April 18, 1925), p. 845.
2. Michael Moritz and Barrett Seaman, *Going for Broke: Lee Iacocca's Battle to Save Chrysler* (New York: Anchor Press/Doubleday & Company, 1984), p. 20.
3. Iacocca with Novak, *An Autobiography*, p. 157.
4. Moritz and Seaman, *Going for Broke*, p. 23.
5. Ibid., p. 41.
6. Peter Vanderwicken, "What's Really Wrong at Chrysler," *Fortune* (May 1975), p. 177.
7. Ibid.
8. Ibid., p. 178.
9. Chandler, *Strategy and Structure*, p. 380.
10. Moritz and Seaman, *Going for Broke*, p. 202.
11. Iacocca with Novak, *An Autobiography*, p. 157.
12. Moritz and Seaman, *Going for Broke*, p. 14.
13. Iacocca with Novak, *An Autobiography*, p. 152.
14. Moritz and Seaman, *Going for Broke*, p. 108.
15. Iacocca with Novak, *An Autobiography*, p. 152.
16. Moritz and Seaman, *Going for Broke*, p. 208.
17. Iacocca with Novak, *An Autobiography*, p. 171.
18. Steven Flax, "Rolling Along," *Fortune* (January 7, 1985), p. 46.

Index